## DATE DUE

| | | |
|---|---|---|
| NO 10'98 | | |
| DE 1'08 | | |
| MY 24'99 | | |
| MY 29'01 | | |
| | | |
| | | |
| | | |
| | | |
| | | |
| | | |
| | | |
| | | |
| | | |
| | | |
| | | |
| | | |
| | | |

DEMCO 38-296

# UNDERSTANDING
# CHINA

# UNDERSTANDING
# CHINA

## A Guide to China's Economy, History, and Political Structure

## JOHN BRYAN STARR

Hill and Wang
A division of Farrar, Straus and Giroux
New York

Hill and Wang
A division of Farrar, Straus and Giroux
19 Union Square West, New York 10003

Copyright © 1997 by John Bryan Starr
Maps copyright © 1997 by Virginia Norey
All rights reserved
Distributed in Canada by Douglas & McIntyre Ltd.
Printed in the United States of America
Designed by Jonathan D. Lippincott
**Second printing, 1998**

Library of Congress Cataloging-in-Publication Data
Starr, John Bryan.
  Understanding China : a guide to China's economy, history, and political
structure / John Bryan Starr. — 1st ed.
    p.   cm.
  Includes bibliographical references and index.
  ISBN 0-8090-9488-6 (alk. paper)
  1. China—Politics and government—1976–   2. China—Economic condi-
tions—1976–   3. China.  I. Title.
DS779.26.S737   1997
951.05—dc21                                                    97-934

For Lynne and Kate

# Contents

# UNDERSTANDING
# CHINA

# Introduction

To the limited extent that Westerners pay attention to what is going on beyond their shores, China commands a disproportionate share of that attention. Moreover, those of us who have some knowledge of what is going on in China tend to have strong feelings about the country, acting as cheerleaders for its successes and harsh critics of its failings. We find it difficult to be indifferent.

There has been a great deal of good news coming out of China in recent years. China has one of the world's fastest growing economies. Indeed, there are those who predict that, at its current rate of growth, China's will be the world's largest economy by 2040, surpassing those of Japan and of the United States. Economic growth has substantially improved the standard of living for most if not all Chinese people. Rural incomes are three times what they were in 1978, the beginning of the current period of economic reform, and urban incomes are up nearly five times. Economic liberalization has been accompanied by some relaxation of the tight control the Chinese government maintained over its population. Most of the Chinese people are enjoying substantially more freedom from government interference in their lives than they did fifteen years ago.

There is also bad news. American enthusiasm for an opening and reforming China ten years ago had the unintended effect of filtering out much of the bad news, but that filter ceased to function when, on the night of 3 June 1989, tanks clattered through Beijing, clearing the streets of demonstrators and killing many hundreds of them in the process. Since then we have been attentive to the repressive measures taken against its own people by a government deeply concerned about the consequences of political instability.

Our attentiveness to China's shortcomings in governance was amplified with the collapse of the Soviet Union in 1991. The demise of what Reagan had called "the evil empire" and the emergence of a new democratic state from its ashes made the resilience of authoritarianism in China all the more repugnant. To those of us with a Manichaean streak, who like identifying a principal adversary, the shoes just shed by the Soviet Union seemed to fit China perfectly.

Economic success has made the Chinese government—and perhaps also the Chinese people—much less malleable and easy to deal with than they once were. They have run up a trade surplus with the United States second only to Japan's. They demand full membership in the world economy but balk at playing by the rules. Recently they have taken actions outside their borders that may be evidence of a dangerous new military expansionism on the part of Asia's largest power.

Complicating any attempt to resolve the contradictions that China presents us with is the fact that, with the death of Deng Xiaoping, the country passed a critical milestone in its recent history and is experiencing all the uncertainties that accompany major change. A succession crisis is virtually inevitable. No socialist system has made a smooth transition following the death of its principal leader. China itself experienced a rocky changing of the guard when Mao Zedong, leader of the Chinese Communist Party for forty years and of the People's Republic of China since the time of its founding, died in 1976. Having maneuvered his way through those rocky shoals, Deng tried three times to put in place a group of capable leaders whom he could trust to carry on his political program. By avoiding the top positions and by retiring early from the positions he did hold, he hoped to make himself thoroughly dispensable and thus easily and smoothly replaced. He failed on all counts. His trusted successors proved insufficient to the task. He had to abandon his efforts to retire to the distant role of éminence grise when student demonstrators called into question his authority and his legacy.

Any succession crisis is difficult to weather, but this one is particularly difficult for China, for it marks the end of a unique political generation, the generation of the leaders of the Chinese Communist revolution and the founders of the contemporary Chinese political system. Rapid change has been a permanent feature of China for the last half century. As a result, members of each political generation after Deng's have had very different lives, careers, and experiences. The people who make up those generations differ in training, perceptions, connections, and aspirations.

Although Deng was not wholly characteristic of his generation, most of his revolutionary cohorts were born in China's hinterlands, ill-educated in a formal sense, and limited in their knowledge of and experience in the world outside of China. The next generation, born too late to have been active in the revolution and civil war, grew up in a China heavily dependent on the Soviet Union. They were educated in schools modeled after Soviet schools, they learned the Russian language, and many of them spent time studying or working in the Soviet Union. They are technologically adept, ideologically cautious, and instinctively bureaucratic. By the time Mao died and reforms began, they were late-middle-aged dogs who found the new tricks difficult to master.

The next generation had their lives and careers shaped by their participation in the chaos of the Cultural Revolution launched by Mao in the 1960s. It rendered many if not most of them at best skeptical, at worst highly cynical. As such, although they are significantly better educated and their opportunities to interact with the outside world were infinitely greater than those available to their elders, the new ideas they have encountered did not engender great optimism in them. Having lost their idealism at an early age, they now find the materialism of contemporary China a comfortable fit.

The youngest generation has come to maturity since the post-Mao reform period began. It is made up of bright, brash, hardworking, and cosmopolitan people, but they are more self-interested than public-minded. Their goal is personal wealth, and that is best pursued in the rapidly expanding private sector. Devoting their energies to solving major problems in the public realm is out of the question.

Given the diversity of these generations, the transition period will surely be protracted. Unfortunately, there does not appear to be a group of capable, intelligent, honest, forward-looking, and enthusiastic political leaders waiting in the wings. But then, China is not the only country about which one can say that.

The purpose of this book is to look beyond the immediate situation and to explore three questions: What are the principal problems confronting China today? What is the capacity of the Chinese political system to deal with these problems successfully? And, given the answers to these two questions, how might the political situation play itself out in the near term?

My answers to these three questions, which I will elaborate on in the chapters that follow, are first that the extraordinarily serious problems that China confronts would tax the capability of the strongest and most able of governments. But, second, the capacity of the Chinese government is severely diminished and its capability is weak. Hence, third, China's near-term future looks rather dark.

At least a dozen critical problems face China's leaders. Each of them threatens the nation's ability to continue on its current trajectory of economic development. Some of them threaten the viability of the state itself. Four of them affect primarily the one-quarter of the Chinese population that lives in cities. Three of them affect primarily the remaining three-quarters of the population that lives in the towns and villages of China's countryside. Three are problems that affect Chinese society as a whole, and the others concern China's relations with the outside world.

Overheated economic growth is the first problem that has affected primarily China's urban population. By most assessments, the overall rate of growth of the Chinese economy from mid-1992 through the end of 1994 was unsustainably high. It was targeted at 6 percent in 1994 but came in at more than double that rate by year's end. By the end of 1995 the rate had slowed to a somewhat more reasonable 10.2 percent: anything more than 10 percent is high in itself, and if the figure is disaggregated, the growth rate in certain sectors was many times that. State-owned enterprise in 1995 grew at a modest rate of 4 percent, but output from collective enterprises grew at 15 percent, and from privately owned enterprises at 52 percent; foreign-invested private enterprises grew at a rate of 37 percent for the year. Stringent measures adopted in the summer of 1993 to try to rein in the economic growth rate have met with limited success and widespread resistance.

Closely related to these rapid growth rates is a second problem, that of high inflation. After more than thirty years of a nearly flat cost of living, inflation began to mount sharply in the late 1980s. It was brought under control in part through a retrenchment program put in place in late 1988 and in part through the slowdown caused by economic sanctions imposed by foreign powers outraged at the massacre of students in Tiananmen Square in June 1989. When the lid was removed again in the early 1990s, the economy and foreign contacts burgeoned and inflation once more became a serious issue, particularly for the urban population, some of whom experienced rates in excess of 30 percent. In the past, a decline in purchasing power has been of enough concern to bring people out into the streets in protest demonstrations. Mindful of this danger, the government took steps to curb inflation and succeeded in cutting the rate in half in 1995. Avoiding a recurrence of runaway inflation is a high priority for the authorities.

The third urban problem is the serious financial straits of most state-owned enterprises. More than half of the hundred thousand industrial enterprises owned by the government are losing money, some at a staggering rate. They are kept alive by government loans and subsidies that, in 1994, amounted to $28.7 billion (equivalent to more than a third of China's total national budget). So-called triangular debt—that is, money owed by state-owned enterprises to other state-owned enterprises—amounted to $71 billion that year (equivalent to one-third of the total output of the state-owned industrial sector). The government has avoided the obvious solution—allowing money-losing enterprises to go out of business—because it would put so many workers out of a job. It is a solution the government also avoids for ideological reasons. China claims to be a socialist system "with Chinese characteristics." Whatever its characteristics, a socialist system that closes down its state-owned sector risks becoming an oxymoron.

Employment-related issues are the fourth problem the Chinese state faces in the urban economy. The official unemployment rate stands at 3 percent and is not in itself a cause of concern, but concealed unemployment is. Because of financial problems, many state-owned enterprises have put their workers on reduced hours or temporary furlough. Underemployment of those who remain on the job is a related problem. One reason for China's financial crisis in the state sector is that its workforce is excessively large. Estimates vary, but they suggest that up to one-fifth of the state-sector workforce is superfluous to production processes. Enterprises are attempting to downsize gradually; about two million workers lost their jobs in 1995. While the private and collective sectors are growing rapidly, they cannot absorb all those who are jobless or underemployed.

The most serious employment-related problem facing municipal authorities concerns the more than 100 million workers who have come from the countryside into China's cities in search of more lucrative work. These floating workers are hired on a short-term basis, most frequently as day laborers in construction. Because they are not official residents of the cities they are living in, they are not entitled to housing or social services and tend to camp out wherever they can find shelter—often in exurban shantytowns.

As a large group of people outside the organizational web that controls the population, the floating workers are a novel anomaly in China. Municipal officials look on them as a dangerous necessity. On the one hand, they are needed to do the unskilled labor that even the unemployed among urban residents spurn as too hard and too ill-paid. On the other hand, they are blamed for an increase in violent crime in China's cities, and it is assumed that they will be a dangerous source of political unrest if they can no longer find regular work.

There are serious problems in the countryside as well. First among them is the growing gap in the standard of living between urban and rural China. Average urban income has always exceeded that in the countryside, but during the early years of reform the gap began to close. Beginning in the mid-1980s, the gap widened once again and is now as large as it has ever been, and, worse, with the agricultural economy growing at about 3 percent and the urban economy growing at more than 20 percent, it is certain to widen still further. The difference between rural and urban incomes used to matter very little, since country people were only dimly aware of living conditions in the cities, and even if they knew that life was better there, they were prevented by the government from moving. Neither of those conditions prevails today.

A second source of dissatisfaction in the countryside is excessive taxation. Although taxes are nominally restricted to 5 percent of household income, the local governments' need for additional revenue leads them to impose every imaginable kind of fee, fine, toll, and levy so that peasant households are regularly paying between 15 and 50 percent of their income to the local authorities. This would be unsatisfactory to most citizens under any circumstances, but it is especially galling here because a significant portion of that revenue ends up being used by local officials in ostentatious personal expenditures.

To add insult to injury, local governments frequently experience cash-flow problems that interfere with their ability to pay farmers for the commodities they have contracted to sell to the state. Farmers bring their harvested crops to state purchasing depots where, instead of cash, they are given chits, or "green slips," redeemable for cash when the cash flow improves; meanwhile the money that would have gone to pay the farmers for their grain is often invested by entrepreneurial officials in speculative ventures that promise a large return. These unredeemed green slips are a major source of dissatisfaction in the rural communities and have led on many recent occasions to demonstrations—occasionally violent ones.

Then there are issues affecting all Chinese people, whether they live in the city or the countryside. Two are interrelated: How will it be possible to feed a growing population on a rapidly shrinking amount of arable land? The government is dealing with a fraction, the numerator of which is agricultural production, the denominator of which is population. Its task is to increase the numerator and keep the denominator as small as possible.

The government's population-control program, or "one-child policy," addresses the denominator. And though the government credits the policy with reducing the rate at which the population is growing, the average family in China still has 2.3 children; the one-child policy is only fully effective when draconian measures are used to enforce it, measures that serve to alienate further a population already highly dissatisfied with its government. At its current rate of growth, the Chinese population will reach 1.5 billion by 2015, having trebled in less than a hundred years.

As for the numerator, grain production currently stands at 480 million tons per year. That is a substantial increase over what was being produced forty years ago, but the growth rate in production has begun to slow. Per-acre yields are already impressively high, and many observers are skeptical that they can be raised much higher. Meanwhile, arable land, already a scarce commodity in China, is being taken out of cultivation with alarming speed. China feeds 20 percent of the world's population on less than 7 percent of the world's arable land; recent economic development has resulted in substantial quantities of this land being taken out of cultivation and used for factories, roads, and houses. Finally, like that of all developing societies, the Chinese diet is evolving. As the living standard improves, consumption of meat and eggs is increasing, raising the demand for grain. Taking all these factors into account, pessimists forecast a grain deficit in 2030 so large that it will be impossible for world grain exporters to fill it.

Another grave issue that affects not only the Chinese population but the rest of the world as well is that of environmental degradation. Two-thirds of all factories in China are polluting the air and water in violation of the state's environmental regulations, which are hardly as strong as in Western countries. Nine-tenths of Chinese cities do not meet Chinese clean-air standards. A quarter of China's freshwater is polluted, and 90 percent of the water flowing through cities is impotable. At its current rate of economic growth, by 2025 China will produce three times the amount of greenhouse gases currently produced in the United States. As though this domestic agenda were not a sufficient challenge, China has problems in its interaction with the outside world. The most immediate challenge is to handle the transfer of Hong Kong's sovereignty from Great Britain to China in such a way as not to disturb the delicate equilibrium on which the remarkable success of that territory rests. Over the period since the Sino-British agreement on Hong Kong was signed, considerable rancor developed on both sides; reactions in Hong Kong to the Tiananmen Square massacre in 1989 fundamentally altered China's view of that city and Hong Kong citizens' view of their future. These changes are expressed in some of the specific provisions that filled in the vague outline of Hong Kong as a Special Administrative Region contained in the Joint Declaration of 1985. Hong Kong has thrived, many argue, because of its government's light hand on the tiller of the economy. Will the Chinese government prove willing and able to maintain an equally light hand? It is normally heavy-handed in its own domestic affairs; even if it were willing, will it be *able* to lighten its touch in dealing with Hong Kong?

The relationship between Taiwan and the mainland is closely related. Hong Kong is intended to be a model of the Chinese government's ability to keep the promise of "one country, two systems" that it has extended to Taiwan as well. A successful transition in Hong Kong, so the argument goes, will arouse confidence in Taiwan that, under Beijing's rule after reunification, its political, economic, and social systems will remain unchanged.

Beginning in 1987, the Taiwan government began a process of opening up contact with the mainland. That process has eventuated in a sizable amount of trade and investment closely linking the two economies. Informal talks between the two sides aimed at facilitating their relations began in 1993, but the process of coming together was interrupted in 1995 by a strong reaction on the

Chinese side to what the Taiwan government calls its "flexible diplomacy": what the Taiwan authorities depict as efforts at securing informal recognition of Taiwan's standing in the world as a political and economic power, the Beijing authorities construe as moves in the direction of a declaration of independence, which is absolutely unacceptable to them, and they have pledged to use force to ensure that it does not come about.

All too closely intertwined with relations across the Taiwan Strait is China's relationship with the United States. With the Shanghai Communiqué in 1972, the United States attempted to recuse itself from this entire issue, but in the ensuing years, politicians in all three capitals have worked to prevent that from happening. Chinese leaders have sought U.S. assistance in bringing Taiwan to accept their terms for reunification. Taiwan authorities have sought U.S. endorsement of their claim to being other than merely a province of China. And some Americans, mindful of the special relationship between the United States and Nationalist China, argue for a revival of American guarantees for Taiwan's interests.

The Taiwan question is but one of a series of conflicts between Beijing and Washington that in 1996 brought Sino-American relations to a low point reminiscent of the near rupture of relations following the Tiananmen massacre in 1989. Americans are repulsed by the Chinese government's violation of the human rights of its citizens and alarmed by the mounting deficit in U.S. trade with China. Chinese see the United States as reviving a Cold War policy of containing China and thwarting its taking a deserved place as a nascent world power.

The last foreign-policy issue with which the Chinese government must deal is its relationship with Japan. What is now a complementary economic relationship is very likely to become a competitive one as China's economy expands. China's armed forces are growing and flexing their muscles, and Japan feels pressure to respond in kind. Its doing so will confirm long-standing Chinese concerns over a revival of the Japanese militarism of which China was the victim in the first half of the twentieth century. In short, the two nations must come to a new strategic and economic understanding that takes into account the altered circumstances in which they both find themselves at the turn of the millennium.

It is hard to imagine a government that would have the vision, the political capital, and the tenacity to address successfully this daunting agenda. The Chinese government at present is far from that ideal. It has suffered a serious loss of credibility in the eyes of its own people. It is deeply enmeshed in corruption and seems incapable of disentangling itself. It is weakened by rigidity in the face of change and by its absolute refusal to countenance organized opposition. It is vying for authority, often unsuccessfully, with insubordinate cities and provinces. Finally, it is beholden to its army to the point that it is unable to countermand military initiatives, many of which exacerbate rather than help to solve the problems the government confronts.

The Chinese Communist Party (CCP) has as little political credibility today as it has ever had since its founding in 1921. It came to power in 1949 with a tremendous reservoir of popular support. It added to that reservoir with reforms it undertook in the early 1950s, then soon lost credibility with a series of misguided movements undertaken at Mao's insistence that had disastrous consequences for the Chinese people. The Cultural Revolution had a devastating effect on the reputation of the Party. So complete was the loss of popular confidence that even a reversal of the Party's policy line and a partial repudiation of its past mistakes were not enough to repair the damage.

Most Chinese people are quick to acknowledge that the reform policies put in place by Deng Xiaoping in 1978 have put modern

China in a position to realize its great potential for the first time and have substantially improved their standard of living. Paradoxically, however, these successes have done little to bolster the Party's reputation, most probably because most people inseparably associate the Party with the Marxist-Leninist rhetoric that they find so irrelevant to their lives. And Deng's own reputation suffered a serious blow when it became clear that it was he who had instructed that martial law be declared in Beijing, he who ordered distant but loyal troops into the capital, and he who determined that Tiananmen Square must be cleared of protesters at any cost.

The collapse of the Communist Party in the Soviet Union appears to have given the CCP's credibility an unanticipated boost. One might have expected the CCP, an illegitimate party with an illegitimate elder leader, like virtually every other communist party in the socialist bloc, to collapse of its own weight. Unlike those other parties, however, the CCP had been remarkably effective in ensuring that no other organization in the country could take its place. There was no Solidarity, no Protestant Church, no nationally elected parliament. Because no other institution stood between the Chinese people and a disorder such as that which they witnessed in Eastern Europe and Russia, they accorded the Party a limited vote of confidence: living under the CCP was preferable to living in anarchy.

China's burgeoning economy has multiplied the already numerous opportunities for corrupt behavior on the part of government and Party officials, and few have missed the chance of taking advantage of them. From village councils to the Party's politburo, officials have been profiting from their positions. Campaigns are launched to stamp out the pervasive corruption, but the officials put in charge of the campaigns are themselves deeply involved in corrupt behavior; the campaigns stagnate, and even the Party newspaper opines that "a certain amount of corruption is inevitable." With their eyes firmly fixed on personal gain, not the public weal, officials are hardly in a position to tackle the complex problems facing them.

The capability of China's political system is further diminished by an advanced case of arteriosclerosis. Conscious that its status is precarious, the Party-state has become more and more rigid, less and less tolerant of disagreement and dissent, more and more prone to act on its habits of repression. At a time of rapid economic and social change, the Party has grown less flexible, less open to political reform. Always a society ruled by men and not by law, China finds itself with a group of late-middle-aged leaders who give lip service to the principle of subordinating themselves and their actions to a fully developed code of law but who, when push comes to shove, ignore the law in favor of arbitrary and often self-serving action.

Meanwhile, political power and authority have shifted noticeably from the center of the Party-state to its periphery. Central government and Party organs have relinquished power, and provincial and local governments have gained it. The economy's market reform has been accompanied by an appropriate loosening of central control. Problems arise, however, because this loosening has occurred without a clear-cut or uniform allocation of authority between center and regions. Each region has negotiated its own arrangements, and none is prepared to give back what it has successfully obtained. Meanwhile, regional interests have begun to diverge from those of the center and, adding to the complications, among themselves. There is a real possibility that, were any one or a combination of these political problems to reach crisis stage, the center might not hold.

The glue that the Party-state has come to rely on since 1989 to hold China's political system together is the People's Liberation Army. It is the only organization with national scope that is capable of supporting a collapsing Party-state or of taking its place.

Given that fact, the Party-state finds itself beholden to it in a way that is unparalleled since the violent phase of the Cultural Revolution threatened to spin out of control in early 1967. China's military budget is growing, and it is acquiring substantial, new, and sophisticated equipment. To help support its growth, the Army has become a major player in the Chinese domestic economy and has extensive connections in the global economy. At the same time, actions it has taken in Burma, in the South China Sea, in the Taiwan Strait, and elsewhere raise the question whether China's foreign policy is being made in the Foreign Ministry or by uniformed officers.

The People's Liberation Army paid dearly for its decision to respond to Deng's orders in 1989 at Tiananmen Square. Its public image suffered, and it found all of its carefully cultivated contacts with foreign military establishments suddenly severed, leaving it without the technology, training, or intelligence it had come to depend on. In exchange, it has received substantial budget increases each year, but only now is it beginning to rebuild its credibility and contacts, and it would be very reluctant to repeat this unhappy scenario. On the other hand, military officers are patriots—indeed many are xenophobes—and unlikely to sit on the sidelines were China to come apart at the seams or sink into anarchy. Whether or not their intervention into the political sphere would be successful is another question.

I begin this book with an exploration of China's geography, illustrating some of the natural constraints on the country's growth and pointing up the unevenness of the endowments of its regions. Then I describe the political system as a power grid, with central agencies constituting the vertical elements and regional agencies the horizontal elements. When center and region are at odds with each other, as is often the case, the grid thwarts rather than facilitates the implementation of central directives. Next, the description of

China's economy in transition focuses on three questions: Who owns what? Who works where? And who is making the economic decisions? The final chapter in this initial section is devoted to China's armed forces—their strategic capability, role in the economy, and political potential.

Subsequent chapters take up the problems I have briefly outlined in this introduction: urban concerns, problems in the countryside, and the problems that affect the country as a whole, such as environmental pollution, population growth, and the tendency toward regional fragmentation. Three chapters are devoted to the status of rights and freedoms in China: human rights and the rule of law, intellectual and artistic freedom.

In the closing section of the book, I consider China's interaction with the outside world. Separate chapters on Hong Kong and Taiwan are followed by a final chapter on China's strategic, economic, and political relations with its neighbors and with the United States. The conclusion takes a cautious stroke or two through the dangerous waters of predicting China's future.

This book originated as a seminar on "issues in contemporary Chinese politics" that I offered at Yale University for seventeen years beginning in 1978. More immediately, it derives from a series of lectures that I gave under the auspices of the Patricia Prescott May Academic Lectures series in Greenwich, Connecticut, in 1994–95. I am grateful to my Yale students and to those who attended the May lectures for what I learned with and from them.

# Geographical Inequalities

A s a first step toward understanding China, one can hardly do better than to spend some time with a good atlas. It is vital to understand China's diversity, and a key element in that diversity is its geography.

Superimposing an outline of the United States on an outline of China shows us two important geographical similarities between the two countries. China's territory, covering some 3.7 million square miles, is nearly identical in size to that of the United States, which covers just over 3.6 million square miles. The two countries are located at more or less the same latitude; New York and Beijing are at roughly the same latitude, as are New Orleans and Shanghai.

A topographical map, on the other hand, shows us important geographical differences between China and the United States. Only about a third of the United States is taken up with mountains and desert, and the remainder is reasonably flat and easily habitable, but in China, these proportions are reversed. The difference in the amount of land available for cultivation in the two countries is even more striking: 40 percent in the United States versus only 10 percent in China.

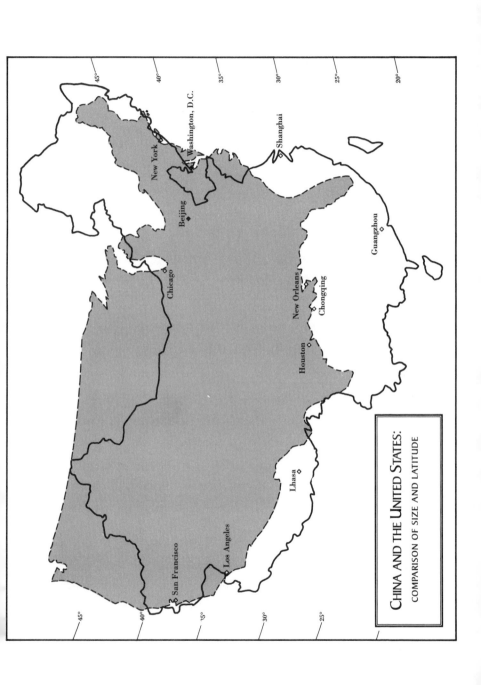

CHINA AND THE UNITED STATES:
COMPARISON OF SIZE AND LATITUDE

In any country rivers serve as arteries for transportation and sources of both irrigation and energy. Silting improves the fertility of river-basin fields, but flooding destroys crops and homes and often claims lives. The major river systems on the North American continent run from north to south, while China's three major river systems all flow from west to east. The northernmost is the Huang He (Yellow River), which runs for more than three thousand miles from the western territory of Tibet to its mouth in Shandong Province. The river takes its name from the color of the extraordinary amount of silt it carries, deposits of which continually raise its level; it now flows well above the level of the North China plain and is contained between high dikes.

The second major river system, the Yangzi or Changjiang (Long River), also originates in Tibet. It is somewhat longer than the Yellow and has ten times the discharge. It is navigable by ocean-going ships from its mouth near Shanghai as far upstream as the city of Wuhan. About three hundred miles upstream from Wuhan, ground was broken in 1993 for the very large and controversial Three Gorges Dam, among the purposes of which is to extend the navigability of the river to the city of Chongqing, in Sichuan Province, to produce hydroelectric power, and to regulate the flow of the river to control downstream flooding.

The Xi Jiang (West River) in Guangdong Province, the third of China's major river systems, is the shortest of the three, flowing 1,650 miles before merging with the Zhu Jiang (Pearl River) in the delta, at the mouth of which are located Guangzhou (more familiarly known to Westerners as Canton) and Hong Kong.

China's most fertile agricultural regions are located in the deltas of the Yellow, Yangzi, and West Rivers. A fourth area of high fertility is located along the upper reaches of the Yangzi River in the Sichuan basin, just south of the center of the Chinese landmass.

.    .    .

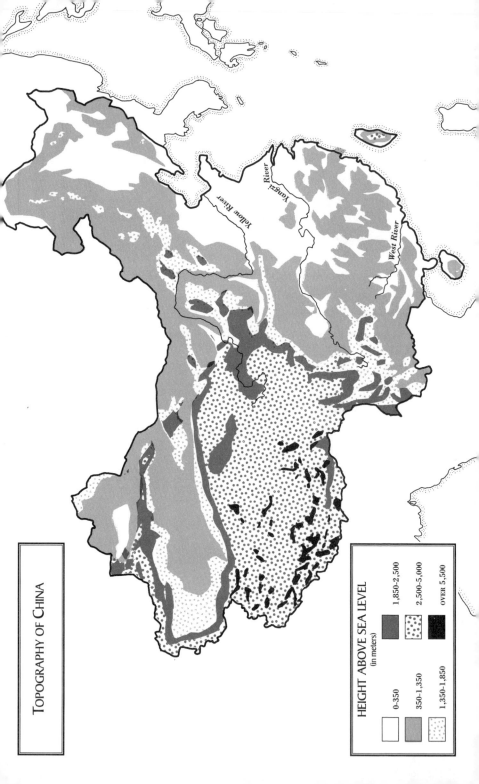

TOPOGRAPHY OF CHINA

Yellow River

Yangzi River

West River

HEIGHT ABOVE SEA LEVEL
(in meters)

0–350

350–1,350

1,350–1,850

1,850–2,500

2,500–5,000

OVER 5,500

A striking difference between the American and the Chinese landmasses is found in the nature of their western borders, which in the United States is of course an ocean coast, while in China it is marked with mountains, plateaus, and deserts. This difference accounts for major dissimilarities in the prevailing climates of the two landmasses. American weather is governed by the movement of the jet stream carrying moisture-laden Pacific storms across the continent. China's weather is determined by monsoon winds that, between December and March, blow northwest to southeast; coming from the Siberian landmass, the air crossing the northwestern provinces is very dry and provides little rainfall. Then, during the summer months from April to November, the monsoon winds reverse themselves, and, now moving across the South China Sea, they are heavily laden with moisture, which descends as rainfall on China's southeastern coast; the winds are relatively dry by the time they reach the northwestern provinces. Annual rainfall on the southern coast exceeds seventy-five inches, but along the Mongolian border, it is no more than five inches.

Temperatures along the southeastern coast of China are moderate enough even in the winter that there is a year-round growing season, and as many as three crops of rice can be harvested. North of the Great Wall, by contrast, the growing season is only 140 days, and farmers consider themselves fortunate to harvest a single crop of spring wheat.

Coal accounts for nearly three-quarters of all energy consumed in China. Oil currently supplies about 20 percent and hydroelectric power the remaining 5 percent of the country's energy resources, percentages about the same as in the United States. The important difference is that about half the energy supplied by coal in China is supplied by natural gas in the United States.

Energy resources and raw materials are somewhat more equally

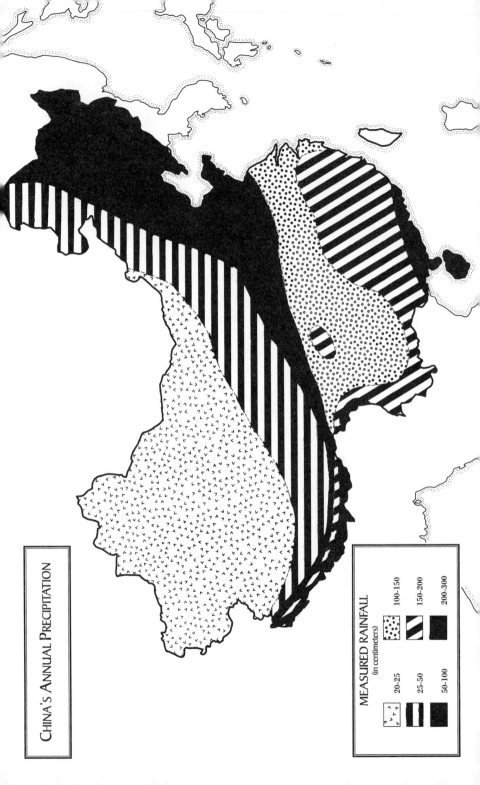

CHINA'S ANNUAL PRECIPITATION

MEASURED RAINFALL
(in centimeters)

20-25
25-50
50-100
100-150
150-200
200-300

distributed across China than is its scant supply of agricultural land, for coal is found in substantial quantities across the eastern half of the country as well as in Xinjiang, while principal onshore oil fields are located in Gansu, Xinjiang, Shanxi, Sichuan, and Heilongjiang. Annual coal production is running at a rate of just over one billion tons. The vast majority of China's coal is bituminous, or soft, the burning of which contributes heavily to air pollution. Weaning China of its heavy dependence on soft coal is a necessary first step toward solving its serious environmental problems.

Before the beginning of exploration in the Tarim Basin in Xinjiang in 1993, the Chinese estimated their onshore oil reserves at 75 billion barrels. Early estimates of the Tarim Basin reserves were as high as 180 billion barrels—which would have more than tripled their reserves—but most recent estimates are as low as 4 to 5 billion barrels. Meanwhile, offshore oil exploration undertaken with foreign assistance has been under way for more than twenty years. Assessing China's offshore reserves is complicated by a lack of reliable survey data and by issues of territorial rights; estimates have varied from a low of 37 billion barrels to a high of more than 200 billion barrels. Combining onshore and offshore reserves, then, China may have as little as 116 billion barrels or as much as 455 billion barrels. (To put these figures into perspective: the onshore and offshore oil reserves of the United States are about 156 billion barrels, those of Saudi Arabia about 260 billion barrels.)

In the late 1970s, when China began to interact with the world economy, Chinese planners estimated that oil would double its share of China's total energy consumption and reach about 40 percent by the early 1990s and that revenues from oil exports would be sufficient to fund imports of Western and Japanese technology. But the ensuing development of the economy increased domestic demand for petroleum at a rate that exceeded the rate of increase in oil production: whereas total economic growth has averaged in excess of 10 percent per year, oil production is increasing at about 7 percent. Thus, oil occupies about the same position in China's energy pool that it did twenty years ago, and, as of 1994, China became a net importer of oil.

Hydroelectric power is China's third source of energy, providing about 5 percent of the total. The existing electric-power grid serves the eastern third of the country quite effectively, the western two-thirds less so. Total electric-power generation in 1994 was 928 billion kilowatt hours, but 80 percent of that power was thermal generated, using soft coal. Electric-power generation is increasing annually at a rate of about 10 percent, but the ratio of coal-burning thermal-generated electricity to hydroelectric power has remained constant for fifteen years.

The Three Gorges Dam project is projected to produce some 85 billion kilowatt hours of hydroelectric power when it is fully operative in 2015. In theory, that could help reduce the use of coal by 50 million tons per year. But in fact, at that point the annual electrical energy needs of eastern China alone are projected to be between 900 billion and 1 trillion kilowatt hours, so it is most likely that power from the new dam will simply augment the supply of thermal-generated electricity, not supplant it.

The distribution of China's population accords closely with the location of fertile soil and adequate growing seasons. Approximately 75 percent of the population lives on 15 percent of the landmass, being most heavily concentrated in the fertile river basins, where densities in excess of two thousand people per square mile are not uncommon. (This compares with a population density of fewer than four hundred people per square mile in the northeastern United States, the most highly populated area.) Compared to the river basins, western China is sparsely populated, but even these wide open spaces have a fair number of people. The auton-

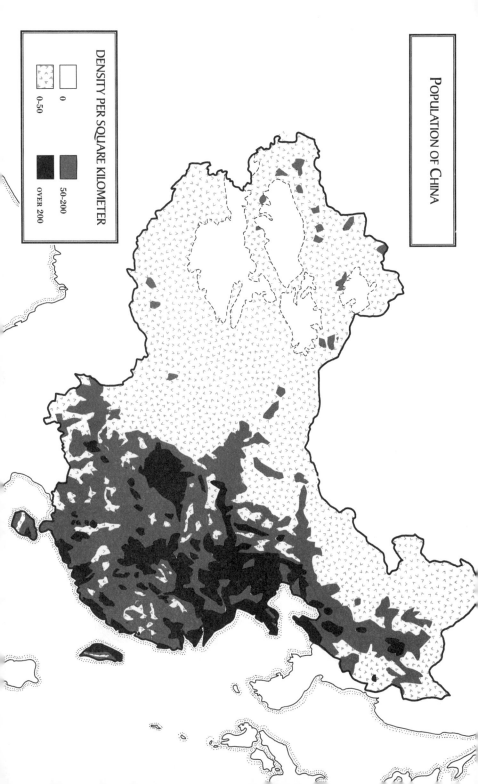

POPULATION OF CHINA

DENSITY PER SQUARE KILOMETER

0

0-50

50-200

OVER 200

omous region of Xinjiang, China's largest province, is also its least densely populated, with some twenty-six people per square mile. (By comparison, Wyoming and Alaska have five and one per square mile, respectively.)

Some 300 million people—one-quarter of the Chinese population—reside in China's 570 cities, and the density of the network of these cities generally conforms to the pattern of population density shown in the map. This is a more even distribution than is the case with many other countries at a comparable level of economic development, and for three distinct reasons.

As the territory over which China's sovereignty extended began to expand as early as the third century B.C., the central government established administrative seats from which its officials exerted control over the populace. By the beginning of the nineteenth century, a network of some two thousand cities and towns covered all of what we now think of as Chinese territory, with, at the center of each, a walled compound housing the local representative of imperial authority. Each administrative seat was part of a hierarchy organized according to the respective ranks and positions of the imperial officials. Beijing, the imperial capital, stood at the apex of this hierarchy, provincial capitals formed its mid-levels, and county seats formed its base.

A second reason for the rise of urban aggregations in China was commercial. The exchange of agricultural goods and handicraft products and, subsequently, the exchange of both of these for manufactured items led to the rise of itinerant merchants, moving periodically from village to village, and then to a whole stratum of society devoted entirely to commerce. While some villages were centers of commercial activity only occasionally, others, by virtue of their location, proved more durably convenient for marketing purposes. Market days in these villages became more frequent; eventually the markets became permanent. Thus was created a hierarchy of commercial centers that was integrated with, but at the same time distinguishable from, the hierarchy of administrative centers.

Whereas the administrative centers were laid out from the top down in a reasonably orderly fashion so as to exert imperial control as uniformly as possible over China's hinterlands, the network of market towns grew naturally from the bottom up. The former were called *cheng*, a word that also means "wall" and that conjures up an image of a formally laid-out and enclosed urban space; market towns were called *zhen*, which connotes an outpost or garrison without a formal layout or walls. Administrative centers were large—the smallest had a population of between three and ten thousand, while the market towns were much smaller, the lowest ranking among them being mere hamlets of as few as five hundred people, half or more of whom were full-time farmers.

The third force that gave rise to urban agglomeration in China came much later in the country's history and resulted from the government's unsuccessful effort to prevent or at least limit foreigners' commercial and cultural contact with China. One result of the series of defeats that the Chinese endured in the modern period at the hands of Westerners superior in modern armaments and the tactics to employ them was that for the first time in its history China was forced open to the influence and influx of non-Chinese. Because Western nations were themselves in rivalry with one another for slices of what came to be called the "Chinese melon," the Chinese used this rivalry to their advantage in order to restrict the points of Sino-Western contact to a few locations, which came to be known as treaty ports. Unlike administrative and marketing towns, treaty ports were part of neither a hierarchy nor an effective network. To the extent that the Chinese government was able to control their designation, they were located where contact between Chinese people and nefarious foreigners would be minimal and easily controlled. To the extent that Western powers succeeded in imposing their preferences, they occurred where

Western entrepreneurs found maximal ease of access to what they sought in China: cheap labor, cheap raw materials, cheap maritime transport, and abundant consumers.

Today, even the smallest of China's 570 cities seem very large to Americans; at the other end of the scale, 15 cities in China have more than 2 million people.

## China's Fifteen Largest Cities

| | Nonagricultural population (in millions) | U.S. cities population (in millions) |
|---|---|---|
| Shanghai | 8.9 | |
| Beijing | 6.6 | New York 7.3 |
| Tianjin | 5.0 | |
| Shenyang | 4.0 | |
| Chongqing | 3.8 | |
| Wuhan | 3.8 | |
| Guangzhou | 3.7 | |
| Harbin | 3.1 | Los Angeles 3.5 |
| Chengdu | 2.8 | Chicago 2.8 |
| Changchun | 2.5 | |
| Nanjing | 2.5 | |
| Dalian | 2.4 | |
| Xian | 2.4 | |
| Qingdao | 2.3 | |
| Jinan | 2.2 | |
| | | Houston 1.7 |

*(Sources: China Statistical Yearbook 1996 and American Almanac 1994–95)*

China is by modern standards inadequately interconnected, with only about seven hundred thousand miles of highways and roads, about 90 percent of which are paved—about one-sixth of the highway network in the United States. Moreover, the roads are unequally distributed: dense in China's eastern provinces and sparse in the west. About 13 percent of the country's freight traffic and just under half of its passenger traffic is carried on these roads and highways, and highway construction is a high priority in the country's economic development program. Between fifteen thousand and twenty thousand miles of new highway are being added annually, much of it at the expense of China's limited supply of arable land.

The rail network covers about thirty-five thousand miles, only a quarter of which is double tracked. (The United States currently has a rail network four times that size.) This rail system carries about 40 percent of the country's freight and passenger traffic (coal accounting for nearly half the freight). As China's economy expands, its railways are operating at or close to capacity and are meeting less than 60 percent of the demand for rail transport; major construction is under way to add six thousand miles of track by the turn of the century, the largest of these projects being a second north-south rail corridor connecting Beijing and Guangzhou and paralleling the existing line to the east that was opened to traffic in 1996. Projections suggest that the railroad system's share of passenger and freight traffic will decline to about 30 percent each over the next fifteen years, with highways and airlines attracting away passengers and trucking absorbing the difference in freight traffic.

China's system of navigable inland waterways, both rivers and canals, is twice as long as its rail network. More freight is carried on inland and coastal waterways than on either road or rail.

The roughly six hundred commercial air routes (a number that shows an increase by a factor of five in the fifteen years since the economic reforms began) in China now cover almost the same distance as that covered by highways, though the volume of air transport remains small. Until the mid-1980s air transport was handled by a single state-owned corporation, the Civil Air Administration of China (CAAC); in the past decade, CAAC has broken up into more than a dozen local companies, which have taken over domestic and some international routes; CAAC is now an exclusively international airline. A shortage of equipment and trained personnel has hampered the expansion of air transportation, which in any case has a dauntingly bad safety record. Currently, only about 6 percent of China's passenger travel and less than 1 percent of freight movement is completed by air.

As with the network of roads and highways, so with waterways, railways, and air routes: eastern China is well linked; western China is much less accessible.

Mountains and deserts rendered interaction with China's neighbors to the north and west problematic throughout the nation's history, and the ocean on the east was also a barrier to, rather than avenue for, interaction. Capable of an autarkic existence, China chose to cut itself off from contact with the outside world for much of its long history. Exceptions to this habit of isolation are seen with the expansion of maritime trade during the Tang and Song dynasties, in the tenth and eleventh centuries, and with the opening of the overland Silk Route, connecting China to Central Asia and the Middle East, during the Yuan dynasty in the thirteenth century.

In the nineteenth century, the European nations, Japan, and the United States began to push on China's closed door. They initially came to buy tea and silk; later they began to think of China as a potential market for Western manufactures and a source of inexpensive labor to produce those goods. Almost all the intercourse into which China was reluctantly forced took place at ports on the eastern littoral, a pattern that was revived when China rejoined the world economy in the late 1970s. The vast preponderance of China's now extensive interaction with the outside world occurs in the major coastal cities that were once treaty ports—Tianjin, Dalian, Shanghai, Fuzhou, Xiamen, and Guangzhou. To be sure, there is cross-border economic interaction with Russia and the former Soviet Central Asian republics to the north and west, and with Burma and Vietnam in the south. But this economic activity pales by comparison with the volume of transactions initiated in the coastal provinces.

In ethnic terms, the Chinese population is unusually uniform. Despite great cultural differences among various groups, more than nine-tenths of the population consider themselves to be of the same Han ethnicity. The remaining population is divided among fifty-five distinct minority nationalities, each with its own language. This small fraction of the total population, however, inhabits nearly two-thirds of the Chinese landmass, including northern, western, and southern China.

Beneath the ethnic uniformity of the Han Chinese population lies a strong sense of local loyalty that is reinforced by habits of language, cuisine, and a remarkably persistent regional stereotyping. The Chinese term *difang guannian*, best translated as "sense of place," has great importance in the individual Chinese psyche, despite the homogenizing tendencies of a rapidly modernizing society. Ask an American where he or she is from, and you are likely to get some variation of a current zip code as an answer. Ask that same question of a Chinese, and you are likely to receive an answer that will call into question your command of the first lessons of elementary Chinese.

"Where are you from?" I have asked a new acquaintance. "I am from Shanghai" comes the answer. "Shanghai is changing very rapidly," I respond. "When is the last time you visited there?" "I've never been to Shanghai," he replies, and I wonder where my simple conversation went astray. As it turns out, my Chinese is not at fault. My friend has, in fact, never been to Shanghai, nor has his father. It was his *grandfather* who was born in Shanghai and who left at the age of twenty never to return; yet at some important level, my friend continues to consider himself a Shanghainese and to identify with the fortunes of his "native" place.

Local dialects are an important ingredient of this persistent sense of place. All of the Han population share the same written language, and about three-quarters of them speak a more or less mutually intelligible version of the language that we Westerners often refer to as "Mandarin." The remainder, who live in the southeastern quadrant of the country, speak mutually unintelligible dialects that adhere to seven major dialect groups and countless local subgroupings. The northern dialect, or Mandarin, forms the basis of what the Chinese call *putong hua* (the common language), which is taught in schools throughout China, is used as the medium of spoken communication in official life, and until quite recently was the only language spoken in radio and television broadcasting.

Diet and cuisine vary by region in China, as they do in many countries, and constitute an important part of this strong regional self-identification. The most significant distinction is found between the northern provinces, where wheat is the principal grain, and the south, where rice predominates. Northern cuisine is best known for its flavorful sauces; southern cuisine features fresh ingredients with light, often sweet sauces that enhance the fresh flavors. South-central Chinese cuisine makes copious use of the red pepper. Fish and seafood figure prominently in the food of the coastal provinces; pork and chicken predominate inland. In areas inhabited by Muslim minorities, lamb is the preferred meat. Throughout China, grain and vegetables are still the principal sources of protein, though with growing affluence a preference for meat is increasing—a trend viewed with concern by those worried about feeding a growing population on a limited supply of arable land.

The enduring regional identities have created, over the centuries, regional stereotypes that Chinese people never abandon. As is the case in other parts of the Northern Hemisphere, northerners in China are often thought of as reserved, formal, and aloof; southerners, by contrast, are seen as more outgoing, volatile, and spontaneous. Residents of Beijing, like those who live inside our Washington Beltway, have a reputation for being highly political and power seeking; like New Yorkers, people from Shanghai consider themselves, and are considered by others, sophisticated, cosmopolitan, and managerially capable. Residents of Guangzhou are often characterized as having a highly developed commercial sense; natives of the south-central provinces of Sichuan and Hunan, perhaps because of their peppery cuisine, are called hot tempered and impetuous.

The People's Republic of China is divided administratively into twenty-two provinces and five so-called autonomous regions, where the majority of the population are non-Han. In addition, there are four "directly administered cities"—Beijing, Tianjin, Chongqing, and Shanghai—which with their surrounding counties are treated, for administrative purposes, as equivalent to provinces. The provinces are divided into counties, of which there are just over two thousand nationwide, and cities. Under the supervision of the county governments, rural political and economic administration is conducted at the level of the township or town. Each county has, on average, some two dozen townships and towns, with a national total of thirty-three thousand townships and about half that number of town governments. There are about eight hundred thousand village governments, the lowest level of rural administration, or about two dozen per township. The average village population is a little over one thousand individuals—though the villages vary significantly depending on whether they are located in densely or sparsely populated regions.

Translating China's geographical inequalities into economic terms, one begins to sense the significance of regionalism in China today.

POLITICAL MAP OF CHINA

HEILONGJIANG
Harbin ◇
JILIN
Changchun ◇
LIAONING
Shenyang ◇
INNER MONGOLIA
Hohhot ◇
Beijing ◆
Tianjin ◇
HEBEI
Shijiazhuang ◇
Ji'nan ◇
SHANDONG
JIANGSU
Nanjing ◇
Shanghai
SHANXI
Taiyuan ◇
Zhengzhou ◇
HENAN
Hefei ◇
ANHUI
ZHEJIANG
Hangzhou ◇
Nanchang ◇
JIANGXI
Fuzhou ◇
FUJIAN
Taipei ◇
TAIWAN
SHAANXI
Xi'an ◇
HUBEI
Wuhan ◇
Changsha ◇
HUNAN
GUANGDONG
Guangzhou ◇
HAINAN
Haikou ◇
NINGXIA
Yinchuan ◇
GANSU
Lanzhou ◇
QINGHAI
Xining ◇
Chengdu ◇
Chongqing ◇
SICHUAN
Guiyang ◇
GUIZHOU
GUANGXI
Nanning ◇
YUNNAN
Kunming ◇
XINJIANG
Urumqi ◇
TIBET
Lhasa ◇

Consider the data on economic output broken down by province and organized into three geographical areas: the coastal provinces, central China, and the western territories. It shows that the significant advantages enjoyed by the coastal provinces are quite recent. Whereas Shanghai was and is the front-ranking economy in each of the years for which information is provided, other provinces and cities have altered their relative positions over the last forty years. The southern coastal provinces of Guangdong and Fujian, for example, stand out as late bloomers.

The table shows that in 1994 the thirteen top-ranking performers are all in coastal China. On the other hand, the ranking of per capita national income for the other two regions is less clear-cut. The central provinces are not uniformly more productive than those in western China, though they are growing faster, with one or two notable exceptions.

The information in this table substantiates the hypothesis that the policies of the economic-reform period have worked to magnify China's geographical inequalities. Before, development policy in China operated according to a different logic. Mao Zedong's first principle of economic development was egalitarianism. Mindful of the regional differences and geographical inequalities, he argued that resources should be preferentially allocated to the poorest regions, allowing them to develop to the level already achieved by the richest; only then would the richest regions be encouraged to move forward, and the pace of their development would be kept to a rate that could be matched by China as a whole.

The inauguration of reform policies in the late 1970s shifted away from this Maoist egalitarianism. Deng and his like-minded colleagues believed that egalitarian development for China was inevitably development at an unacceptably slow pace. Arguing that the Chinese people could not be persuaded to "delay gratification" any longer, the reformers adopted a policy of "building on the best." Resources once devoted to developing China's poorest

# Comparative Output, Growth, and Investment by Region and Province, 1952±94

| | 1952 Per capita output* | Rank | 1983 Per capita output* | Rank | Growth 1979–83 (%) | Rank |
|---|---|---|---|---|---|---|
| *Coastal China:* | | 1 | | 1 | | 1 |
| Beijing | 187 | 5 | 337 | 3 | 47 | 10 |
| Fujian | 72 | 21 | 70 | 20 | 51 | 5 |
| Guangdong | 89 | 16 | 85 | 13 | 50 | 7 |
| Hainan | n.a. | n.a. | n.a. | n.a. | n.a. | n.a. |
| Hebei | 95 | 13 | 86 | 12 | 27 | 24 |
| Heilongjiang | 238 | 3 | 137 | 5 | 33 | 22 |
| Jiangsu | 95 | 14 | 152 | 4 | 70 | 2 |
| Jilin | 164 | 6 | 121 | 6 | 44 | 13 |
| Liaoning | 222 | 4 | 106 | 8 | 35 | 19 |
| Shangdong | 72 | 20 | 100 | 10 | 46 | 11 |
| Shanghai | 771 | 1 | 683 | 1 | 34 | 20 |
| Tianjin | 479 | 2 | 362 | 2 | 50 | 8 |
| Zhejiang | 98 | 12 | 117 | 7 | 85 | 1 |
| Average | 199 | | 181 | | 44 | |
| *Central China:* | | 3 | | 2 | | 2 |
| Anhui | 56 | 29 | 65 | 26 | 51 | 6 |
| Henan | 65 | 24 | 66 | 23 | 7 | 28 |
| Hubei | 101 | 11 | 106 | 9 | 65 | 3 |
| Hunan | 76 | 18 | 75 | 15 | 41 | 15 |
| Jiangxi | 93 | 15 | 65 | 25 | 46 | 12 |
| Shaanxi | 75 | 19 | 74 | 17 | 31 | 23 |
| Shanxi | 81 | 17 | 96 | 11 | 40 | 16 |
| Sichuan | 65 | 25 | 67 | 22 | 48 | 9 |
| Average | 77 | | 77 | | 41 | |
| *Western China:* | | 2 | | 3 | | 3 |
| Gansu | 65 | 26 | 71 | 19 | 13 | 26 |
| Guangxi | 69 | 22 | 55 | 27 | 35 | 18 |
| Guizhou | 66 | 23 | 45 | 29 | 43 | 14 |
| IMAR | 126 | 7 | 74 | 16 | 40 | 17 |
| Ningxia | 109 | 10 | 71 | 18 | 19 | 25 |
| Qinghai | 109 | 9 | 67 | 21 | 7 | 27 |
| Tibet | 67 | 27 | 66 | 24 | 7 | 29 |
| Xinjiang | 110 | 8 | 81 | 14 | 57 | 4 |
| Yunnan | 60 | 28 | 54 | 28 | 33 | 21 |
| Average | 87 | | 65 | | 28 | |

Note: Figures for 1952 and 1983 show industrial and agricultural output. Figures for 1994 show gross domestic product, which, in addition to industrial and agricultural output, includes output of the commercial and service sectors.

* The national average equals 100.

*(Sources: China Statistical Yearbook 1985 and 1996)*

| | 1994 Per capita GDP* | Rank | Growth 1993–94 (%) | Rank | 1994 Foreign direct investment (billion $) | Rank |
|---|---|---|---|---|---|---|
| Coastal China: | | 1 | | 1 | | 1 |
| Beijing | 261 | 2 | 14 | 15 | 137 | 7 |
| Fujian | 137 | 8 | 22 | 1 | 3.71 | 3 |
| Guangdong | 162 | 4 | 19 | 4 | 9.46 | 1 |
| Hainan | 123 | 9 | 12 | 17 | 0.92 | 11 |
| Hebei | 86 | 14 | 15 | 11 | 0.52 | 14 |
| Heilongjiang | 113 | 11 | 9 | 26 | 0.35 | 17 |
| Jiangsu | 148 | 7 | 17 | 6 | 3.76 | 2 |
| Jilin | 95 | 13 | 14 | 12 | 0.24 | 20 |
| Liaoning | 156 | 6 | 11 | 19 | 1.44 | 6 |
| Shangdong | 114 | 10 | 16 | 7 | 2.55 | 4 |
| Shanghai | 388 | 1 | 14 | 13 | 2.47 | 5 |
| Tianjin | 208 | 3 | 14 | 14 | 1.02 | 9 |
| Zhejiang | 157 | 5 | 20 | 3 | 1.15 | 8 |
| Average | 165 | | 15 | | 2.23 | |
| Central China: | | 3 | | 2 | | 2 |
| Anhui | 64 | 24 | 21 | 2 | 0.37 | 16 |
| Henan | 63 | 25 | 14 | 15 | 0.39 | 15 |
| Hubei | 85 | 15 | 15 | 10 | 0.60 | 13 |
| Hunan | 69 | 21 | 11 | 21 | 0.33 | 18 |
| Jiangxi | 61 | 26 | 17 | 5 | 0.26 | 19 |
| Shaanxi | 60 | 27 | 9 | 27 | 0.24 | 21 |
| Shanxi | 72 | 18 | 9 | 25 | 0.03 | 28 |
| Sichuan | 64 | 22 | 11 | 20 | 0.92 | 10 |
| Average | 67 | | 13 | | 0.39 | |
| Western China: | | 2 | | 3 | | 3 |
| Gansu | 49 | 29 | 10 | 23 | 0.09 | 22 |
| Guangxi | 71 | 19 | 16 | 8 | 0.84 | 12 |
| Guizhou | 40 | 30 | 9 | 28 | 0.06 | 25 |
| IMAR | 77 | 16 | 10 | 24 | 0.04 | 27 |
| Ningxia | 69 | 20 | 8 | 29 | 0.07 | 23 |
| Qinghai | 74 | 17 | 8 | 30 | 0.02 | 29 |
| Tibet | 51 | 28 | 16 | 9 | n.a. | n.a. |
| Xinjiang | 101 | 12 | 11 | 22 | 0.05 | 26 |
| Yunnan | 64 | 23 | 12 | 18 | 0.07 | 24 |
| Average | 66 | 22 | 11 | | 0.14 | |

regions were reallocated to its most promising regions—that is, the coastal provinces.

Moreover, the reform policies themselves, substituting market forces for central planning in the national economy, gave a significant advantage to the well-endowed coastal regions, since they favored areas that could generate capital through agricultural surpluses, or had surplus labor with skill levels appropriate to new industrial processes, or had access to domestic and foreign markets in which new products could be sold, or, finally, could develop global connections to potential sources of investment capital. The coastal provinces possessed all of these characteristics, the provinces in central China some of them, and the poorest provinces in western China few if any. So the coastal provinces, perfectly positioned to take full advantage of the policies of market reform and opening to the world economy, benefited accordingly. As we shall see, the central provinces are just beginning to be able to take advantage of the reform policies, and in the west they are still unable to do so.

While it is useful to think of coastal China as a single, well-endowed economic region, it is important to understand that its provinces are rivals for scarce resources, particularly as regards their foreign economic relations. As is clear from the table, foreign investment is concentrated almost exclusively in these provinces, and many of them have been disproportionately successful in cultivating economic ties with a specific foreign nation: as a result, after a decade of growth one sees a pattern that looks like the "spheres of influence" into which foreign powers carved China a century ago.

Hong Kong is the principal source of foreign investment in China, contributing about two-fifths of the $48 billion placed in China by foreign powers in 1995. These Hong Kong investments are heavily concentrated in Guangdong Province, where in 1991 80 percent of the $17 billion in outside investment came from

Hong Kong. Taiwan is second, contributing just over 6 percent, according to 1995 figures, much of it in Fujian Province. Shandong Province has been especially successful in attracting South Korean investors, while foreign investment in the northeast—in Heilongjiang, Jilin, and Liaoning Provinces—is dominated by Japan.

But these linkages differ in important ways from the spheres of influence in nineteenth-century China. First, the nations most active in "carving the Chinese melon" a century ago—Britain, Germany, France, and the United States—are neither the most important investors in the Chinese economy today nor have they concentrated in particular areas. Second, the spheres of influence were created by means of decisions made by foreign governments and firms, while in the current situation, Chinese economic actors are as involved in soliciting investment as are the investors involved in selecting the areas of China where they will invest.

This brief geographical foray gives us a background for trying to understand the major issues with which China's political and economic systems must contend in the near term. One of them involves that critical fraction that will determine China's ability to realize its economic potential: the numerator being food supply and the denominator population. A second set of issues are those concerning energy resources—how they will be developed and the effect of that development on China's environment and that of the world. A final issue is whether or not the geographical inequality among regions of China and the infrastructure put in place thus far will make for divisiveness.

# II

# Patterns from the Past

The Chinese phrase *henduo yiqian* means "a long time ago." A literal translation reads "a long way in front of me," which suggests a very different sense of the direction one faces to look at the past from the one we are accustomed to. It calls to mind the image of a Chinese historian seated beside the stream of events looking toward its source, while behind him the stream runs on into the future.

What are the patterns Chinese people discern as they look upstream toward their past, and how do these patterns inform their understanding of the present? As so often in an ancient culture, the patterns are as much myths about Chinese history as they are accurate accounts of past events. Common wisdom about the Chinese past is that China has always been a strong, unified state headed by a single, powerful individual, a minimal state with maximal reach: that is, a relatively small state apparatus that succeeded in extracting substantial revenues and labor from a large population. The bureaucratic system undergirding the state is believed to have been remarkably stable, having functioned without significant change for two millennia from its founding in the second century B.C. to its demise at the turn of the twentieth century. And the changes that did occur over this extraordinarily long span of history are believed to have been cyclical rather than linear; the system evolved, but it evolved through a series of deteriorations and restorations, as new dynasties looked to re-create the system as it had existed in a more perfect form at some point in the past, not to build a new order.

A key component in the Chinese view of their past is the idea of a unified state with a strong central government led by a single ruler exerting control over subordinate, weaker local governments and neighboring states. The geographical scope of this idealized state was very large: what the Chinese consider to have always been inalienable Chinese territory is in fact all the land inside China's borders when the reach of the empire was at its broadest, that is, in the eighteenth century A.D., during the middle years of the last dynasty. But when the contending principalities living in what is now Chinese territory were first unified under the control of the Qin emperor in 221 B.C., the empire occupied only a third of today's China—as far north as the Great Wall but not beyond. Its capital was in the city of Xianyang (present-day *Xi'an*), and its territory extended westward to the center of what is today Gansu Province. The first Qin emperor aspired to control all the land as far south as present-day Guangdong and Vietnam, but his armies' hold on that territory was tenuous at best.

The Chinese empire expanded and contracted, and the fluctuations were periodically interrupted by conflict and fragmentation. While the Chinese may look on the latter as temporary aberrations from the unified, centralized imperial norm, they in fact persisted for about a quarter of the time—five of the twenty centuries about which we are speaking. Nor were these times of regional fragmentation in the far-distant past. The century prior to 1950 was marked by a sharp decline and eventual collapse of central control and its replacement by dozens of heavily armed and contending satrapies.

Twice China was overrun by foreign invaders—once in the thirteenth century by the Mongols and again in the seventeenth century by the Manchus—and in each case the received wisdom would have it that the conquerors were engulfed and assimilated by their nominal victims. The Yuan and Qing dynasties, respectively, are made to fit the pattern of China's own dynasties; in fact it was under Manchu rule that the Chinese empire reached its maximal territorial grasp. The island of Taiwan, for example, was brought under Chinese control only during the last dynasty in the late seventeenth century; Tibet, briefly under Chinese suzerainty during the Tang dynasty in the seventh century, also came under the tenuous hold of Chinese authorities at about the same time. When officials in Beijing speak of Taiwan and Tibet as always having been an inseparable part of China, these facts are conveniently ignored.

A dominant thread in this pattern from the past is the strong emperor. There were norms for the emperor to observe and rites to perform, but only two real constraints on his power: his personal capacity, and the size of the empire under his rule and the necessity it imposed on him to make use of others to carry out his wishes and his will. And the proof of the pudding was always in the eating. If the dikes were mended, the borders secure, the people well fed, and commerce thriving, the emperor was ipso facto doing his job. A bad harvest, a natural disaster, a foreign threat, or hard times, by contrast, were signs that there was trouble at the center, under which circumstances those adversely affected might well consider mounting a rebellion aimed at displacing the incompetent monarch. But this was an extreme solution to the problem of misrule and occurred only a dozen or so times over two millennia. Most of the time an arbitrary emperor was restricted only by the length of his reach.

. . .

In China's traditional domestic sphere, a minimal state structure effectively controlled a massive society by making only limited demands on it, expecting society to control itself through its strong family system. The traditional order consisted of four interdependent elements: the family; the upper class—or gentry, as it is most commonly known; a group of bureaucrat-officials who were recruited to office by means of a civil-service examination; and the imperial throne itself. And it endured for so long because it involved a carefully constructed division of labor and a finely calibrated balancing of power and authority among these four elements.

The foundation of traditional Chinese society was the family, ideally consisting of several generations united under a single roof. But this ideal was feasible only for the best off in the best of times; for most people most of the time, the family was two parents and their children.

The Chinese have taken relationships within the family as paradigms for relationships within society and, indeed, for China's relationships with the world beyond its borders. They were described and subsequently canonized in the works of Confucius, the great scholar-teacher who died just a little less than a decade before the birth of Socrates. Confucius, an ethicist not a metaphysician, argued that there were more than sufficient problems to address in this world so he had no time to devote to issues about the next world. Comfortable in his position on the banks of the stream of events and looking upstream, Confucius, as a teacher, aimed to find a way to restore harmony to human relations.

The paradigmatic relationship in Confucius's mind was that between father and son, and he depicted it as reciprocal. It is the responsibility of the son to obey and respect his father in all circumstances, of course, but the father, too, has obligations. The father must serve his son as a moral exemplar, to teach moral behavior by modeling rather than by relying on rules and harsh punishments. Confucius then applied this model of reciprocity to other relationships within and outside the family—between siblings, between marriage partners, and, ultimately, between ruler and subject.

The father-son paradigm also informed China's sense of its relationship to the outside world. Just as the father's authority is based on his superior grasp of and ability to exemplify ethical principles, so China's authority among its neighbors was believed to be based on its superior grasp of ethical principles and its monopoly on a civilization that exemplified them. By these lights, China was the center of the civilized world and owed its neighbors the obligation of sharing its civilization by example, just as its neighbors owed it obedience and respect, which was symbolized by an elaborate ritual of bringing tribute to the emperor at various intervals. This Sinocentric worldview made for great stability in East Asia for a very long time. It also made it difficult for China to take seriously the idea that there might be value in ideas or approaches outside its own sphere of cultural influence.

The relationship between the commoner family and the gentry class was also a reciprocal one. The family was responsible for providing for its own subsistence, and beyond that, it was relied on for a surplus of both labor and product that could be tapped by the gentry for its private purposes and by the government for its public purposes. It was also expected to instill in its younger members a respect for order, discipline, and hard work.

Although the nuclear family was theoretically self-sufficient, in practice there were situations in which it needed to call upon external resources. In normal times, this might take the form of mutual-assistance arrangements with one's neighbors; in hard times, there was the extended family and, beyond it, the clan. Exploring the familial web far enough, one might well encounter a relative, however distant, who had secured membership in the gentry class: the resources of the extended family, especially where there were gentry connections, might be tapped for financial assistance in straitened times, for providing an education to a promising young scion, or for adjudicating a civil dispute that had turned uncivil.

Defined in narrow terms, members of the gentry class were those men who had passed a civil-service examination and had thus received a degree. Degree holders numbered, on average, about a half million men. If we add the members of their immediate families, the gentry class would have numbered no more than about five million in a society that grew gradually from about fifty million to about one hundred million people.

As we have seen, the gentry as a class depended on the nuclear and extended families into which all Chinese society was organized, and they, in turn, depended on the gentry. Similarly, the gentry and the bureaucracy were engaged in an interdependent and reciprocal relationship. Although gentry membership, strictly speaking, required a civil-service degree, landownership and the revenues derived therefrom were the gentry's economic mainstay. The imperial bureaucracy relied on the gentry to manage the local agrarian economy in such a way as to make available to the state the revenues and labor power it needed for public works and payroll. Also, by virtue of its monopoly on knowledge of the canon on which the examination system was based, the gentry identified and instructed future recruits to the bureaucracy. Finally, for reasons we shall explore in a moment, local representatives of the bureaucracy were strangers in the territories they administered and thus depended on local gentry for the information needed to administer successfully.

But the gentry were equally beholden to the bureaucrats. While receipt of a degree entitled a man and his family to membership in the gentry, every degree holder aspired to hold an office. A position within the bureaucracy not only enhanced the status of the gentry family but added significantly to its wealth. Beyond this, the bureaucracy's monopoly on political power was a necessary complement to the gentry's economic power. It was the bureaucracy that organized and supervised the public works—roads, dikes, and canals—upon which the successful functioning of each local economy depended.

The bureaucracy was composed of men who had been appointed to their official positions by the throne. Its size varied substantially over time, but a reasonable figure to keep in mind is about thirty thousand officeholders. The lowest level in the bureaucratic hierarchy was the county magistrate, of which there were some two thousand. A magistrate, assisted by a staff of clerks, runners, and personal servants, would have been responsible for governing on average between twenty-five thousand and fifty thousand people. It was his responsibility to investigate crimes and prosecute criminals, adjudicate civil disputes that could not be resolved within the family system, collect taxes, mobilize a workforce for public works, and raise a temporary militia in times of civil unrest.

Because he set examinations, awarded degrees, and appointed officials, the emperor legitimated and controlled the bureaucracy, but the bureaucrats were the eyes, ears, arms, and legs that made it possible for him to govern China's vast territory and to control and extract tax revenues from its large population. From the emperor's perspective, the danger lay in the possibility that the bureaucracy would come to rule in his place rather than in his name. A carefully constructed system was devised to prevent local alliances from forming that might impinge on the power and authority of the center. To be avoided at all costs was a confluence of political, economic, and military power held simultaneously by men with strong ties to a particular piece of territory. The law of avoidance, designed to prevent such a confluence, proscribed bureau-

crats from serving as officials in their home locales. A newly
appointed magistrate thus arrived at his post as a stranger. With
no local ties and more often than not speaking a dialect different
from that of the staff and clientele at his new post, the magistrate
came to rely heavily on the local gentry (with whom he could
communicate in Mandarin) for intelligence about the community.
   State bureaucrats held a monopoly on political power within
each local community. Although officeholders profited from their
offices through legitimate and extra-legitimate emoluments, local
economic power rested securely in the hands of the gentry. And,
though the local magistrate was authorized to call up a militia,
once the disturbance was extinguished militia members returned
to their civilian pursuits. A standing army was the exclusive purview of the throne. Political, economic, and military power were
thus controlled by three separate and interdependent elements of
China's society.
   A key ingredient in the glue that kept this carefully balanced
traditional system together over so long a period was the idea that
one's position in the social order was not fixed for all time. A
limited amount of social mobility was endemic, but more important
to the system's stability was the pervasive *myth* of social mobility.
The fortunes of many families—whether rich or poor—in fact remained much the same across many generations. (As is the case
in our own highly mobile society, there were obstacles to overcome
in moving up and advantages to being on top.) But the myth held
that a family's fortunes were likely to change radically every fourth
or fifth generation: a peasant's great-great-grandson might well
become a bureaucrat, and the bureaucrat's great-great-grandson
might well end up tilling the fields. To sort out the myth and the
reality of social mobility, we need to take a closer look at the
rungs of what one historian called the "ladder of success in imperial China."
   To begin the process of upward mobility, a commoner family

needed two things: the first was a son with intellectual promise, and the second was enough wealth and labor power to do without him in the fields. The next step would be to find a teacher to assist the son in the tortuous process of becoming literate and acquiring an introduction to the classics on which the examination system was based. Here a family connection to the gentry—however attenuated it might be—was of great value. The teacher in all likelihood was himself a recent product of the examination system, a degree holder but not yet an officeholder who might well spend years training others before securing his own position in the bureaucracy.

The young man's education was largely a matter of modeling and memorization. One learned to write characters by reproducing perfectly and frequently models of calligraphy. One learned the classics by committing them to memory. One prepared for the examination by repeatedly practicing the complicated, formalistic essay style in which answers were to be couched.

Examinations were given at the local level every three years. Those who passed were granted the degree that brought elevated status and respect. The top few candidates in the local examinations were then admitted to examinations administered by the central government, successful passage of which brought still higher degrees and greater likelihood of appointment to office. Those who failed the local examination were entitled to take it again . . . and again. Those whose persistence exceeded their proficiency might well continue to sit for examinations into late middle age.

The successful scholar, degree in hand, would then begin what for many was a long, often tedious process of securing office. Respected for his intellectual attainments, he might find employment as a tutor or, even better for his résumé, as the secretary to an official. In this latter capacity the scholar would encounter for the first time the practicalities of governance, which neither his education nor the examinations had been concerned with. Whatever extra income he had would be invested in buying more land, for it was in his capacity as a landlord and lender that a member of the gentry who did not hold office was able to advance his family's interests.

Office holding, when it finally arrived, was the capstone on the upwardly mobile scholar's career. His status and that of his family were enhanced and their wealth augmented by the emoluments of office—both legitimate and illegitimate ones (commonly known as "squeeze"). Once again, it was additional land into which that wealth was most likely to be invested.

The reverse process, the descent of the ladder of success, was predicated on two important features of China's state and society: the first, a political feature, held that with the exception of that of the emperor himself no position was hereditary; the second, a social feature, was that primogeniture was not practiced and a father's estate was divided equally among his sons. Given these facts of life, a son had to go through the same process his father had gone through—education, examination, and appointment to office—in order to hold on to the family's position in society. Of course, the deck was stacked in favor of the already well-endowed, and the chances of success were much greater for the scion of an elite family than for the scion of a commoner family. On the other hand, wealth and status often encouraged an effete lifestyle that dulled interest in and ability for a classical education. Failure to pass an examination put the entire generation at risk. Without income from office holding, the family would be hard put to maintain the extravagant lifestyle of China's upper elite, and landholdings, rather than being augmented with the investment of a surplus, would be sold to make up the deficit. Also, with the passing of each succeeding generation, landholdings were equally divided among the sons; the progeny were likely to find themselves obliged to work for a living until such time as, with a combination of wit, drive, and a cash surplus, the family might begin the process of ascent once again.

Marxist historians in China have worked hard to persuade themselves that the system described here was feudal in character and thus that Chinese society was moving through the same historical stages that Marx and Engels used to describe European history. As is clear from this brief description, however, the Chinese experience differed significantly from that of feudal Europe (or feudal Japan, for that matter), where a family permanently retained its status in the social order. Though fact may have fallen far short of myth, there *was* mobility in the Chinese system, and status was ultimately based on achievement, not on birth and only indirectly on wealth. Moreover, estates were more likely to be dissipated when all the sons were obliged to share the bequest with their siblings.

In the same way that the fortunes of a Chinese family might rise and fall over time, so the fortunes of an imperial dynastic house were seen to wax and wane. Giving a sense of continuity over a vast span of history, these changes were seen as fitting a cyclical, not a linear, pattern. Throughout, a Confucian set of ideas about governance, with a strong emphasis on the value of restoring an ideal system of right rule from which actual practice had slipped over time, dominated this cyclical pattern.

The idea that the imperial family had the "mandate of heaven" as its source of political legitimacy dates from as early as the Zhou dynasty in the twelfth century B.C. The idea of an anthropomorphic deity had been dominant during the Shang dynasty, which preceded the Zhou, and it gave way under the Zhou to the vaguer concept of "heaven" as a "supreme spiritual reality," as one student of Chinese philosophy describes it. It was heaven that bestowed the right to rule, and the ruler and his offspring retained that right or mandate so long as they ruled virtuously and effectively. A lapse in virtuous rule meant that the mandate would be withdrawn and placed in the hands of another, more virtuous emperor.

A corollary to the idea of the mandate of heaven was the "right to rebel." Under circumstances of misrule, since the mandate was about to be withdrawn from the ruler anyway, it would not be wrong to speed the process by mounting a rebellion. This "right," however, was granted only in retrospect—that is, if the rebellion was successful, it proved ipso facto that the mandate was about to be withdrawn, and if it failed, its very failure demonstrated that heaven was not ready to shift the mandate.

With nine major dynasties and numerous minor ones over two thousand years of Chinese history, the mandate shifted many times. Intriguingly, however, the new incumbent on the imperial throne, whether rebel or foreign invader, invariably made it his business to restore the system to the way it had existed at some better point in the past and never undertook to change it in any fundamental way. No doubt this had something to do with the strong restorationist theme in Confucianism, which served so effectively as the basis of the state ideology, but it also had to do with the fact that the carefully articulated and balanced social-political system had proved such a remarkably effective and efficient form of administration for a large, unwieldy empire.

The apex of the dynastic cycle was marked by good times, when the central government was at its strongest, taxes were collected, and the appropriate sum of tax revenue made its way to the capital. China's borders were secure, public works were undertaken and maintained, and the baneful effects of natural disasters were effectively addressed. In short, the economic health of the empire was sound, and the authority of the central government relative to that of local officials and the gentry was strong.

Conversely, at the nadir of the cycle, marked by bad times, the empire's economic health was seriously threatened, poverty was widespread, and the people were underfed, overworked, and over-taxed. The central government was weak and ineffective, tax revenues were insufficient, and a disproportionate share of them stayed in the hands of local officials and never got to the central coffers. External threats to the empire were not effectively repulsed. Natural disasters occurred with what appeared to be increasing frequency, and their devastation of the lives and livelihood of the people went unmitigated by government action. With the authority of the central government weakened, local power holders were emboldened and their excesses went unchecked. Superstition surged: since heaven was known to express its dissatisfaction with the unvirtuous ruler through natural signs, people anticipated floods, droughts, earthquakes, and—everyone's favorite among the portents—birds flying backward. At this point, the mandate was transferred through rebellion or invasion, and the process of restoration and rebuilding began again.

Since restoration occurred with such unvarying regularity, one might have expected it to occur once again when the authority of the Qing dynasty began to wane in the mid–nineteenth century. How do we explain the fact that the Qing was replaced, when it finally collapsed in 1911, not with another dynastic cycle but with a long, intensely painful period of linear change—a period that has yet to draw to a close?

One very important feature of China in the nineteenth century that had not been true at the time of other dynastic nadirs was the size of the population, for its population growth rate had remained constant and very low for centuries. Estimates of the population in early times are, naturally, subject to large errors, but historians generally agree that the population in the Han dynasty (at the beginning of the Common Era) had reached about 60 million people; a thousand years later, at the time of the Song dynasty, it passed 100 million; and by the middle years of the Ming dynasty, five hundred years thereafter, it stood at perhaps 150 million. During the course of the Qing dynasty, which ascended to the throne in 1644, China's population roughly trebled, and it stood at close to 450 million by the late nineteenth century. Historians attribute this population surge from the mid-seventeenth to the mid–nineteenth centuries, which mirrors a growth in world population during the same period, to advances in agricultural techniques that permitted higher yields from agricultural land. It had to do as well with the introduction of new crops, including corn, the sweet potato, and the peanut. Whatever the cause, the result of this extraordinary spurt of growth was that China's population quickly exceeded the capacity of the land to produce an adequate food supply; the development of a transportation network lagged far behind the growing population, and a food shortages in one area could not easily be relieved by shifting surpluses from another.

A second new factor was a series of steps taken by the throne to put down a virulent rebellion that came very close to overthrowing the dynasty. Rebels, led by a group claiming to have Christian connections, proposed to replace the Manchu dynasty with a "heavenly kingdom of great peace." So great was the threat from these Taiping rebels that the throne agreed to undo the careful separation of political, economic, and military power that had given China such remarkable stability. Responding to the demands of a capable general, Zeng Guofan, the throne agreed to suspend the law of avoidance and the prohibition on mounting a permanent military force under local command. Zeng Guofan succeeded in defeating the Taiping threat but in the process became the first in a long sequence of local warlords who held full political, economic, and military authority over a discrete piece of Chinese territory.

A third factor in the nineteenth century was the arrival on China's shores of Western powers intent on opening it up as a source of raw materials, labor power, and new markets, and using weapons and technology that gave them significant advantages over their Chinese adversaries. The defeat of the defending forces time and time again at the hands of foreign powers discredited the central government, reminding its subjects of the foreign origins of the Manchus and sapping their authority.

Along with their guns, and later their railroads and factories, Westerners brought their ideas. The first response of Chinese intellectuals was to try to accept the guns, railroads, and factories and reject the ideas—the scientific and philosophical systems— that had given rise to them. Maintaining a "Chinese essence" while borrowing "practical things" from the West was a last-ditch defensive stance against the threat of wholesale Westernization. It was quickly overwhelmed, and Western ideas about social and political relationships soon damaged the credibility of the Confucian canon to the point that it could no longer serve to underpin the mounting of a new dynasty and the restoration of the old order. Instead, restoration gave way to a long, intensely painful process of revolution.

The uniquely long history of Chinese civilization is looked on by most Chinese as a source of great pride. Much effort was expended in an attempt to preserve this heritage in the face of changes encountered as China has entered the modern world. But more and more, others in China look on themselves and their compatriots not as enriched, but rather as imprisoned by China's past. Perhaps the most vivid version of this counterview was a film series aired on Chinese television in the summer of 1988 titled *He Shang* (River elegy, or River dirge), which used familiar images from China's past—the Yellow River, the Great Wall, the dragon—to symbolize the restrictions and limitations imposed by tradition and juxtaposed these earth-tone images with that of the blue Pacific, symbolizing the freedom of the outside world. Only by looking beyond China and its past to the world outside, the series said, could the confining restrictions of that past be overcome and the country's great potential realized. Even those Chinese who agreed with the film's premises found the starkness of the images disturbing, and those who disagreed were vitriolic in their condemnation of such an attack on China's splendid past.

# III

# China's Political System:
# The Party-State and the Power Grid

A mericans like to think of the Chinese political system as the opposite of the U.S. system. Ours is a democracy; theirs is authoritarian or even totalitarian. Ours is a rule of law, theirs a rule of men. Ours protects the rights of the individual; theirs regularly infringes on these rights. In some instances, these generalizations are supported by strong evidence, but in others, they obscure similarities and common problems. In still others, they fail to take account of the substantial changes that have occurred in the past twenty years. But in each instance, the comparison is made between an American ideal (often very different from American practice) and Chinese practice (often falling far short of Chinese ideals).

When, as students, Americans learn about their political system, they are taught to think about four relationships: that among the executive, legislative, and judiciary branches of government, between the federal government and state and local governments, between political parties and the government, and between civilian and military authority. Civics texts refer to the system of checks and balances that governs and regulates the relationship among the three branches of the federal government, designed to prevent any one from assuming an inappropriate ascendancy over the others. Laid out in our Constitution, these checks and balances have been elaborated and refined over time, with the three branches pulling and tugging, each trying to influence the other two.

The relationship between the federal government and state and local governments is still in flux. The idea of states' rights is an active political rallying point, reminding us that local governments existed before the federal one, which was created through an agreement reached among them. The terms of that agreement, spelled out in detail in the Constitution, include the important provision that what is not specifically set out as the prerogative of the federal government remains that of the states. Two hundred and more years of practice, a range of issues inconceivable to the framers of the Constitution, and the addition of thirty-seven new states have all served to modify the balance between federal and local power.

The relationships between our political parties and the government and between (or among) the political parties themselves, postdate the framing of the Constitution, and custom more than law regulates them. Though there is an ideological core in each of the two major parties, they are not particularly ideological and play to the middle when they are out to win elections. Also, they are not selective: voters are free to choose (and to change) their party affiliation or to participate in the electoral process as independents. Each party tries to control the government by getting its candidates elected to the presidency or to a majority in Congress, but its ability to do so is limited by the actions of the opposition party. The existence of a vital opposition is critical to our definition of an effectively functioning democracy.

As for the relationship between civilian and military authority, we accept that our system is based on the principle that military forces must always be subordinate to civilian leadership. So ingrained is this idea in our political process that, although we go through periodic bouts of concern over military spending or over the influence of the Pentagon on our foreign policy, intervention by our armed forces into our political life has never been a serious threat.

Considering these four relationships in the Chinese political system we find similarities—many superficial—and profound differences. China's political system has three branches—a legislature, an executive branch, and a judiciary—but in practice there are really two, since the Chinese judiciary functions more as a department of the executive than it does as an independent check on the other two arms of the government. Similarly, the legislature has only very recently come to see itself as a potential check on the operations of the executive branch and the judiciary. The branches are not equal partners, and there is no provision in the Chinese constitution for checks and balances to maintain an equality. Indeed, the constitution itself and its function in the political system reveal perhaps the most important differences between the two systems. China has had five constitutions since the People's Republic was founded in 1949, and the document is probably best understood as a mission statement or policy platform with a finite duration. It was not intended, nor does it function, as a set of fixed principles against which specific laws and practices are measured and overturned if found to be at odds.

In general the Chinese system relies much less on relationships fixed by law, constitutional provisions, or regulation. Rather, negotiated relationships between and among individuals and organizations dominate the political landscape—which helps to account for the very different relation between the national government and regional and local governments. China's is not a federal system, and the central government deals with provincial and municipal governments by means of myriad ad hoc agreements made after complex bargaining negotiations.

In practice, the center-local relationship is a power grid in which the vertical elements are the bureaucratic departments of the central systems and the horizontal elements are the provinces and cities. In many if not most instances, the vertical and horizontal elements work at cross purposes, stymieing rather than facilitating political activity.

The most important difference between the American and the Chinese political systems concerns their political parties. The key function of setting government policy in China since 1949 lies outside the government entirely and is monopolized by the Chinese Communist Party (CCP). There is no interaction among or between political parties, for the CCP succeeded long ago in eliminating its rivals and has effectively prevented the emergence of any force that could even begin to be a nucleus for political opposition.

A selective organization, the Party chooses its members on the basis of their suitability for leadership in its political life. One in every twenty-two Chinese are Party members, for a total membership of about fifty-seven million. (In contrast, one in every 2.2 Americans is registered with a political-party affiliation, and the total party affiliation is roughly double the size of China's Party.) Functioning somewhat like a board of directors for the country, the CCP defines its function as that of making all the critical decisions, which the government must then carry out. Unlike a board of directors, however, the CCP has created an organizational structure operating in parallel to that of the government bureaucracy, so that Party members oversee the work of the bureaucrats at every level.

With respect to the relationship between military and civilian authorities, there are, once again, substantial differences between the two political systems. Like the United States' Founding Fathers, the leaders of the newly formed Chinese state in 1949 had been active in the revolution that brought them to power, but unlike our Founding Fathers, the Chinese revolutionaries were slow to distinguish between military and civilian authority. The blurring of the lines was especially acute in regional and provincial governments, where, in most cases, the officer who had "liberated" an area stayed on as head of the new government.

As military and civilian authority gradually became differentiated, the Party continued to exert control over the army in the same way that it exerted control over the government bureaucracy. Twice, though, as we shall see, it found itself obliged to call on the army to intervene on its behalf in civilian affairs, in the aftermath of which the armed forces retained a hand in political decision making.

Today, because of the effectiveness of the Party's efforts to eliminate any organization that might challenge its monopoly on political life, the People's Liberation Army (PLA) is the only organization in China with a nationwide reach that can pick up the pieces if the CCP should falter. For all these reasons, any account of the power grid in China must include a careful look at the PLA.

The Party likes to think of itself, ideally speaking, as an elite organization that selects its members from the best that Chinese society has to offer. Selection criteria have changed over the years, but political correctness—a knowledge of the current line and an ability to apply it to day-to-day decisions—has been a constant despite many changes in the current line. Currently the Party also emphasizes technical competence, managerial skills, and entrepreneurial ability. Its legitimacy is based on its monopoly on these desirable leadership qualities and on the policies that derive from them.

But the reality is quite different. Although Party membership is at an all-time high, members are unequally distributed among the population, with a substantially heavier concentration in the city and sparser concentration in rural communities. Moreover, the Party is having difficulty attracting China's best and brightest. Although it is true that for every thirteen individuals who apply for

Party membership, only one is accepted, the quality of the applicant pool is not what the Party would like it to be. Moreover, there is evidence that the applicant pool is artificially inflated: individuals who have no intention of accepting an offer of Party membership are induced to apply to fulfill their employer's quota. For Party membership is no longer the exclusive avenue of upward mobility. An ambitious young Chinese with imperfectly developed entrepreneurial skills and business contacts can get a leg up in the process of career advancement by joining the Party, thereby acquiring political clout that might be translated into economic gain. But for those with a full set of skills and contacts, Party membership is superfluous, and the CCP does not attract the most successful of China's young entrepreneurs.

But this should be no surprise, since the Party's political authority has been progressively undermined over the last thirty years by the irrationality of its policies, the corruption of its leaders, and its failure to put forward a compelling vision for China's future. It came to power in 1949 with a reputation for honesty and a promise to end inflation. It set up a government that contrasted with its predecessor's in its dedication and in its young officials' freedom from corruption. Inflation was brought under control by 1952, and prices remained quite flat for thirty years. The substantial changes brought about in Chinese society and economy in the first years of the CCP regime appeared reasonable to most Chinese people and helped to improve the welfare of the vast majority.

Within a decade, however, people began to question the probity of the Party's leaders. The Hundred Flowers Campaign was the first of a number of events that served to undermine the Party's legitimacy. Confident of its achievements and its reputation, the Party called in 1957 for criticisms of its first eight years in power: "Let a hundred flowers bloom!" Mao cried. The attacks on those who responded to this invitation—imprisonment and forced labor for thousands of so-called Rightists—seemed irrational and out of proportion. Then the further excesses of the Great Leap Forward in 1958 and the destructive anarchy of the Cultural Revolution thereafter took even more of a toll on popular confidence in Party leaders.

One would assume that the considerable successes of the economic reforms undertaken after Mao's death would have restored at least some of the Party's lost legitimacy. Interestingly, this does not seem to be the case. The Party is not given credit for the transformation of the Chinese economy and its subsequent rapid growth, perhaps because they are the results of the effective abandonment of the Marxist-Leninist principles on which the Party rests. At best, the Party is credited with stepping out of the way and giving people with entrepreneurial skills free rein.

Paradoxically, it is not what has happened in China, but rather what has happened in Russia that has bolstered the CCP's somewhat shaky position. Many Chinese people see the economic chaos and near anarchy of Russian society today as resulting from the collapse of the Communist Party of the Soviet Union, and to avoid the same outcome in China they are willing to put up with a corrupt and discredited Party as the only alternative to chaos.

According to the textbook description of the relationship between the Party and the government in the Chinese political system, the Party proposes and the government disposes; the Party makes policy, and the government carries it out. In real organizations, things seldom function according to the textbook, and the line separating policy making from policy implementation is often difficult to draw. Certainly the reality of the relationship between the Party and the government in China shows this confusion, since all the key Party leaders also occupy senior positions in the government. Decision making is monopolized by a small handful of powerful individuals, and while the Party's constitution provides that the Party Congress is responsible for setting political policy, in fact that authority rests with a half dozen or so Party leaders who, at any given time, are members of the Standing Committee of the Political Bureau of the Party's Central Committee. In the recent past, even this small group had to refer all major decisions to other, retired elder statesmen, notably to Deng Xiaoping as the primus inter pares of that group.

The Party has two means for ensuring that its policies are implemented by the government officials. The first is the power of appointment, since at each government level appointments are the responsibility of the Party organization at the level just above. (Provincial officials are appointed by the Central Party organization; provincial Party organizations, in turn, appoint officials at the county and city level.) Secondly, the performance of officials appointed by the Party is then monitored by Party organizations. In organizations and enterprises at each level of the government, a Party committee monitors political correctness and ensures that policies are carried out. It is thus next to impossible to separate the roles of policy making and policy implementation.

During the early 1980s, the goal of the political reform movement that went hand in hand with economic reform was to address and rectify this situation. Party and government were to be separated and double-hatting eliminated wherever possible. The functions of and relations between the two structures were to be clarified, with the government acting independently in day-to-day affairs and the Party confining itself to broad policy making. But these efforts at reform came to an abrupt halt in 1989 when, in violation not only of the principles governing Party-government relations but also of Party rules for decision making and discipline, Deng Xiaoping moved from behind the scenes to mobilize support for the declaration of martial law in Beijing and, subsequently, to use the army to clear demonstrators from its streets.

Several factors have conspired to keep the reform effort on hold since then: the siege mentality brought on by the domestic and international reaction to the massacre in Tiananmen Square; the mounting concern over the imminent passing of the elders responsible for that episode; and the lessons drawn by Party leaders from the collapse of communist parties in Eastern Europe and the Soviet Union. Indeed, the principal task since 1989 has been to maintain Party control at all costs.

The CCP's dominance of China's political system has led many observers to favor the term "Party-state." It seems irrelevant to try to distinguish Party from government when the government is so lacking in independent authority. And many in China agree, finding it futile to draw distinctions when they are so blurred in practice. On the other hand, others in China have begun to demand that the rule of law be extended and that the Party and its leaders be subject to it, which implies the idea that the blurring of functions is inappropriate. Indeed, one could argue that a strong state, operating with an effective legal system and set on eliminating political corruption, would have significantly greater legitimacy than the Party currently enjoys. But until that goal of eradicating corruption begins to be addressed effectively, it makes sense to continue to use the term Party-state to describe China's system.

The executive branch of the Chinese government is headed by a State Council, or cabinet, whose members are the heads of the ten commissions and thirty-one ministries that make up the 4.5 million-strong central bureaucracy. The focus of most of the ministries and commissions is the economy, its reform, and its relations with the world economy. There are, in addition, ministries devoted to noneconomic functions, such as public health and foreign affairs. In principle, commissions have a more comprehensive function than ministries, and some are intended to coordinate the work of several ministries. This is certainly the case with the State Planning Commission or the State Science and Technology Commission. On the other hand, there are ministries with an equally broad coordinating role, such as the Ministry of Finance, and commissions with a relatively narrow purview, such as the State Education Commission.

Each ministry or commission stands at the top of a system of bureaus and offices located in provincial capitals and county seats. In all there are probably some ten million bureaucrats in these vertical systems, each of which has a specialized function, overseeing a narrow sector of the economy or society. The smooth operation of these vertical systems is complicated by the fact that bureaus and offices of central ministries and commissions report not only to them, but also to the local government of which they form a part. The Shanghai education bureau, for example, reports both to the Shanghai municipal government and to the State Education Commission: its staff appointments are made by the latter, but its budget is set by the former. When push comes to shove, the interests of the local government often take precedence over those of the central ministry or commission.

In theory, communication flows smoothly and regularly up and down within each system. Communication between systems, however, is often difficult or impossible to arrange except at the uppermost reaches. A construction project in a county seat, for example, requires the approval of a number of local bureaus of different systems, and the project manager will find it hard to get officials in one to talk to those in others; it seems much more effective to refer the question up one or two levels in the bureaucracy—in some cases, even as far as the central government itself—where differences between systems can be hashed out and approvals coordinated.

China's unicameral legislature, the National People's Congress (NPC), is routinely described in the Western press as a rubber-stamp parliament. In fact, until very recently, every proposal initiated by the Party and drafted by the executive branch was given unanimous approval by the three-thousand-odd delegates to the

NPC at their annual meetings in March. This led observers (and presumably many of the delegates as well) to wonder what purpose was served by their being regularly called together.

Early in his career, Mao was a great believer in citizen initiative. Defining what he called the "mass line," he said that correct ideas originate among the people, ideas that are then refined by those with a full command of and adherence to ideological principles. These refined ideas, now policies, must then be taken back and explained to the people who were their original inspiration. So legislatures in the Chinese political system embodied this principle. Congress meetings gave leaders the chance to hear what delegates had to say, and delegates, in turn, could have policies explained to them by the central authorities. Rather than bringing a group of representatives together to *initiate* laws and policies, the NPC was conceived of as a group of representatives who would *learn about* laws and policies. While this exercise may have been educational, it was certainly not legislative in the sense we use the term in our own political arena.

Delegates to the NPC now seem less and less willing to accede to this narrow definition of their function. Since the early days of the post-Mao reform period, the NPC, through its Standing Committee, has actively participated in drafting the new laws needed to introduce a full-blown legal code for Chinese society. Increasingly, they have taken to speaking out during NPC meetings, and at their 1995 session, up to a third of them cast negative votes— once an unheard-of act of defiance—against government measures and candidates they found unacceptable. Although these are important steps in the development of an independent legislature, one should not overemphasize the progress made to date. Casting a vote against the prime minister's annual report or against the candidacy of a new vice premier is a far cry from having routine oversight and comprehensive budgetary control over the work of the executive branch of the government.

Delegates to the NPC are elected to five-year terms, but not directly by the constituents whom they represent. The process is indirect: delegates to people's congresses at the city or county level are directly elected by constituents, and in addition to these, congress delegates are selected to represent local organizations and interest groups; these local congresses elect delegates to provincial congresses; and delegates to the NPC are elected by these provincial congresses or by national organizations and interest groups.

The trend of legislators' taking their jobs seriously affects congresses at all levels. Indeed, delegates to local congresses, who are in frequent face-to-face contact with their constituents, are even more serious than their national counterparts about securing the initiative in local political battles.

China's judicial system was not intended to serve as a check or a balance on the bureaucracy or legislature, nor does it so function. Its principal purpose is to serve as part of the apparatus of social control, alongside the police and the prosecutors' offices. Substantial changes were made to the criminal procedure law effective at the beginning of 1997. Before that, criminal cases were not brought to trial until the defendant had been proven guilty to the satisfaction of the court and the prosecutor, who worked closely together in investigating crimes. At trials, evidence was heard, and a panel of judges, some of them drawn from the local community, rendered its decision. Only at this point did the defense make its case, which was generally limited to presenting evidence in mitigation prior to sentencing. The new procedures have introduced the presumption of the defendant's innocence until proven guilty and an enhanced role for the defense lawyer in criminal trials. Now, as before, the public is encouraged to attend most court proceedings, which are intended to provide uplifting lessons in civic behavior.

Verdicts are subject to appeal, and the Supreme People's Court is the final court of appeal. It is not the function of the Supreme

People's Court or of any lower court, however, to rule on the constitutionality of the law violated by the defendant in the case. Hence, the court cannot serve as a check on the work of the government or legislature. The court system's principal function is, rather, to apply policies, laws, and regulations to specific cases.

China is divided into several regional systems. The seven military regions are features of the military command structure with no equivalent in civilian affairs, where the pyramid goes from the top—the central government headquartered in Beijing—to the provinces. There are thirty-one governments at the provincial level (thirty-two if one chooses, as does the government in Beijing, to regard Taiwan as a province), twenty-two of which are provinces; four city governments (Beijing, Tianjin, Chongqing, and Shanghai); and five "autonomous regions." These are provincelike units, the population of which contains substantial numbers of non-Han people (there are also smaller "autonomous" units within several provinces), but these ethnic minorities' autonomy from central control is largely fictive. Most of their local officials are drawn from the minority populations, the minority languages are used in government and education, and the populations are exempt from the one-child policy. On the other hand, though the ethnic-minority population as a whole is quite small, the autonomous regions are strategically located, many of them contain important deposits of oil and minerals, and Beijing worries about ethnic ties that cross China's national boundaries. So, many Han people have been moved into the autonomous regions, the regions are heavily garrisoned by the PLA, members of the ethnic-minority elites are brought into China's central and coastal provinces for schooling in political orthodoxy, and Beijing is quick to suppress any expressions of genuine autonomy.

Provinces are divided into counties and cities. The average Chinese county, of which there are approximately two thousand, is about a third larger than the average American county, of which there are approximately three thousand. Counties in China are administered from a county seat and are divided into townships, each of which is made up of a number of villages. The cities are similarly divided into districts, and districts into neighborhoods.

At the lowest level of the political system is the *danwei*, usually translated as "unit." In its heyday in the 1960s, the unit was a key element in the CCP's system of social control, and virtually every Chinese person was affiliated with a unit. The workplace was the unit for fully employed people; the school, for students; the neighborhood, for the unemployed. The unit was supposedly nurturing: its function was to provide for all of the needs of its members. But it was also the job of the unit to keep tabs on the lives of its members, and files on unit members contain biographical data, employment history, criminal records, and information on political attitudes. Moving from one unit to another almost never happened, and when it did, approval in advance from both the old and the new units was required, and the person's file was transferred as well.

With the gradual emergence of a labor market, more and more Chinese find themselves cut loose from both the support and the watchful eyes of their units. Today 100 million or so floating workers are not affiliated with units, nor are the approximately 25 million who work in the private sector. Even those who remain formally enrolled in a unit find that it is much less encompassing than it once was. The weakening of the *danwei* system is a major reason for most Chinese feeling that their government is less intrusive in their daily lives than it once was.

There is no formal division of authority between the center and the provinces or between the provinces and their counties and cities. Instead, the relationship among central, provincial, and local governments is thrashed out in case-by-case agreements that are subject to renegotiation as conditions and needs change.

In theory, certain powers are vested in the superior level over its subordinates. The most important among these is the power to appoint and dismiss officials. Here the dilemma for the central authorities is analogous to that confronted by the throne in earlier times: an outsider in a given locality is more likely to be loyal to the central-government officials who appointed him but less likely to have the connections that will make him effective in office, while the reverse is true of a local person.

Secondly, the government at each level reserves the power to draw up budgets and levy taxes in their subordinate units. The central government determines what is taxed, the rate at which it will be taxed, the proportion of tax revenue that will go to the provinces, and the government expenditures for which local authorities will be responsible. Provincial governments do the same for counties and cities under their jurisdiction.

Thirdly, the central government reserves the power to allocate and redistribute resources among the provinces; provincial governments do the same for counties and cities. Certain key resources—energy important among them—are allocated in this way. Governments in well-off provinces are taxed to help less well-off regions. This Robin Hood function of the central authorities was used most actively under Mao Zedong, among whose first principles was that of equality of opportunity for rich and poor regions of China.

Local governments, on the other hand, are not without resources of their own. First, they have the choice of cooperating with or making life impossible for appointed officials. Second, though the central government levies taxes and determines the distribution of revenues, until very recently local authorities actually collected the taxes and forwarded a portion to the central government.

Third, and most important, local officials can thwart central directives by inaction. When local officials engage in this tactic, China's power grid experiences gridlock. As those who have had dealings with Chinese bureaucrats are well aware, no phrase comes quite so quickly to a bureaucrat's lips as *kaolu yixiazi* ("I'll have to look into that a bit") or *yanjiu yanjiu* ("That needs some further study"). As we shall see presently, the bureaucratic style favored by the Chinese tends to result in a glacial pace of decision making and execution.

Writing in the middle of the Chinese Communist Revolution and the war against Japan, Mao described the relationship between military power and political power: "Political power grows out of the barrel of a gun, [but] our principle is that the Party commands the gun and the gun must never be allowed to command the Party." Control of the People's Liberation Army in China today rests in the hands of the Party's Central Military Commission, under which the Ministry of National Defense exercises operational and administrative control.

The Ministry's General Staff Department has operational command over the approximately three million active-duty troops via seven military regional commanders. Administrative command is exercised by the General Logistics Department. Finally, the General Political Department stations political officers at each level of command so as to ensure that "the Party commands the gun."

This relationship among Party, government, and army fundamentally altered on two occasions. At the height of Red Guard activity during the Cultural Revolution, the situation became anarchic, with both Party and government under attack and in no position to restore order; the PLA restored order and then set up and continued to participate in new political structures—"revolutionary committees," as they were called. The year 1969 marked an apex of military involvement in China's political system, with military officers exercising political control at every level of the system, including the Party's Central Committee. Some officers no doubt enjoyed their foray into politics and were reluctant to return to their barracks when, in the early 1970s, the regime tried to demilitarize the political system. But many others were eager to relinquish their political responsibilities, realizing that they were discharged at the expense of military readiness: China's poor showing in a border war with Vietnam in 1979 proved their point.

In a second moment of Party weakness during two incidents of civil unrest in 1989, the armed forces again intervened in the political realm. In Lhasa in March, when Tibetans demonstrated against Chinese control of their region, which had been complete ever since 1951, and interference with their religious practices, the army put down the demonstrations and martial law was declared. Two months later, Party officials, unable to respond effectively to the challenge posed by massive numbers of students and workers occupying the streets and central square of Beijing, once again asked the army to intervene. But the military involvement in politics that had followed the earlier episode was not repeated in the 1989 aftermath; the only evidence of a shift in the balance of power was in the military budget, which increased significantly each year thereafter. Today, however, many of China's neighbors are concerned by evidence of Chinese military expansionism and believe that the PLA and not the Foreign Ministry is calling the shots in China's foreign policy. They attribute the Party's inability to control the PLA to its indebtedness to and continuing dependence on it.

This, then, is the grid of political power in China: imperfectly formed branches of government with significantly unequal power and with no effective balance or check on one another. Within the bureaucracy, the highly specialized and vertically structured departments are incapable of communicating with one another easily. Meanwhile, the crosshatched horizontal elements of the grid— provinces, counties, and cities—though unable to defy the central government openly for long, can at least stick wrenches in its wheels and stall forward movement. Overlaying everything, and active at each node, is the Party, which regularly oversteps its bounds, lacks the confidence of the people, and is utterly unwilling to submit itself to criticism, opposition, or legal regulation. Finally, waiting in the wings, a highly patriotic army may find itself, *faute de mieux*, holding China together if political authority collapses.

Four characteristics of the political process in China are especially to be noted: consensus, bargaining, networking, and saving face.

Americans seem very comfortable with a simple majority— whether in a Supreme Court decision, a vote in Congress, or a local referendum on a school budget. Although as individuals we may not be satisfied with a given outcome, we do tend to regard it as legitimate if a majority has decided it. The Chinese vastly prefer consensus to a simple majority, and they prefer that this consensus be achieved at the lowest possible level in the political hierarchy: if one level finds it impossible to reach a consensus, the decision is bumped up to the next level. While strategies for building consensus are much the same as those for building a majority, it usually takes longer.

Bargaining, an almost universal characteristic of political interactions, in American political life usually focuses on issues that will have to be voted on: "I need your vote and this is what I'm prepared to do to get it." In the Chinese context, where voting is less common than consensus-building, bargaining is more diffuse: "I will be more inclined to lend you my support on your issue if you agree to lend me your support on mine." Given the scarcity of goods and an imperfectly developed market, exchanges of goods and services as well as support are also subject to political bargaining. Political bargainers in China pay careful attention to their relative rank and status, which affect both the process and the outcome. Political transactions often seem to be conducted with all the attention to protocol of an ambassadorial dinner party or a military change-of-command ceremony, and politicians seem to relish the bargaining. Case-by-case bargaining is almost always preferable in China to applying a uniform rule equally to every case.

Networking, too, a practice common in both American and Chinese political contexts, is vitally important. Business people newly introduced to China are taught the word *guanxi* (relationships), as though it were a powerful mantra unique to the Chinese setting. But "whom do I know who can . . ." is a formula that springs as quickly to the mind of a Westerner as it does to that of a Chinese. The difference is the degree to which it is appropriate to be proactive: a skillful practitioner of *guanxi* actively cultivates relationships that might be helpful at some unknown point in the future. Westerners may look on someone who does them an unbidden favor with some suspicion, but a Chinese person is likely to greet the unbidden favor without surprise and to assume that a request for a quid pro quo cannot be far behind.

Students of the Chinese psyche conclude that Chinese people have a greater aversion to conflict and disorder than do Americans. And it is unquestionably true that finding oneself shamed in public—losing face—is for a Chinese person an experience to be avoided if at all possible. Since open conflict is likely to result in loss of face for one of the parties, passive resistance accompanied by a perfectly opaque demeanor are the weapons of choice for the conflict-averse Chinese.

As a result of all these characteristics, the political process in China may often seem agonizingly slow and mystifyingly obscure to Westerners. Americans have a reputation for being blunt and impatient even among Europeans; it is no wonder they find it hard to make sense of Chinese bureaucrats.

The Chinese political system, then, far from being the well-oiled totalitarian machine it was once reputed to be, is a highly complex and inefficient structure that tends to thwart much more than it tends to foster effective governance. The central authority is meant to be ascendant over regional authority, and Party authority is meant to be ascendant over government authority, yet the system operates with a substantially weakened central authority and a party whose power and legitimacy are seriously eroded. Unless it changes significantly, the system lacks the capacity to address and resolve the many serious problems it now confronts.

# IV

# China's Economy:
# Who Owns What, Who Works Where,
# and Who Makes the Decisions?

Thirty years ago an ideological controversy erupted into public view after simmering bitterly within international communist circles for years. In 1963, a year before he was overthrown, Soviet premier Nikita Khrushchev scoffed at his erstwhile Chinese allies' view of communism:

To follow their line of thinking, it transpires that if a people walks in rope sandals and eats watery soup out of a common bowl that is communism, and if a working man lives well and wants to live even better tomorrow that is almost tantamount to the restoration of capitalism!

Mao Zedong denounced Khrushchev as a proponent of what he sneeringly labeled "goulash communism."

Twenty years later, however, Deng Xiaoping struck a remarkably Khrushchev-like note when he described the rationale behind his economic reforms:

Socialism means eliminating poverty. Pauperism is not socialism, still less communism. The superiority of the socialist system lies above all in its ability to develop the productive forces and to improve the people's material and cultural life.

Deng's first priority was to reform the Chinese economy so as to improve the standard of living. A second priority, always at a significant distance from the first, was to reform the political system. He was not an ideologue. He often sounded more like an American pragmatist than a Chinese revolutionary. His approach is encapsulated in his comment, "It does not matter whether the cat is white or black; if it catches mice it is a good cat." During the Cultural Revolution, the regime denounced him as one of those who would abandon socialist goals and take China "down the capitalist road." Still needing to protect himself against such charges when he returned to a position of authority in 1977, he enunciated what he called his "four cardinal principles." They were, he said, the irreducible nucleus of what had been the full-blown (some might well argue overblown) ideology of his predecessor, Mao: any reform measure was acceptable so long as it did not call into question the leadership of the Communist Party, the dictatorship of the proletariat, the correctness of Marxism-Leninism, or the goal of socialism.

In practice, Deng operated with just two principles that became, if anything, more fixed as he aged: reform measures were legitimate if they promoted rapid economic growth and if they did not weaken the Party's control of the political system; everything else was subject to compromise. This was particularly true with respect to the "socialism" of the fourth cardinal principle, which, in Deng's hands, became "socialism with Chinese characteristics."

As it exists today, "socialism with Chinese characteristics" is an economy moving rapidly and sometimes painfully from central planning to market decision making. It is an economy with a large but shrinking state-owned sector, a substantial and growing collective sector, and a rapidly burgeoning private sector. Liberal use has been made of capitalist methods to jump-start and then fuel truly remarkable growth over the last two decades.

The government is still the most important player in the Chinese economy, with about a hundred thousand state-owned industrial enterprises employing a workforce approaching fifty million. These enterprises operate as small, semi-independent communities within China's cities, the largest including as many as a half million people if managers, workers, service personnel, dependents, and retirees are taken into account. These state-owned factories were once all directly controlled by one or another government ministry. Forty years ago, ownership of most of them was turned over to provincial or municipal governments. Management schemes for them have come and gone over the years. At certain points, the factory manager has been given decision-making responsibility; at other times, his authority has been eclipsed by that of the factory's Party secretary. Today, as a result of reforms initiated a decade ago, the factory manager most usually is under contract to produce a given level of profit for a fixed period of time.

Prior to the beginning of the reforms, all profits from all enterprises reverted to the government at year's end. In cases where the enterprise had a deficit rather than a profit, the deficit would be made up with a government subsidy. With the reforms, the remittance of profit was abandoned and replaced by taxes, the rates set so as to leave a portion of the profits with the enterprises, and managers were permitted some flexibility in deciding how after-tax profits should be distributed. At the same time, the subsidies to make up deficits were replaced with bank loans on which interest is charged.

The state sector also includes about two-thirds of China's wholesale distributors, two-fifths of the country's fourteen million retail outlets, and all but a small handful of banks, schools, and hospitals. Most urban housing stock is owned and managed either by individual enterprises and units or by municipal governments. Finally, although the state sector is all but completely absent from the rural economy, about two-thousand-odd state farms employing some five million workers account for eleven million acres—about 4 percent of the total land under cultivation. These farms are mostly in remote areas where land is being reclaimed for cultivation and people are being resettled—in some instances for disciplinary reasons, in others to alter ethnic balances.

Despite the positive effects of the recent industrial reforms on productivity, the state sector is in trouble. So serious is the deterioration that many argue that a political and economic crisis will result if it is not immediately and effectively addressed. The state sector's share of industrial output is declining each year, slipping in 1993, for the first time in forty years, below 50 percent. Although figures vary, at least half and probably closer to two-thirds of the state-owned enterprises are operating at a loss. To avoid putting their workforce into the ranks of the jobless, the state is subsidizing these losses rather than allowing the enterprises to go bankrupt.

A collective enterprise, in Chinese parlance, is one that is owned and managed by the people who make up a *danwei*, a workplace or residential unit. The largest number of collective enterprises are owned by rural townships, but collectives are also found in schools, neighborhoods, and even army units. There are more than 25 million collective enterprises in China, with a workforce of close to 500 million people.

The business of the collective enterprise may be farming, manufacturing, transportation, or commerce. Resources are mobilized, the enterprise established, and the product produced and sold on the basis of decisions the group makes on its own. Members are also responsible for deciding how profits are to be divided—how much will be reinvested and how much distributed as compensation. Finally, they also decide how members are paid—whether on the basis of the amount of their initial investment, the level of their skills or expertise, the amount of work they do, or the difficulty of the tasks they perform.

In legal terms, title to the assets of a state-owned enterprise is vested in "the whole people"—all the citizens of the country (or province or city). Title to a collective's assets is vested in its members. The collective is licensed and taxed by the local government. It may or may not have business relations with state-owned enterprises, either buying its raw materials from or selling all or a portion of its product to them. In some cases collectives have been formed within state-owned factories in order to diversify their product lines, to provide work for the underemployed, or to augment sagging profits. A more radical solution to the problem of losses in state-owned enterprises is to sell off a losing enterprise to its workers.

Virtually all agricultural production in China is collectively owned and managed, but reforms have rendered the collective nature of these arrangements ambiguous at best. The more than 95 percent of cultivable land in China that is not controlled by state farms is collectively owned by citizens of villages and townships where the land is located. The "household-responsibility system," initiated as one of Deng's first economic reforms in the late 1970s, called for leasing the right to use plots of this land to individual households according to a contract stipulating the amount of grain to be produced on the plots. Contracts were awarded on the basis of the household's probable ability to fulfill the terms given its size and the number of able-bodied workers in it. Everything produced on the leased plot over and above the contractual amount can be disposed of by the household as it wishes—sold to the state (ordinarily at a higher price than that received for the contracted grain), sold on the free market, or consumed by the family.

Contracts were initially signed for a one-year term. To encourage farmers to invest in improving the land, the terms were extended to three, five, fifteen, and, in some instances today, even fifty years. Contracts can be inherited, bought, and sold. With key decisions thus being made at the household level and with the distinction between use rights and ownership rights blurred as a result of the extension of contracts over long periods, the "collective" nature of this economic activity becomes attenuated indeed.

There are some thirty-three thousand townships in China. The average township has about 750 collective enterprises, 10 of which are involved in agricultural production, 300 or so in industrial production, a roughly equal number in the service sector, and the remainder in construction and transportation. In addition, more than 2 million collectively owned industrial enterprises are located in China's cities, and probably an equal number are engaged in service trades.

Although still small in terms both of number of workers or enterprises and of output, the private sector is the fastest growing part of the Chinese economy. Close to half a million private enterprises are located mostly in China's cities. They employ, on average, fewer than fifteen workers each and hold less than forty thousand dollars in registered capital, though a few are much larger.

Also included in the private sector for statistical purposes are the more than 200,000 foreign joint ventures. By the end of 1993 the cumulative total of foreign investment in China had reached $60 billion, and, most significantly, goods produced by foreign-invested firms accounted for more than a quarter of China's exports.

Furniture, personal effects, and individual bank accounts are all privately owned by both rural and urban Chinese. In addition, rural residents own their own homes, though they have use rights, not title, to the land they live on.

About three-quarters of the Chinese population live in the countryside. Among these 900 million people, there is a workforce of
about 550 million, up to 100 million of whom elect to seek temporary work in the city. Of the 450 million who remain in the
countryside, close to 70 percent are employed in agriculture (including farming, forestry, fisheries, and animal husbandry). These
310 million agricultural workers are almost all under contract in
the household-responsibility system and are thus part of the collective sector. The remainder work on state-owned farms. There is
a substantial surplus of labor in Chinese agriculture: it is estimated that at least 70 million workers could be redeployed with
no reduction in agricultural output.

## Employment in China
Total = 1.2 billion people

| URBAN | RURAL |
|---|---|
| 25% = 300M | 75% = 900M |

| 7M unemployed | 170M workforce | | 100M "floaters" | 450M workforce | |
|---|---|---|---|---|---|
| STATE | PRIVATE | COLLECTIVE | STATE | PRIVATE | COLLECTIVE |
| 110M | 30M | 30M | 5M | 10M | |
| | | | | INDUSTRY | AGRICULTURE |
| | | | | 125M | 310M |

| SECTORS: | STATE | PRIVATE | COLLECTIVE |
|---|---|---|---|
| % of workers | 18 | 6 | 76 |
| % of output | 36 | 15 | 49 |
| Percent rate of growth, 1995 | 4 | 52 | 15 |

(Source: China Statistical Yearbook 1996)

In part to absorb some of this surplus labor, in part to raise household income, and in part to boost the production of manufactured goods, reformers have actively encouraged opening up collective factories owned and managed by township and village governments. There are now nearly two million of these township and village enterprises (TVEs), employing a workforce of more than 125 million. They tend to be small outfits with low capitalization, thrown together quickly with little or no regard for their ill effects on air and water.

The private sector in the countryside is less well developed than it is in the city. About two million rural residents are employed in privately owned enterprises. Another 8 million are self-employed, primarily in handicrafts and other sideline activities.

Many rural households find that it makes good economic sense to keep a hand in several sectors. Holding on to the farming contract means access to fresh food and a certain amount of security, but a household's income can be significantly augmented if one or more of its members works in a TVE or a privately owned enterprise and further augmented, with luck, if a family member moves to a city and finds a job as a day laborer in construction, transportation, or a service industry.

Rural income has increased threefold since the reforms began in 1978. This does not match the fivefold increase in urban incomes during the same period, and the gap between city and countryside is ever more pronounced and aggravating to rural residents. Moreover, rural amenities by no means match those available in the city: schools are poor, and the tuition, while reasonable enough, is an expense that many find onerous. Medical care is less accessible than it once was and has significantly increased in cost. Finally, because they are a part of the collective sector, very few rural residents are covered by retirement programs and must rely on their children to support them when they leave the workforce.

The remaining 300 million Chinese people are urban residents. About 170 million of them are in the workforce and 7 to 10 million are unemployed. About 65 percent of urban workers work in the state sector: 50 million in state-owned industrial enterprises, another 50 million in the commercial and service sectors, education, and health care, and approximately 10 million as government and Party bureaucrats. Among the many problems plaguing the state-owned industries is that of excess staff. Some estimates place the number of surplus workers in state-owned factories as high as 20 million.

Jobs in the state sector used to be much sought after because of good pay, excellent fringe benefits, and a tenure system that made it virtually impossible to be fired. Workers receive a wage based on an eight-grade scale set by the state; during the last ten years, wages have been augmented by bonuses designed to reward productivity and performance, though in practice they are often given to workers regardless of their output. In addition, state-sector employees receive heavily subsidized housing, health care, primary and secondary education for their children, stipends that help to offset living costs, and generous retirement packages. For most factory managers, coordinating this benefits package is as great a responsibility as overseeing the production process. In addition to supervising an assembly line, they must also oversee schools, clinics, housing blocks, and retirement communities, all of which are a part of their domain. Covering the costs of this generous benefits package has pushed many state-owned enterprises into the red.

Collective enterprises in China's cities employ about 30 million workers. The remaining 30 million work in the private sector, 3 million of them in foreign joint ventures. China's collective and private enterprises have considerable flexibility with respect to whom they hire or fire and how much they pay their workers, but most of these enterprises offer no fringe benefits, and when they do it is much less than state enterprises offer. So to attract qualified workers, they must offer higher wages. Because a nationwide social-security system has yet to be implemented, only state employees are guaranteed retirement incomes. And while some of the most profitable collective and private enterprises offer retirement packages, most do not.

In recent years, China's urban population has been augmented by nearly 30 percent with the arrival of as many as 100 million floating workers. Until ten years ago, moving from countryside to city was virtually impossible, given a rationing system initiated in 1959 that limited any person's access to necessities, such as grain, cooking oil, and cotton cloth. Every household had an officially registered residence, and ration coupons were issued at one's place of residence and could only be redeemed locally. When economic reform made these necessities available on the free market, the rationing system no longer worked as a means of controlling geographical mobility, and a small but rapidly expanding labor market was born in which enterprises can recruit freely and people can choose where they work.

Rural residents who go to China's cities in search of more lucrative employment tend to take the first jobs they find. Most employment is short-term, and, although quite high paying, there is no job security and, of course, no benefits package. Moreover, the floaters are not officially city residents and hence have no claim on public services. Because they cannot live in regular housing, most of them go to squatter settlements in the suburbs. If they fall ill, they must cover the costs of their own health care. While many of them have come to the city alone, those who bring their families cannot put their children in public schools. Their presence in the cities is tolerated because they are a relatively low-cost and obligation-free labor force for the burgeoning construction projects under way everywhere, but they are potentially disruptive.

.    .    .

In his pursuit of economic reform, Deng Xiaoping had an opponent with a great deal less faith in the virtues of market forces. Chen Yun, an advocate of the centrally planned economy, is famous for his description of the economic plan as a birdcage and the economy as a bird within the cage. Chen believed in enlarging the birdcage to allow the bird more room to move about, a pragmatic approach to economic problems that at key points in his career enabled him to help bring China back from the brink of economic disaster. Still, it would never have been acceptable from Chen's point of view to open the door of the cage and allow the bird to fly free.

Chen's influence was at its height during the 1950s, at which time the Chinese economy, like the Soviet one after which it was modeled, operated under a comprehensive plan. In any economy, decisions have to be made about how national resources—land, raw materials, labor, and capital—are allocated. In an ideal market economy, these decisions are made on the basis of supply and demand; in an ideal planned economy, they are based on the plan.

The Chinese economy has never been wholly governed by plan, in part because of a lack of experience and expertise, in part because of a lack of solid statistical data, in part because of a bias in favor of decentralized decision making, and in part because of a proclivity to throw the plan aside periodically in bursts of ideological fervor. Nonetheless, the State Planning Commission drew up annual, five-year, and in some cases ten-year economic plans embodying decisions about the allocation of national resources. Flexibility was limited by China's "givens." In 1949, with the triumph of communism, the new regime found itself with a reasonable resource base and a surplus of unskilled labor, but China had a shortage of land, capital, and skilled labor. Land, as a resource, was taken out of play in the plan, inasmuch as title to all of it was vested in either the state or the rural cooperatives and no rents were charged for it.

The principal focus of the plan was on state-owned industry, which, at the height of Chinese central planning in the late 1950s, accounted for nearly 90 percent of industrial output. The plan stipulated the amount of raw materials to be extracted and processed, the amount of energy to be generated, the amount of manufactured goods to be produced, the prices at which producer goods and products would be exchanged, the allocation and wages of the labor required to achieve these goals, and the amount and destination of investments. But agricultural production, too, was governed by national quotas, in turn divided into provincial, county, and, ultimately, commune or collective quotas: the prices at which quota grain was purchased and sold were determined by the plan; state-owned enterprises conducted the wholesale and retail trade.

Peasants had private plots, also, on which they were allowed to grow goods for their own consumption or for sale on the rural free markets once they had fulfilled their obligations to produce for the state quotas. Handicrafts they produced as a sideline were either sold on the market or distributed through the collective. Rural free markets were subject to close regulation and during the high tide of the Great Leap Forward were shut down entirely.

Functioning on the margins of the economic plan were collective enterprises, which gradually increased their share of industrial output from one-tenth to nearly one-quarter of the total by the late 1970s. The small private sector had been largely eliminated by the late 1950s and was reborn only after the reforms were launched.

A labor market was almost completely eliminated in China in the late 1950s. Skilled labor was scarce, and if its movement had not been subject to government regulation, workers would have bid up the cost of their services to unacceptable levels. Also, since unskilled labor was overly plentiful, particularly in the rural sector, and per capita income was consistently higher in the urban economy than in the rural one, free movement of labor would have resulted in a massive immigration of rural workers into the already crowded cities.

The shortage of skilled labor was addressed by expanding gradually the secondary and postsecondary training facilities for scientists, technicians, and skilled workers. Through a job-assignment system, graduates of these institutions were channeled into the state sector where they were needed. Once assigned, employees were given what amounted to lifetime job security, but the quid pro quo was that lateral moves were virtually impossible to effect. Meanwhile the risk of urban in-migration by underemployed rural workers in search of higher pay was avoided by implementing the rationing system described above. Permission to shift one's household registration from the countryside to the city was almost never granted: where you were born was likely to be where you spent your life; where you began working was likely to be where you retired.

This centrally planned economy was by no means a total failure in its three decades from 1950 to 1980. In fact, economic performance in China was worst during the Great Leap Forward and the Cultural Revolution when the plan was set aside and a campaign mentality replaced it. The economy grew at an average annual rate of 8.6 percent; industrial output led this growth with an average annual rate of 10 percent; while agricultural output, growing more modestly, was outpaced by population growth. Still, the end result was an abysmally low per capita gross national product and a living standard that fell far short of the expectations aroused by promises of a bright socialist future. When he launched his program of economic reforms, Deng Xiaoping's proposal was to expand that portion of the economy in which market forces were decisive while at the same time keeping the central plan for the state sector. He hoped that a vibrant, rapidly growing market-driven sector would, by its success, persuade his skeptical colleagues and potential successors of its merits.

Agriculture was the first to experience the introduction of market forces. Deng's household-responsibility system re-empowered the household, giving it the authority to decide how it used its labor and strong incentives to increase productivity. But prices and production quotas were still in government hands: like all commodities, grain had had a very low price, limiting the exposure of the government, which supplemented the urban population's income by selling grain below cost; without quotas, this low price would have encouraged farmers to turn to more lucrative crops.

There have been recent experiments with allowing the market to determine grain prices and allowing prices to determine the amount produced. But this strategy resulted in a very sharp rise in the price of grain—a more than 50 percent increase in 1994 —that seriously exacerbated urban inflation. Regulating grain prices helps to reduce inflation, but overregulation undermines the incentive needed to increase grain production. Today more agricultural produce is traded on the free market than in state stores. Free market prices are higher, but the quality, supply, and variety of fresh meat and produce available to city dwellers has increased markedly over the last decade.

The success of the household-responsibility system in increasing agricultural output was useful to the reformers in building support for their efforts when they turned to China's cities. The straightforward solutions that had worked so successfully in the countryside were, however, ill-suited to the complex urban economy. Among the first reform steps was permission to revive the private sector. Very small privately owned enterprises in the service sector were the first to appear: food stands, tailor shops, cigarette vendors, and the like. These small businesses gave jobs to many people returning to the cities after having been sent to the countryside during the Cultural Revolution and provided goods and services that were unavailable in state-owned stores and restaurants. At first, there was a limit on the number of nonfamily members each business was permitted to hire, though exceptions were made where needs existed that were not being filled by state-owned enterprises. But soon there were a number of very large enterprises, some of them operating under the same name and management they had had thirty years before.

The collective sector was encouraged to expand as well. Workers in state-owned enterprises, schools, hospitals, and government offices were encouraged to form collectives that, because of their smaller size and greater flexibility, could develop new product lines, employment practices, and markets. Their immediate success promoted the merits of the market to otherwise conservative skeptics and encouraged them to explore the ways the state-owned businesses could take advantage of it.

By the mid-1980s, reform of the state-sector economy began in earnest. It was at this point that taxes replaced the remission of profits and enterprise managers became responsible for their profits, losses, and investment decisions. These reforms were interrupted by the retrenchment measures taken to slow the overheated economy in 1988–89; efforts to revive them in the early 1990s were hindered by mounting losses.

Meanwhile, the Chinese economy was being opened up to the outside world. Trade expanded rapidly and the government actively encouraged foreign investment. China's experience in the world economy had been very limited, self-reliance having been a guiding principle and foreign trade having been closely controlled by the central government and confined, for the most part, to the socialist world. Although trade in the mid-1950s had amounted to nearly a quarter of China's national income, the proportion had sunk to a mere 6 percent when the Cultural Revolution drew to a close in 1970.

The "open policy" of the reform era called at first for substantial importation of technology, which would be funded by the export of oil. When China's oil reserves proved insufficient for this, and exploration and drilling operations too time-consuming, the strategy shifted to one of encouraging technology transfer through foreign investment in joint ventures; special economic zones were set aside where preferential regulations were put in place to attract this investment, the first four in Guangdong and Fujian Provinces in 1979; similar arrangements were extended to fourteen coastal cities and to the island of Hainan five years later. (The most recent addition to the list of zones and regions is the Pudong area in the city of Shanghai.) The third stage in this process was a substantial expansion of production for export, led by the foreign-invested industrial sector.

We can see, then, that the critical decisions about allocation of land, raw materials, labor, and capital, once made by the Party-state and incorporated in an economic plan, are being made, after nearly twenty years of reform, by the market. Contracts involving use rights to agricultural land can now be bought and sold, so there is the beginning of what amounts to a real-estate market in the countryside. State-owned enterprises and governments in the cities are selling housing stock to the tenants so as to reduce the heavy burden of providing subsidized housing. Use rights and sometimes title to land are also involved in some joint-venture contracts. In the case of deficit-producing state enterprises where the only attractive asset of value is the land on which the factory is located, foreign investors, after signing a deal, level the factory buildings in order to put the land to more profitable use. In effect, the state is raising capital by liquidating some of its landholdings and, in the process, creating a real-estate market for the first time in more than forty years.

The dual-allocation system for raw materials—a portion allocated by the government, a portion allocated on the basis of supply and demand—has been dismantled, and today the market determines commodity allocation. Only a few key commodities—steel, coal, and oil and electric power—are still allocated to state-owned enterprises, and even here the prices, held artificially low to maximize industrial profits, are gradually being raised to the world-market level.

Price reform is of course a sensitive issue in an economy as vulnerable to the effects of inflation as China's. Nonetheless, 95 percent of retail prices, 90 percent of agricultural prices, and 85 percent of capital goods prices are now market determined, though when urban inflation gets out of hand, the government still tends to regulate food prices, since the price of food accounts for as much as 70 percent of the consumer price index.

The government has been reluctant to give up control of the allocation of labor, and a genuine labor market has been slow to develop. Nonetheless, decisions about movement in the workforce are much more likely to be made outside the government than they were twenty years ago. Though it is still very difficult for anyone to move from one job to another within the state sector (those with scarce skills or good performance records find their current employer reluctant to let them leave, and those without these qualifications are unlikely to find a new employer willing to agree to their transfer), many workers have chosen to leave the security of their state-sector position entirely and *xia hai*—plunge into the sea of private or collective enterprises. Of course one loses the benefits package, including access to housing, a health plan, and a retirement plan, but the advantages are higher salaries and greater freedom to change jobs or even residence.

Others seek to have the best of both worlds by keeping their state-sector position and taking a second job in the collective or private sector. Factory workers, many of them involuntarily placed on short hours or on furlough, find part- or full-time work in private or collective enterprises; doctors with positions in hospitals or medical schools take on private patients; government employees, capitalizing on their access and connections, set themselves up as business consultants, moving, sometimes with less than perfect precision, along the fine line that divides ethical practice from corruption. And this tendency to function in several sectors is as common in the countryside as it is in the city: moonlighting has so many advantages as a strategy that it would not be surprising to find that most Chinese families today have more than one employer and a foot in more than one sector.

Allocation of capital is the last decision to be opened up to market forces. As a part of the urban reforms a decade ago, state-owned enterprises were to be weaned from their dependence on subsidies to cover deficits or to fund expansion: government funds would continue to be available but only in the form of interest-bearing loans, for the eventual repayment of which enterprises would be held accountable.

The subsequent poor performance of most of China's state-owned enterprises and the government's unwillingness to suffer the political consequences of adding the employees of bankrupt businesses to the ranks of the disgruntled unemployed have frequently rendered this reform moot. Subsidies continue to flow into state-sector business. Nominally called loans, they accumulate as uncollectible assets in the banking system, precluding more productive use of capital.

A reform of the banking system aimed at addressing this problem was undertaken at the beginning of 1993. Vice Premier Zhu Rongji, dissatisfied with its implementation, dismissed the head of the People's Bank of China six months later and temporarily took over its administration himself. The goal was to make the People's Bank of China a central bank, to create a series of policy banks that would address the problem of uncollectible loans in the system as a whole, and to direct the flow of credit away from speculative projects and toward projects that would serve the development of the overall economy. The lack of appropriate levers of control has made the problem of regulating the part-planned, part-market Chinese economy so intractable.

What, exactly, is socialist about "socialism with Chinese characteristics," then? A cold-eyed response to the question would have to be "Not much at all." The elements most commonly associated with a socialist economy are public ownership of the principal means of production, economic activity largely determined by government decision as contained in an economic plan, a heavy dose of egalitarianism, and a high level of government attention to the welfare of the working population. All these elements are in the process of being dismantled in China under the current program of economic reform. And however negative the consequences, there is little likelihood that China will return to socialist solutions.

# The Chinese Armed Forces

The People's Liberation Army (PLA) is a major force in the Chinese economy, a potential participant in its politics, and a growing cause of concern to other nations in Asia.

The nominally civilian hand that controls the gun in China is that of the Central Military Commission. In the restructuring of the political system that occurred in the mid-1980s, it was anticipated that there would be both a Party and a government military commission—the one to oversee military policy, the other to implement it. But in fact there is a single seven-member Party commission, which was chaired by Deng Xiaoping himself until 1989, when he relinquished the position to Jiang Zemin. The commission hardly constitutes *civilian* control, given that all its members save Jiang Zemin are uniformed officers and include the former head of the PLA navy and the Minister of National Defense.

Taking its orders directly from the Central Military Commission, the Ministry of National Defense is divided, as we have seen, into three major departments: the General Staff Department, with operational command of the three million active troops, which takes responsibility for operational planning, intelligence, and procurement; the General Logistics Department, responsible for finance, supply, maintenance, and transport; and the General Political Department, which is there to ensure the political correctness of the military forces and to draft regulations and run personnel matters—assignment, promotion, and retirement. In addition, there are a Discipline Inspection Commission and a Commission on Science, Technology, and Industry (COSTIND).

As in the civilian political structure, where provincial and local government officials often thwart the implementation of directives issued by the central government, regional commanders and their subordinate garrison commanders often thwart the commands issued by the central military authorities. In the first twenty-five years of the People's Republic, the regional commanders were the generals whose troops had been responsible for "liberating" the areas under their command. Concurrently holding positions in local Party and government organizations, they became well-connected fixtures, advantageously placed to implement, modify, or ignore central directives.

But this monopoly on local power was broken by Premier Zhou Enlai, who shortly before his death in 1976 succeeded in reassigning most of the regional commanders to new posts. Such reassignments have continued to recur periodically since then, and they reduce the resources with which the regional commanders are able to resist central directives, though not their tendency to try to do so.

The PLA, including the army, navy, and air force, has a troop of about 3.2 million men and women—about 25 percent smaller than the force level of the late 1970s, when the PLA had been increased in size in anticipation of a 1979 border war with Vietnam. Since 1985, approximately a million troops have been demobilized, returning the army to its pre-Vietnam size. This force is somewhat more than twice the size of the American military, which, as of 1995, had about 1.5 million people in uniform. And beyond the

uniformed personnel, the Chinese military establishment includes
about 4 million military dependents and several million civilian
employees and workers. Also, the People's Armed Police (PAP),
administered as a branch of the PLA, with about 700,000 members, is the first line of defense in the case of civil unrest. (It was
because PAP was so unsuccessful at this in the spring of 1989
that the PLA was called in.) In the aftermath of the Tiananmen
massacre, PAP was strengthened substantially, its budget augmented, its riot-control equipment upgraded; and a large number
of demobilized PLA troops were reassigned to PAP.

China's armed forces and the military budget that supports them
are among the world's largest, and the budget has been expanding
rapidly. A portion of the funds has gone for new equipment from
foreign suppliers, including planes and submarines (negotiations
were also begun but not completed to purchase an aircraft carrier),
and other Asian powers naturally enough see this upgrading of the
Chinese arsenal as related to a possibly aggressive and expansionist new policy.

The military budget passed annually by the National People's
Congress is alone not sufficient to underwrite the modernization
of China's armed forces, and indeed it accounts for only a portion
of the revenues available to the PLA, which uses its extensive
system of factories not only to meet its own logistics needs but
also to produce weapons for sale abroad and consumer goods for
domestic sales, profits from which supplement the official budget.

The official budget is four times larger today than it was before
the reforms of the late 1970s. But given the rapid growth of China's
national budget and gross national product, military expenditures
have actually declined sharply in relative terms. Still the rate of
growth of the military budget compared to that of total government
expenditures, recently as high as between 15 and 20 percent each
year in contrast to 5 percent, alarms China's neighbors. (The year

1995 was an exception on both counts, with military expenditures up 23 percent and the total budget up 18 percent.) Some have argued that the budget increases accorded the PLA constitute a quid pro quo for services rendered when the PLA came to the aid of the Party elders, but others take a longer view, seeing the current expansion as compensation for the 1980s, when military budgets shrank in real terms. The reform goal had been described as the "four modernizations"—that of agriculture, industry, science and technology, and the armed forces—and Deng told the PLA that he took the sequence in which these were listed seriously: military modernization had to wait until Chinese industry and technology could supply the needs of the PLA. Past experience, with the armed forces heavily dependent on Soviet equipment, training, and technical assistance, was not to be repeated. So the military budgets of the 1980s reflected these priorities, first decreasing after the post-Vietnam demobilization, then averaging less than 4 percent annual growth while the national budget increased at four times that rate. Taking the effects of inflation into account, one can see that the PLA actually lost ground over the decade 1978–88; prices doubled while military expenditures increased by only 25 percent, giving a net effect of a 1.2 percent loss per year.

Another way of putting it is to say that budget increases since 1989, which have averaged a bit over 16 percent, have done no more than allow the armed forces to recoup their position at the beginning of the reform period. An index of real growth in military expenditures using 1978 as 100 shows a figure of just 100.28 after the large budget increase of 1995.

As one might imagine, this decline in military expenditures had a serious effect on morale, as military pay fell seriously behind civilian wages. By 1988 an officer earned only a little more than half of what an average urban worker earned; a new conscript's pay was a fifth of that. This discrepancy naturally affected military recruitment. Once, the PLA had been a highly desirable avenue of advancement for rural young people, offering training, better pay, and, perhaps most important, geographical mobility, and there was stiff competition to get in so recruits tended to be very capable young people. Today, with so many lucrative employment opportunities in the countryside, few qualified young people are attracted to a military career.

The official military budget tells only a part of the story—by far the smaller part, some argue. The "real" Chinese military budget is harder to estimate because it is not a matter of public record, and, depending on the accounting practices one employs, the numbers vary widely, but $30 billion is roughly the midpoint between the lowest and the highest estimates.

On the expenditure side, this real budget, larger than the official budget, includes a range of goods, services, and even salaries that are usually included in the reporting of military budgets in other countries. (For example, research and development—estimated by some to be as high as $5 billion per year—is not included in the official budget.) Some observers have assumed that procurement of military equipment from foreign suppliers—a major item in recent years—is also off-budget, but more recent research indicates that it is included in the official budget.

The PLA has two major sources of income, not reported in the official budget. The first, the sales of weapons to foreign purchasers, is estimated to have been nearly $2 billion annually by the late 1980s. With the end of the Iran–Iraq War, to both sides of which China supplied arms, and with pressure from the United States and other nations to restrict these arms sales, China has reduced the volume, but they probably continue to generate up to $1 billion annually. Profit from the second source of off-the-books income for the PLA, the sale of civilian products produced in military-controlled factories, may add as much as an additional $1 billion per year to PLA revenues.

The armed forces are responsible for some ten thousand factories that employ about seven hundred thousand workers. Most of these are administered by the General Logistics Department, others by the General Political and General Staff Departments. This network of military factories is the legacy of a policy initiative of Mao Zedong to make the army self-sufficient in food and supplies and to promote the development of China's hinterlands. Locating military factories in remote areas had two advantages: the army's sources of supplies would be dispersed and thus more impervious to enemy attack; and industrialization of the hinterlands would contribute to Mao's paramount goal of egalitarian development of China as a whole. At the peak of its expansion, this so-called third line of defense-managed factories numbered thirty thousand and employed nearly three million workers.

Today enemy attack is a less-than-present danger, and the goal of egalitarian development has been abandoned in favor of a policy of "building on the best," so the third-line factories seem more a liability than an asset. Efforts have been under way for some years to relocate them nearer lines of communication, redirect their production, restore their profitability, and close those that cannot easily be transformed. In the last decade the central military authorities have inaugurated a range of new enterprises, among them a commercial satellite-launching service. Their expanded economic activities not only augmented the lean budgets of the mid-1980s but also gave work to some of the one million soldiers demobilized then.

Of the ten thousand PLA-managed factories, probably a third are losing money each year—a performance record significantly better than that of the rest of the state sector. Those that are turning a profit are the ones that sell to civilian consumers. At the beginning of the reform period, about 8 percent of the output of military-managed factories was destined for the civilian economy, but by 1992 the proportion had risen to 65 percent and is currently

85 percent. One estimate has placed the market share of these consumer goods at 20 percent and has suggested that the PLA has set a 50 percent market share as its target by the turn of the century.

In addition to these state-sector factories, the armed forces have also spawned a plethora of collective enterprises attached to regional and local military commands and operated by uniformed troops or their dependents. Profits from these enterprises, impossible to calculate, generally go directly to the command under which they operate and are mostly used to augment the pay and benefits of the troops.

Finally, the PLA is not immune to the attraction of foreign joint ventures. There are currently more than two dozen such foreign-invested military firms.

The most immediate effect of all this economic activity, a substantial augmentation of the funds available to the military, is difficult to assess. A 1994 study of the Chinese army concluded that the net effect of off-budget income and military expenditures debited to other accounts in the official budget increased China's military spending fivefold to a figure in the neighborhood of $40–$50 billion per year. Were this true, it would place China second after the United States or third after Russia in military spending, with its military outlay at 7 percent of gross national product (GNP), a rate nearly twice that of the United States. Others more cautiously argue that the PLA does not have direct access to all the profits from production attributed to its enterprises and suggest that the real military budget is no more than twice the official one—about $15 billion per year, or 3 percent of GNP.

Whatever the total revenue generated by military entrepreneurship, it is clear that only a small portion is being allocated to upgrade and expand the Chinese arsenal. Most of the off-budget income is used, instead, to augment military pay, so as to offer a marginally competitive standard of living for military personnel and to help ward off the effect of inflation on their real income, and in investment to expand the already huge PLA-controlled economic empire, for example in Hong Kong real estate. The Army's economic activity has important unintended effects. It enmeshes the armed forces deeply in China's new market economy and its connections with the world economy, and where they were once regarded as a conservative force opposed to economic reform, many military officers would now find their personal and professional interests seriously prejudiced were the reforms to be reversed. Secondly, it affects combat readiness: time, energy, and thought spent managing businesses are time, energy, and thought not spent in military training. The PLA's capability to defend China's borders and its national interests is, then, hardly strengthened by encouraging the military to augment its revenue through entrepreneurship. People taking this view argue that the official budget should be augmented so that the Army can devote its attention to its primary mission, and indeed, there is evidence that the substantial increase in the official military budget for 1995 may have been accompanied by a series of measures designed to curtail some of the Army's more ambitious business ventures.

The term "praetorian rule" is sometimes used to describe a situation that results from a nation's military force seizing control from a government it regards as inept or corrupt. Under what circumstances might the PLA be tempted to establish praetorian rule in China and how capable would it be of doing so?

The Party has been very effective in preventing the emergence of any national organization that could mount strong political opposition. There is no church, no labor union, no political party in China that could do what these organizations have done in Eastern Europe and the former Soviet Union when Communist Party control unraveled. The Chinese people, told that their choice is one between Party rule and anarchy, have reluctantly but firmly chosen

Party rule. But in fact, there is a third choice: the PLA could step in should the Party collapse in the same fashion that the Communist Party of the Soviet Union collapsed in August 1991.

The Army has a number of characteristics that lend themselves to its serving as a praetorian administration. Most important, of course, is its arms. It is also highly patriotic and its intense patriotism could motivate it to intervene politically, were there a real danger of the collapse of central authority and a breakup of the Chinese state into competing regional entities. And the PLA enjoys credibility. While many people in China have come to question the credibility of the Party, fewer question the legitimacy of the Army. As a corollary, the PLA has a reputation for being less corrupt than the Party.

In 1989 the military rallied in Beijing to enforce martial law and save a regime on the brink of collapse because of its commanders' personal loyalty to Deng Xiaoping. It is highly unlikely that they would agree to do so again on the same terms. No other political leader has personal connections equivalent to those that Deng used to secure its compliance, and the negative consequences of the 1989 intervention were very serious, losing the PLA respect in the eyes of many of China's urban population and highly valued contacts with foreign military leaders as well. The next time out it will be patriotism rather than loyalty to the Party or to particular leaders that brings the military into the political arena. Although they could use new Party leaders as a cover for their actions, they would function as an alternative to the existing Party, not as a crutch for it.

But could the PLA succeed in restoring central authority? The PLA and PAP have a virtually total monopoly on armed force in Chinese society. As the legitimacy of the Party and the central government has declined and the independence of local and regional governments has increased, the implicit threat of the use of this armed force has become politically more and more important.

But the PLA was ill-equipped and ill-trained for what it did in the streets of Lhasa and Beijing in 1989. Upgrading PAP in budget, equipment, and training after those episodes was intended to rectify its shortcomings in civil enforcement, but it is easy to imagine the seven-hundred-thousand-strong PAP, backed by the three-million-strong PLA, stretched very thin were they forced to restore and maintain order over any significant portion of China.

Public respect for the Party and the PLA derives from their having fought a successful revolution. Respect for the Party seriously eroded over decades of disastrously counterproductive economic and social policies, but respect for the PLA suffered no such decline in the 1950s and 1960s—indeed, its reputation was enhanced by its effectiveness when the Cultural Revolution threatened anarchy. But China's urban population lost respect for the military at the time of the Tiananmen massacre; that this loss of respect did not go beyond the cities was due to a surprisingly effective propaganda blitz about the "counterrevolutionary incident," which portrayed the PLA as victim rather than perpetrator. Hence, while neither Party nor Army is popular in the cities, in the populace as a whole respect for the PLA almost certainly outweighs respect for the Party.

From early on, this has been based in great part on the PLA's reputation for scrupulous honesty, tight discipline, and incorruptibility, especially during the revolution and civil war, but after 1949 as well. As corruption has come to taint China's politics more and more, and as politicians have failed to curb it, the PLA's reputation for honesty has frequently been called to public attention. But unfortunately, that reputation is not what it once was. During the Cultural Revolution, the PLA became deeply involved with national and local political machines, which gave it new opportunities to engage in corrupt behavior. More recently, corruption is flourishing where the political realm intersects with the economy, and the PLA's heavy involvement in entrepreneurial activity is the source of most of the current perception of corruption in the ranks.

In some respects, the PLA is ill-suited or ineffective as a praetorian force. It is a specialist organization, not an organization of generalists, and it is short on experience in civilian administration. Although it is reasonably unified, exercising the responsibilities of civil administration would very likely divide it along several fault lines. Because its mission is that of national defense, there is no reason to expect that its officers would be especially good at directing economic development or political and economic reform. There is no question that a military caretaker government in China would look after the interests of the armed forces, but there are serious questions as to its ability to look after the national interest.

The PLA has had more experience than some armies in civil administration, but that experience is now twenty years old, and only a handful of officers on active duty remember it. One could argue that, since economic issues dominate China's political agenda and since the PLA is acquiring substantial managerial experience in business, it is better suited to be a caretaker than it was during the Cultural Revolution. Still, a PLA-led regime would have to depend on the technical and managerial expertise of those on whose behalf it was caretaking.

Also, within the officer corps there are strong differences of opinion over the question whether the PLA should ever take on political assignments. There are, in addition, divisions of the kind found in most military forces: rivalries among the services and differences of viewpoint based on age, rank, and time in service. Finally, the central military authorities and the regional military commands are divided along parallel lines to those of the center-region political divisions.

The long-standing division between so-called reds and experts in the PLA dates from the immediate aftermath of the Korean War, when some officers began to argue for a new strategy to replace the guerrilla doctrine of the revolutionary years and for a new professionalism to accompany the transition from guerrilla band to national defense force. Mao disagreed. He argued that the strategy of drawing an invading enemy into the heartland of China and defeating it by guerrilla warfare was still appropriate. Moreover, he believed that the Army was, most importantly, a paragon of political virtue to be emulated by society; yet to emphasize professionalism, he thought, was to undermine political correctness, for expertise was acceptable only if matched with and tempered by "redness."

The PLA's military professionalism was, perforce, ignored during its decade-long involvement in politics during the Cultural Revolution. Many officers attributed its miserable performance in the border conflict with Vietnam in 1979 to that involvement. They argued that the PLA could become an effective national defense force only if it attended exclusively to training, developing new strategy, and updating and upgrading its arsenal. (Their case was strengthened during the Gulf War in 1991, when Iraqi troops were defeated so rapidly and their equipment, some of it supplied by China, proved so ineffectual against American weapons.) Their position is that the PLA is not now combat-ready for the kinds of conflict in which it is likely to find itself engaged. To them, any expenditure of time or money that does not directly enhance combat readiness is inappropriate, whether spent on managing a factory or doing the job of a provincial Party secretary.

These professionals in the PLA are interested in defining as sharply as possible the respective roles of China's armed forces, Party, and government and working to ensure that each confines itself to its designated part. They appreciate the benefits of having contacts with the military establishments of other countries, and they are eager to maintain these, since they provide the PLA with access to technology, training, and strategic and tactical thinking; they tend to be less xenophobic than some of their colleagues.

The PLA's "nonprofessionals" (for lack of a better term: certainly reds is no longer appropriate) take a more benign view of noncombat-related military activity. Some of them are nostalgic for the heady days when the government called in the PLA to restore order, wield political power, and pull China back together; others have a strong personal and professional interest in being economic buccaneers, and they don't mind blurring the roles of Party, government, and army. They see more to be lost than gained by the PLA's having contact with foreign military establishments: for them, to respond to the Pentagon's request for mutual "transparency" in military affairs is to reveal state secrets in a treasonable fashion.

The professionals' hesitation to intervene politically might in a given circumstance be overcome by patriotism, were the situation sufficiently dire and the alternative sufficiently unsatisfactory. But any eagerness to divest themselves of political responsibility as quickly as possible would put them at odds with their more politically inclined colleagues.

To a degree, the split between professionals and nonprofessionals parallels a split among the services. Interservice rivalry, which after all is found in most military establishments, is encouraged to the extent it builds loyalty and enhances morale and is played out through strategic-planning bargains and, more sharply, around the table when military appropriations are decided on. In the case of the PLA, the army is by far the largest service, with 2.3 million soldiers; the air force numbers about 470,000; and the navy some 260,000. As one might expect, the technological level of the weapons and equipment used by the navy and air force is far higher than that of the ground forces, and so is the educational level of their soldiers and officers. Troops assigned to the ground forces are generally more conservative and less professional than their navy and air force colleagues.

Current strategic doctrine in the PLA calls for rapid deployment forces capable of responding quickly to domestic or international incidents. This doctrine, relying heavily on the navy and air force, has given those two arms prominence and necessitates the upgrading of their equipment and training. Moreover, they appear to have strong and effective spokesmen at the highest level. Admiral Liu Huaqing, once head of the PLA navy, now occupies influential positions on the Politburo Standing Committee and as vice chair of the Central Military Commission.

Divisions along lines of age, rank, and time in service are more acute in the Chinese army than in other, more established armed forces. For one thing, the PLA has only quite recently implemented a regular retirement system for senior officers, and there is a greater age spread between the oldest and youngest soldiers than in the Pentagon, for example. Also, because of the significant difference in military operations during the revolution and civil war, during the Korean War, and in the more recent border conflicts with India and Vietnam, the military "generations" in the PLA have had substantially different experiences.

Ranks and rank insignia were eliminated in the PLA, prior to the Cultural Revolution, so as to level differences among the troops and emphasize the belief in the virtue of egalitarianism. Lip service was paid to equality, but the absence of formal designations and badges had little lasting effect, and the ranks were restored in 1988.

The fissures between China's central military authority and that of the regional military commanders weakens the PLA's ability to staff any caretaker government needed in the future to help mend a regionally fractured state. The regional commanders' habit of ignoring directives that run counter to their local interests, very like the habits of civilian authorities at the provincial level, will significantly reduce the adhesive properties of the caretakers' glue.

In sum, were civil authority to collapse or a regional breakup threaten, along with a loss of central government control, the PLA would very likely intervene to form a caretaker government. It would do so out of patriotism and knowing that, as the only national organization capable of taking the place of the CCP, anarchy might result if it did not. Once in power, it would be likely to rule in the name of a purged and revivified Communist Party and to pursue a policy of continuing Deng's economic reforms and his open policy toward the world economy, since its officers would consider their own economic interests served by these policies. But there would be strong pressure to make the caretaker government a short-lived affair from the professional officers, who would consider the adverse effects on combat readiness and be sensitive to international pressure to restore civilian rule. Rebuilding confidence in China's central authority would be the major undertaking, with an effective crackdown on corruption and the equal enforcement of laws and regulations as important first steps. But apart from its possibly greater discipline, there is little to inspire confidence in the PLA as a better problem solver than those whom it would replace.

During the 1980s, the PLA was told that upgrading its equipment had to wait until China's own industries could supply the new equipment; the policy was implemented by an initial reduction in the military budget and then only very small annual increments to it, which, given the effects of inflation, did not offset the continued downsizing of the military budget. But two events occurred at the beginning of the 1990s that turned this situation around: the PLA began to augment its budget through arms sales abroad and through production for the domestic civilian market; and the collapse of the former Soviet Union put large quantities of military equipment on the market. The PLA took full advantage of this coincidence of events: it signed contracts with Russian suppliers to buy one hundred S300 missiles, seventy-two Su27K fighter aircraft, and four Kilo-class submarines, and conversations were also held about the purchase of SS-18 nuclear missile technology; the cost of these acquisitions is approximately $3 billion to date, part of it paid in cash, part in barter arrangements. In addition, China has made substantial purchases of arms and equipment from Israel, including laser-guided armor-piercing warheads; electronic fire-control systems; optics and cannons for tanks; night-vision, communications, and radio equipment; antitank missiles; and artillery ammunition. The bill for this equipment over the last ten years is estimated to be another $3 billion.

Admiral Liu Huaqing has long sought to add aircraft carriers to the Chinese Navy. Since it is estimated that it will be 2005 before China is capable of launching its own carrier, Liu began negotiations to purchase one under construction in the Ukraine. When these broke down, he turned to France with the proposal that it make a gift of the 35-year-old carrier *Clemenceau* in exchange for China's agreeing to a contract with French ship-builders for its retrofitting (a complicated arrangement designed to skirt the European Union's 1989 arms embargo against China).

The PLA argues that these acquisitions are meant simply to update its antiquated arsenal, but China's neighbors see evidence of expansion, not simple replacement. And they relate this expansion to actions taken to strengthen China's military position outside the national borders. An agreement was signed with Burma in 1994 by which, in exchange for sending military equipment to the Burmese army, China would have access to naval facilities in the Bay of Bengal. A year later, China extended its position in the South China Sea by occupying the Mischief Reef, just 135 miles off the coast of the Philippines. Alarmists saw these events as evidence of a pincers movement designed to encircle and control Southeast Asia. But the Chinese government depicts the two events as unconnected and defends the actions in the South China Sea as intended exclusively to protect Chinese territory.

One can plausibly argue that the PLA is engaging in these

actions simply to justify an expanded military budget. But whatever its motivation, the key question is whether its actions are proceeding under a plan drawn up by civilian authorities and implemented under civilian control, or whether the PLA itself is doing the planning and controlling. There is evidence to suggest that the latter is the case.

Military officers who enjoyed close personal ties to Deng and his senior colleagues occupy key positions in the highest circles of power in the Party and the armed forces. Their influence is enhanced because, as we have seen, the Party-state is heavily dependent on the PLA and PAP. When Chinese arms sales abroad have become an international issue, the foreign minister has left the impression that he has only very indirect and ineffective control over the military corporations making these sales.

In arguing for a larger share of the national budget, the PLA takes advantage of its position of influence within the triangle of Party, government, and military authority, using the resources available to it to upgrade its arsenal, adopting a new strategy that takes account of the structure of power in East Asia and the Pacific, and lobbying effectively for a strong assertion of Chinese sovereignty broadly defined.

# Sources of Rural Discontent

The sheer size of China's rural population is one of its most arresting features—900 million people, more than three and a half times the total population of the United States. Even when it was only a third of its present size during the civil war, Mao Zedong recognized China's rural population as a singular resource that could give the Communist Party the leverage it needed to defeat the city-based forces of the Nationalist Party. And so he set aside the conventional Marxist-Leninist canon and focused his attention on peasant grievances: their desperate poverty and their concern about the depredations committed by the Japanese forces seizing and occupying so much of China's territory. Attending to these concerns, the Chinese Communists mobilized their overwhelming social force and with the help of the peasantry brought about the victory of the Communist Revolution in 1949.

By means of land reform and the creation of collective farms in the years immediately following the Communist victory, rural incomes were equalized and raised. But in other ways the exploitation of the rural population continued. Keeping the price it paid for grain artificially low, the government turned a profit at the expense of the peasantry and then used this profit as the source of capital for industrializing China's cities; city dwellers also got government subsidies for housing and food that were unavailable to the rural majority. And it was the rural population that suffered the most serious consequences of China's disastrously misguided agricultural policies during the late 1950s. In the twenty-five years prior to the reform period, per capita income in the countryside increased less than 50 percent.

Deng Xiaoping began his economic reforms in the countryside for two reasons: he knew that reforming agriculture would be much easier than reforming industry; and if the reform of agriculture were successful, Deng could use that success to persuade his skeptical colleagues to take on the more complicated tasks of reforming industry.

Indispensable to the success of agricultural reform was the household-responsibility system, a system that had originated as an experiment in the early 1960s, when Deng and his colleagues were looking for ways to alleviate the disaster brought on by the Maoist excesses of the Great Leap Forward in the late 1950s. In the experiment, land was taken out of the collective and given to households to farm; what any one household was capable of producing over the quota set by the local government, it was permitted to sell on the rural free market. The experiment had been successful, but it was abandoned once the disaster abated, and Mao later denounced it as unacceptably capitalist in spirit.

The household-responsibility system was resurrected in 1978, once again as an experiment in one or two locations. But almost overnight it was adopted by farming communities throughout China. The incentives it incorporated quickly boosted productivity, output, and household income. When these increments began to slow seven years later, a further round of reform stabilized the contract system and opened the door to the proliferation of small-scale industry in the rural economy.

The combined effect of these reforms was to raise rural incomes by a factor of three over the first twelve years of the reform period. A lot of publicity was given to the first "ten thousand *kuai* households" (households whose annual income had reached twelve hundred dollars). When news of this new phenomenon reached city residents, they found themselves envious of their country cousins for the first time in memory and were more than ready to see replicated in the city some of the entrepreneurial opportunities available beyond the suburbs. And, given their significantly improved standard of living, China's rural residents were generally quite satisfied with their lot at the end of the 1980s. They were somewhat insulated from the inflation which loomed large in the cities, and corruption, which was the second most frequent complaint of city dwellers, had yet to become fully visible in rural communities. This helps to explain why the slogans and speeches of students and workers who rushed into the streets of every major city in China in the spring of 1989 fell on deaf ears in the countryside, why there was so little sympathy among country folk for the demonstrators' demands, and why the demonstrators made virtually no effort to arouse the support of people living outside the cities.

Since the events of the spring of 1989, this quiescent satisfaction in the rural community has disappeared. Urban reforms have eliminated the small entrepreneurial advantages that rural residents enjoyed over their urban compatriots, and today the urban living standard is improving much more rapidly than that in the countryside. The rural majority is reacting to this situation in two ways: they are taking advantage of the relaxed restrictions on geographical mobility in record numbers, and some 100 million underemployed workers have left their rural homes in search of temporary work in China's largest cities; and those who stay in the countryside are nursing their grievances and, increasingly, acting on them. Given their new attitudes and habits, it seems unlikely that they will sit on the sidelines the next time political dissatisfactions spill into China's streets.

Until the 1980s the Chinese countryside was organized into large collective enterprises called communes, a unit (or *danwei*) typically incorporating the people of what had been several villages before collectivization began. The average commune, with a population of about two thousand households, was divided into brigades, each made up of a population roughly equal to that of the average village, or about two hundred households; the brigades, in turn, were divided into production teams of twenty to forty households. The production team or, in some cases, brigade held title to the land and equipment for which it was responsible; members received their work assignments from the production-team leader. Individual householders owned their houses (but not the land on which the houses were built) and personal effects and had use rights to a "private plot" of land on which produce or animals could be raised for home consumption or for sale on the rural free markets.

Compensation within the commune system was based on work points. Work points were assigned based on the difficulty of the task, the capability of the worker, and the amount of time spent at work. Men, who were considered more capable than women at working the land, routinely received more work points for performing the same task for the same period of time. After the harvest, grain was sold to the state according to predetermined quotas, and work points were totaled; whatever amount of the team's profit it had agreed to set aside for compensation was then divided by the total number of work points earned by all the team members. This fixed the value of the work point, and team members then received compensation based on the total points. Only the largest, richest communes could offer their members retirement plans, but all of them offered medical care and primary education at nominal cost.

This compensation system gave peasant households fairly secure if very low incomes, but it provided no incentive to work hard or efficiently, and Chinese agricultural production was essentially stagnant. Productivity was very low, and the growth in total output did not keep up with the growth in population.

During the first years after the Communist Revolution, ownership of land and equipment and the power to make decisions about production were removed from individual households and vested in progressively larger and larger units—first the mutual assistance team, then two stages of cooperatives, and finally the communes. In this process, the size of the decision-making unit in the rural economy grew from a household to an entity encompassing, on average, more than five thousand households. But after the failure of the Great Leap Forward, this process was reversed. Beginning in 1959, ownership and decision making were shifted downward, first to the brigade and subsequently to the production team. The cycle was completed with the reintroduction of the household-responsibility system in 1978. With it, the individual household was re-empowered and once again serves as the locus of production decision making and de facto landownership.

Village governments, which took the place of production-team management groups, put the new system in place. They evaluated their land and divided it into parcels, each parcel containing noncontiguous pieces of good land and less productive land. Households were allowed to bid for use rights on these parcels; better off families with more able-bodied workers were rewarded with use rights to the larger, better parcels. Team implements and draft animals were sold at auction to householders.

The village authorities and successful bidders signed contracts that stipulated three "fixed items": the price the household would pay for inputs, including seed and fertilizer, which were rationed based on the size of the contracted parcels; the expected output of specific commodities, such as grain or cotton, to be produced on the parcel; and the price the state would pay for the contracted commodities. The initial contracts were written for one-year terms. Everything the household produced over and above the stipulated amount of the stipulated commodity it was free to dispose of as it chose—whether for personal consumption, barter, or sale. If it chose to sell its surplus, it could sell it either to the state at a price higher than that paid for contract commodities or directly to consumers on the free market.

The rural working community responded to this new system's incentive for hard and efficient work. The increase in grain production was modest, but total agricultural output grew significantly. The average annual increase in the total amount of grain produced during 1970–77 was 3.6 percent; it rose during the seven years following the introduction of the responsibility system to 5.5 percent; and if we look at total income from agricultural production, we find that the comparable figures are 3.1 percent and 13.9 percent. These figures reflect the fact that, since the contract system encouraged farmers to diversify their crops and since fruit and vegetables were more profitable than grain, much of the over-contract production was devoted to those crops.

Bringing industry to China's countryside was a goal that Mao pursued during the last twenty years of his life. He saw a number of advantages in doing so: peasants would be proletarianized by exposure to the industrial workplace; rusticating industry would bring factories closer to their source of supply and to the rural consumer; and China's national defense would be enhanced by making each part of the country more self-sufficient, so that the occupation or destruction of one area would not affect the economic viability of the rest of the country. Finally, opening up factories in the countryside would absorb the substantial surplus labor power in the rural economy.

The first step in introducing industrial practices into the rural community came during the Great Leap Forward, with the creation of what were called "backyard steel furnaces." Rural residents, like their urban compatriots, were encouraged to collect scrap metal (along with useful tools and utensils that were declared scrap in order to reach the inflated goals of the campaign) and to melt it down to help increase the nation's steel output. The campaign was a failure on all counts. Few proletarianizing lessons could be learned in these ad hoc workplaces, and the lumps of melted metal produced in them were largely unusable.

Alongside the useless steel furnaces, however, workshops and small factories were set up that began the process of creating a "cellular" economy in rural China. During the 1960s and into the 1970s, a major effort was launched to open new factories and to make China's more than two thousand counties as self-sufficient as possible. Some of these factories belonged to the state sector, many were owned and managed by the county government, and others were owned and managed by individual communes. By the mid-1970s rural small-scale industry was producing about 10 percent of China's total industrial output; in certain lines, such as chemical fertilizer and cement, the small-scale factories accounted for more than half of the nation's total production. As we have noted, these efforts were augmented by the PLA, which was active in building a "third line" of factories in remote areas.

The most recent wave of rural industrialization began in the mid-1980s, when the initial surge of growth in rural per capita income brought on by the introduction of the responsibility system had begun to slow. Reformers now encouraged a rapid proliferation of new industrial enterprises under township and village management; these enterprises now have a workforce of more than 125 million and account for nearly a quarter of China's industrial output, producing both for the domestic market and for export.

Unfortunately, there are negative consequences of this otherwise promising development. The little factories occupy what was once arable land and contribute to air and water pollution. Built with the lowest possible capitalization, very few of them conform to China's environmental protection regulations. Local officials eager to reap the benefits of rapid industrialization put pressure on the environmental protection officials to ignore violations or to grant waivers. In the trenches where the war between economic development and environmental protection is being fought, economic development is winning most of the battles.

The household-responsibility system increased farmers' productivity through monetary incentives. But the smallness of the contracted parcels severely limits the ultimate productivity. Actually, with so much underemployment in Chinese agriculture, inefficiency and lack of productivity are not the obstacles to increased production that they would be were labor scarce. Nonetheless, there is talk of rationalizing agricultural production by combining small contracted plots into larger, more efficient farms.

Some consolidation of parcels is occurring spontaneously. In some places, households pool their parcels, labor, tools, and animals and farm the land as informally constituted cooperatives. Since contracts are transferable, others have chosen to sell their contracts and to leave agriculture entirely. People buy up these contracts, hire a staff of farm laborers, and become large-scale agricultural producers, which can realize economies of scale with respect to inputs such as chemical fertilizer, insecticides, and the like. But large efficient farms turn underemployed farm workers into unemployed ones. Their need for jobs frequently encourages local authorities to build more factories, which takes badly needed arable land out of cultivation, thereby reducing total production.

With the introduction of the responsibility system came a structural change in rural administration in which the township took the place of the commune as the lowest level in the government structure. On average, each township is approximately twice the size of a former commune, and its administration serves as the local government, supervising the civic life of the two dozen or so villages under its authority, and as a production company, overseeing numerous collective enterprises (the average township has more than seven hundred of these). The production company is organized into agricultural and industrial departments and perhaps others with responsibility for commercial activities, transportation, and the like.

A second stage of structural change has been proposed. The goal is a bold one: to shift the rural-urban population ratio from its current 75:25 to 50:50, which would require a vast expansion of existing rural villages. Facilities and services will be needed for the more than 300 million people to be relocated from their villages to new, more urbanized residences. The purpose behind this radical social restructuring is to transfer rural Chinese underemployed labor power into industry based in the rural countryside. And it is proposed that once this plan has been implemented, rural town governments will take responsibility for administration of their neighboring townships; since there are roughly half as many towns as townships, this consolidation means that the lowest level of rural administration will be roughly twice its current size.

Whereas in the past the Chinese government could count on peasant acquiescence and could focus on the more volatile political behavior of workers, students, and intellectuals, today it can no longer take for granted the passivity of the peasant.

The most serious set of problems the government faces in the countryside is underemployment, perhaps better conceived of as hidden unemployment affecting nearly one-third of the rural workforce: the direct cause of the outflow of 100 million people into China's major cities. A first priority is to find a way of providing housing and social services for that proportion of the floating labor pool that is actually needed in the urban economy. Its second, more complicated priority is to find jobs to attract the floaters who are not needed back to their homes in the countryside.

A second set of problems is related to the task of ensuring a sufficient food supply for the Chinese people into the next century. The task is best thought of as a fraction, the numerator of which is food supply and the denominator of which is population, the aim being to increase the numerator as much as possible while simultaneously reducing the denominator.

The first aspect of this task is to ensure a steady increase in the production of grain, cotton, and other agricultural commodities, without which the Chinese economy would grind to a halt. The market solution—raising the price paid to the farmer to encourage him to produce more—creates as many new problems as it solves old ones. Under the commune system, farmers had little or no choice as to what to grow, to whom to sell their produce, and at what price. Sloth and natural disaster were the only obstacles to the state's realizing its quotas each year. Natural disasters are a constant, of course; reform policies largely eliminated sloth by means of material incentives. But these same policies created a new hurdle for the government to surmount: producing the basic agricultural commodities has become a money-losing proposition for the farmers.

As part of its package of perquisites for city dwellers, China in years past purchased grain at prices well below what would have been market prices then sold it in the cities at an even lower price, absorbing the difference as an expense item in the national budget. When this expense item grew, the state decided no longer to subsidize grain for cities but to allow its price to rise to market levels: in 1994 the price of grain in city markets rose by 50 percent, a major factor in driving the urban inflation rate close to 30 percent that year. Even when this substantial increase was passed along to the producers, however, it was not enough to encourage them to grow grain if they weren't obliged to by state quotas. Almost anything the rural household chose to plant on its contracted land would yield a better income than grain, given the prevailing prices the state was willing to pay for it. So the state cannot both bring urban inflation under control and raise grain prices to a level that makes it profitable for farmers to increase the amount they produce.

The situation is comparable with respect to cotton production. Raising cotton on contracted land and selling it to the state at the state's artificially low price produces only about a fifth of the income that vegetables bring in. Peasants obliged to grow cotton by terms of their contract have taken to selling it on the black market for three times the state price and claiming a shortfall in the harvest when state purchasers come to claim their contracted amount. Were the government to raise cotton prices, it would be increasing costs for the textile plants, most of which are state-owned enterprises already teetering on the brink of bankruptcy.

Increasing the numerator of the food supply–population ratio is all the more difficult because of the declining supply of arable land. Every day decisions are made in rural communities that reduce the already scarce amount of land available for cultivation. China has about 20 percent of the world's population and only about 7 percent of its arable land: currently about 370,000 square miles, which is 80 percent of the 1950 figure. This means that over the past four decades China has endured a net annual loss of about 1,600 square miles despite its vigorous efforts at reclamation; and the current rate at which land is being taken out of cultivation is about six times that average.

Yet land is being withdrawn from cultivation for good cause. Rural factories produce goods that augment the gross national product and give jobs to workers who would otherwise leave the countryside or be unemployed. But factories occupy land that could be cultivated, and they need raw materials and markets, which means expanding the highway and rail network, eating up still more land. As rural incomes rise, people are eager to expand their living quarters, and although local regulations restrict the proportion of land in a community that can be devoted to housing, these are often stretched or violated. Land is also taken out of cultivation for uses with little or no value for economic development: many odd schemes have proliferated recently, the most egregious of which are two dozen golf courses laid out in 1994.

Given the current growth rate of the Chinese population and its changes in diet, it is estimated that it will take more than 600 million tons of grain to feed that population in 2030. Not only will there be more people to feed, but as household income increases, so does consumption of meat, poultry, and eggs. Grain production in 1996 reached the record level of 480 million tons. To reach 600 million tons by 2030, production must annually increase by 4 million tons. But, with land taken out of cultivation more and more quickly, conservative projections show a drop in grain output of up to 20 percent over the next thirty-five years, which would result in a grain deficit of more than 300 million tons in 2030. The total world grain surplus available for export in 1993 was only about 220 million tons, and many other countries are dependent on that surplus; what will happen when China becomes a grain importer on a massive scale?

The goal of reducing the denominator of the food supply–population ratio is equally daunting. China's efforts to limit population growth to one child per family have fallen short of their target. The average number of children in China's cities is down to just over 1 per family, but the national average is 2.25 children per family. Rural resistance to the birth-control program is attributable to tradition, on the one hand, dictating a preference for a male heir to carry on the family name (multiple births in one family frequently being the result of repeated attempts to have a male child), and on the other hand, the economics of the rural reforms. The household-responsibility system rewards big families in which there are many workers. Because girls cease to contribute to their parents' exchequer once they marry and leave the household, boys are considered a better source of income. And since there are no retirement plans in the vast majority of rural collectives, a couple's only source of old-age security is a large family. The birth-control program is successful in the Chinese countryside only when it is enforced with draconian measures, such as forced abortions or sterilizations or the destruction of homes and property. But such measures serve to alienate the peasant community further.

A final source of government dissatisfaction with the rural population is the very high rate at which they choose to withdraw their children from school. Census figures in 1990 revealed that 205 million people, or 18 percent of the Chinese population, are illiterate or semiliterate, of which 90 percent are rural residents and a startlingly high proportion are females under the age of forty. This is precisely because Chinese families will withdraw children, particularly girls, from school before they have completed their education.

Schooling is not free in the countryside. The tuition is nominal, amounting to about two dollars per term, but informal ad hoc charges can mount to twenty-five times that—a sizable amount when the average household income is less than eight hundred dollars per year. Most parents see little to be gained by paying for a high-school education for a child, since what the child is likely to learn seems largely irrelevant to his or her earning capabilities. This is especially so for girls, whose only chance to make money for the family is during their teen years. Only as the economy diversifies and becomes more complex will this shortsighted attitude give way to an appreciation of a high-school education as an appropriate investment. The government's providing truly free schools in rural communities would help to speed this change of attitude.

But rural people have as many reasons to be dissatisfied with their government as the government has to be dissatisfied with them. They face more and more problems that local authorities are unwilling to address or unable to resolve. In some instances, the local authorities themselves are the problem.

Among the most serious sources of dissatisfaction is excessive taxation. There is a cap of 5 percent on the amount of rural household income that can be taken as tax by the government, but in practice, local officials impose fees, tolls, fines, special levies, and charges that in most areas add up to 15 percent or more of household income, in some cases as high as 50 percent. Were this revenue used to pay for public services and improved infrastructure, rural taxpayers would no doubt continue to grumble but would at least enjoy some benefit. In fact, a substantial proportion of the tax revenues goes into the personal accounts of local officials, along with their take from bribes, graft, and profiteering. All too often this ill-gotten gain is consumed in conspicuous displays of personal excess—lavish banquets, expensive automobiles— that only inflame resentment. Indeed, this corruption is itself a potentially explosive source of rural discontent. Those who lived through the final days of the Nationalist government in the 1940s—days marked by rampant corruption—claim that the situation is worse now than it was then.

Unfortunately, three aspects of Chinese society today combine to create a climate particularly conducive to corruption. The first aspect is a mind-set inherited from the Confucian tradition and its emphasis on understanding society as a web of mostly hierarchical relationships. To make one's way through this web one is supposed to cultivate relationships (*guanxi*) that are likely to be helpful. This Chinese practice of *guanxi*, just as vital in contemporary society as it was centuries ago, lends itself all too easily to the proliferation of bribery and political corruption. The line between the legitimate cultivation of reciprocal friendship and the corrupt practice of bribery is difficult to draw, especially where there is the tendency to inflate the cost of the former.

A second element that encourages corruption is the experience of forty years of socialist rule. The Yugoslav writer Milovan Djilas was among the first Communists to describe a "new class" of privileged bureaucrats to which socialist society could give rise; he did so almost forty years ago. Mao Zedong took up the same theme in his criticisms of the Soviet Union under Khrushchev, and he subsequently applied these criticisms to China itself on the eve of the Cultural Revolution. As managers of state resources, bureaucrats in a socialist system monopolize and misuse those resources for their own advancement. And because they control education and recruitment into the political system, they can perpetuate their personal control by favoring their own choices or indeed their own offspring. Mao argued that this process of embourgeoisement— creating a new bourgeoisie out of corrupt proletarians—could be controlled only by means of a "continuing revolution" that takes power away from the privileged class. The "new bourgeoisie" in China was seriously undermined during the Cultural Revolution, though the perpetrators of that movement abused their power just as much or more than the targets of their persecution. Many who were victimized during the Cultural Revolution then returned to power under the aegis of Deng, himself a target of the movement, and they seem to regard the comforts of their current station in life as fitting compensation for what they sacrificed during the last thirty years. Deng and his immediate circle of senior colleagues avoided an extravagant lifestyle, but their sons and daughters are infamous for taking advantage of their parents' positions to acquire personal wealth and influence.

A third element of Chinese society that is conducive to the

growth of corruption is the economy's current state of partial marketization. Most decisions about allocating resources are made by
the market, but decisions about allocating certain critical resources are still made by Party and state officials. The sharp competition among the state, the collective, and the private sector has
raised the ante in decisions about who gets what quantity of critical items in short supply, a situation rife with opportunities for
corruption.

Corruption, the kudzu of contemporary China, is intractable because the legal system is not able to establish a standard against
which corruption can be measured, and the political system lacks
an independent agency to attack and control it. Central authorities
launch periodic anticorruption campaigns, but the agents on whom
they rely to implement these campaigns are the very officials who
are their most eligible targets. At best, one or two scapegoats are
prosecuted and lose their jobs, but the problem grows worse. In
the summer of 1993, Jiang Zemin, calling on his authority as president of the PRC and general secretary of the Party, announced a
campaign to end corruption; two months later, *People's Daily*, the
organ of the Party's Central Committee, editorialized that "a certain amount of corruption in our system is inevitable." Needless
to say, Jiang's campaign did not achieve its goal.

A third source of rural dissatisfaction with the government is
the periodic cash-flow crises. Eager to take advantage of promising
if highly speculative investment opportunities and not always successful in collecting tax revenues, local governments often find
themselves strapped for cash just when the farmers are ready to
sell their grain to the state and thereby fulfill their contracts.
Rather than getting cash for their grain, farmers have got IOUs
redeemable when the government's cash-flow problem is resolved.
So serious was the cash shortage in 1994 that stories were told of
floating workers in China's cities who purchased money orders at
the municipal post office and sent the money orders home to their

families, who, when they tried to cash them at local post offices, were given IOUs instead.

A fourth source of dissatisfaction, perhaps not immediately felt by rural residents in their daily lives, is over the long term perhaps the most serious of all: the gap between rural and urban incomes. For a brief time in the early 1980s, economic reforms in the countryside resulted in rural household income growing much faster than that of urban households; in 1980 rural incomes had been only one-third of urban incomes; by 1985, when reform of the urban economy began, it had at least grown to one-half of the average urban income. But during the past decade, the gap has begun to widen again, and the ratio is now one to three. Thus rural families are no better off than they were in 1978.

The average urban household income in China's cities stands at about three thousand dollars per year; the average rural income is somewhat less than $950 per year. Seven percent of the Chinese population is living in poverty (defined as a per capita income of less than forty-two dollars per year), and the vast majority of these are rural residents. And the situation is getting worse. The overall growth rate in the urban economy is more than 13 percent, and in the rural sector only about 4 percent.

In the past this rural-urban gap didn't matter a great deal. The state's control over the flow of information and the almost complete absence of geographical mobility meant that much of China's rural population was ignorant of city conditions, and even if they were aware of the differences in living standards, there was nothing they could do. Today the situation is very different. Information about conditions in China's most highly developed cities is trumpeted in the official media, and a large number of rural families have one or more members who are floating workers temporarily living in cities.

Another aspect of the rural-urban gap, of which individual farmers may be less aware but which seriously jeopardizes their long-term interests, is that the rate of capital investment in the industrial sector is substantially higher than that in the agricultural sector. In the early days of the People's Republic it was very different: investment in agriculture constituted nearly a quarter of total investment in China in the late 1950s and early 1960s. By the early 1990s, however, that proportion had dropped to 4 percent, the rationale being that the rural collective sector, powered by reforms, was generating enough capital to allow local governments to take over agricultural investment. The fact of the matter is, however, that this local government investment also declined precipitously during the 1980s, from nearly 40 percent of total local investment to under 10 percent by the end of the decade. Seeking a high return on each investment dollar, local governments are much more inclined to invest in new industries or even real-estate development than to settle for agriculture's low return.

Grain production in China totaled 444 million tons in 1994—a decline of 3 percent from the record harvest of 456 million tons in 1993. Alarmed by this decline, the central government pledged to reverse it and to provide investment funds for agricultural infrastructure and for research and development of new seed strains, new fertilizers, and new pesticides.

Several other problems have caused China's rural residents to lose confidence in their local governments. Environmental pollution is one of them. They are the first to suffer when township and village industrial enterprises flout air and water pollution regulations. (Until very recently, China has had no grassroots "green" movement pressuring the government to address these matters, but there are signs that a citizens' movement with an interest in improving environmental quality is beginning to come together.) Also, crime is on the rise throughout China, and one form of violent crime endemic in the countryside is the abduction of women and of male children, the women taken to be sold as wives or prostitutes, the boys to be sold to families who have not produced a male heir. About fifteen thousand cases of abduction are investigated each year. Although the Public Security Ministry reports an increasing number of arrests and prosecutions in cases of kidnapping and abduction, the crime wave has sapped citizens' confidence in the local governments' ability to maintain civil order.

Inflation, a serious cause of urban dissatisfaction, is a less serious issue in the countryside, since the rate of inflation in the rural community is significantly lower than in the cities. Rural residents own their homes and most of them produce at least a portion of their food, so they are insulated from the two major causes of the increase in the cost of living in the city.

As we have seen, rural China was largely inactive when students and workers in China's cities were demonstrating against the government in 1989; rural residents were generally unsympathetic with their demands for a more open, more effective government. But since 1989, as the sources of discontent described here have taken their toll on rural toleration of incompetent governance, the climate has changed. In 1994 the Chinese press reported more than a thousand instances of protest demonstrations involving the rural population. Public protests occurred in rural communities in more than half of China's provinces. The largest of these drew more than ten thousand rural residents protesting excessive and illegal taxes into the streets of a community near Chengdu, the capital of Sichuan Province.

Mao's comment in 1930 on the volatile character of a discontented peasantry, "a single spark can start a prairie fire," vastly understates the amount of political mobilization and organizational work that it took for the Chinese Communist Party to launch the revolution that overthrew the old order in the Chinese countryside.

A thousand protests do not a revolution make. On the other hand, 900 million people in rural communities who harbor serious doubts as to the capability of their government to address their pressing problems pose a serious challenge indeed to the central authorities in Beijing.

# China's Cities:
# Unemployment, Corruption, and Inflation

Mao Zedong was decidedly not a city person. Born in a small village in rural Hunan, he spent his youth deep in the Chinese countryside. Having concluded that the Communist Revolution was to be won in China by mobilizing the support of the peasants, he proposed to build a peasant army and, using guerrilla tactics, seize control of the countryside; once the Japanese occupation was over and Nationalist troops had been driven out, the Red Army would control the nation, for the cities, cut off from their sources of supply in the hinterlands, would of necessity fall to them. Having decided on this strategy, Mao and his colleagues threw in their lot with rural China for the duration of the revolution; doing so left a permanent mark on them, their party, and the policies they subsequently pursued.

Mao and his colleagues were of the opinion that the countryside was the seat of a kind of primitive virtue, the city, by contrast, the seat of decadence and corruption. The highly disruptive and apparently irrational practice of *xiafang*, or rustification—whereby urban residents were involuntarily removed and made to live in remote rural settings, some for a short time, others for years—was based on this opinion. It was taken as an article of faith that their rural experiences would cure their urban flaws and instill virtue in them.

But Mao's reading of Marx presented him with a picture of urban life that conflicted with his experience. He found persuasive the idea that the proletariat was formed in the industrial workplace, a process that, despite the pain inflicted by capitalists who controlled the workplace, was salutary and necessary, for only the proletariat could lead the ultimate advance toward communism. Although he had limited experience outside China, Mao understood that modern societies are urban and industrial; for China to take its place in the world, preferably at the forefront of modernity, it must first clean up, then build up, its cities. So he looked for a way to resolve these contradictory views of the city. Bringing industry to the countryside seemed to him infinitely better than bringing the peasant to the city. The wave of rural industrialization now under way in China is, in effect, a realization of Mao's vision, though it has been undertaken for economic, not ideological, reasons.

Reforming the urban economy in China was significantly more complex than reforming agriculture. The initial changes in the industrial workplace, begun as early as 1979, were undertaken only on an experimental basis, and full-scale urban economic reform was postponed until 1984. By that time the successes of the household-responsibility system in the countryside and the experiments in the urban sector had built a following for extending the reforms throughout the urban economy.

Reform in the countryside had been greatly facilitated by two factors: that agricultural production as practiced in rural China is a relatively simple enterprise involving little in the way of technology or specialized expertise; and that farm households live where they work, and the family operates as a production unit. These features meant that the farm household was well suited and fully able to take on the responsibility for decisions about farming that had once been made by production-team leaders. Once re-empowered, the household willingly took on this new role. Spurred on by effective incentives that soon raised household income, agricultural workers worked harder and more efficiently, and farm output increased.

But the relationship of the typical Chinese urban household to its work is very different, though some city families live and work in circumstances quite similar to those of a farming family—with all the employed family members working for the same enterprise and living in housing provided by that enterprise. But for most city dwellers the situation is different. People work for different employers and are very likely to commute to their workplaces, where the labor is complex. A household lacks the qualifications to make decisions in the production process, since except in the smallest workshops, industrial production requires collaboration, coordination, equipment, and technology.

The goal of urban reform also differed. Although no one in a position of authority in China would be rash enough to say so, the goal of the rural reforms had really been to restore private enterprise to family farms. Fictions were devised to make this goal conform to "socialism with Chinese characteristics" (for example, households were given use rights but not title to the land in order to preserve the appearance of collective ownership), but despite these fictions, the practical effect was to privatize agricultural production and to supplement it with collectively owned industrial enterprises.

Full-scale privatization of industry was neither the spoken nor the unspoken goal of urban economic reform. Reformers encouraged the growth of private and collective enterprises in order to increase the supply and variety of goods and services available to city dwellers and to give them more jobs, but privatization was intended not to supplant, but rather to supplement a core of revivified state-owned industrial complexes. Hence, while analogies could be drawn from the agricultural reforms and applied to the urban reform process, they were only analogies, not models.

The urban reforms outlined in a document adopted by the Third Plenum of the Twelfth Central Committee in October 1984 set out to change three key relationships of state-owned enterprises: their relations with the state, with employees, and with customers.

The relationship between the enterprise and the state prior to the reforms was one of total dependence: the state owned the enterprise and managed it with goals and targets set in the national economic plan; the enterprise itself had no incentive to maximize its profits and minimize its losses. Profits were recouped in their entirety by the state, and operating losses were made up by state grants.

Drawing an analogy from the distinction between landownership and land-use rights, the urban reform document distinguished between ownership of an enterprise, which would remain in the hands of the state, and its management, which would have full responsibility for running it. In the past, factories were virtual government agencies; once reformed, they would be independent legal entities with the power to transform and develop and with the responsibility for their own profit and loss. Managers were responsible for planning, supply, production, and marketing, for appointing supervisory personnel and recruiting workers, for determining wages and rewards, and for setting prices on their products. At the same time, they were told to trim the bloated workforce and increase productivity.

To establish each enterprise's economic independence, the state proposed that they all pay a fixed-rate corporate tax rather than turn over profits to the state at year's end. It would be up to the manager to decide how much to reinvest and how much to put toward wages and benefits for the workforce. Similarly, the state would no longer subsidize enterprises that operated at a loss,

though loans would be available, within limits. The responsibilities
of the state were thus limited to appointing managers, levying
taxes, extending credit, establishing new enterprises, and consol-
idating, closing, moving, or transforming those that failed.
Sweeping changes were also called for in the relationship between the enterprise and its employees. Until very recently a position in a state-owned enterprise was highly coveted, for the
average annual wage, though only about seventy-five dollars at the
current rate of exchange, was better than what workers received
in other sectors. Actual wages were based on seniority; there was
no relationship whatever between remuneration and performance.
Job security and the benefits packages were also unparalleled elsewhere in the economy, since workers in state-owned factories enjoyed lifetime tenure, popularly known as the "iron rice bowl,"
and once having hired a worker, it was next to impossible to dismiss him or her except in the case of a criminal conviction. The
benefits package met virtually all a worker's needs: housing at a
rent so low that it did not cover the cost of maintaining the housing
stock; subsidies to help with food and transportation; free medical
care; and China's only full retirement plan. The national average
annual expenditure for housing in 1995 was just over thirty dollars, accounting for slightly more than 8 percent of total household
living expenses. (The comparable figures in the United States are
seventy-four hundred dollars and 23 percent. Further comparisons
are shown in the table.)

Workers in the larger state-owned enterprises enjoy what could
be called, to borrow a term from American retirement homes, "total
care"—child care at factory-owned crèches, education at factory-
managed schools, medical care at factory-operated clinics, and
access to tickets for entertainment and travel through factory-run
procurement offices. Retired workers get pensions amounting to
about three-quarters of their last wages, may go on living in

## Comparative Household Expenditures,
## China and the United States, 1995
(in dollars)

| Item | China | | United States | |
|------|-------|------|-------|------|
| | *Amount* | *Percent* | *Amount* | *Percent* |
| Total | 424 | 100 | 32,914 | 100 |
| Food | 211 | 49 | 4,574 | 14 |
| Clothing | 57 | 14 | 1,710 | 5 |
| Housing | 30 | 8 | 7,395 | 23 |
| Household | 36 | 8 | 2,082 | 6 |
| Medical | 13 | 3 | 1,634 | 5 |
| Transportation | 20 | 5 | 5,228 | 16 |
| Recreation, Education, and Culture | 37 | 9 | 2,008 | 6 |
| Miscellaneous | 18 | 4 | 5,135 | 16 |
| Taxes | 0 | 0 | 3,068 | 9 |

*(Sources: China Statistical Yearbook 1996 and American Almanac 1994–95)*

factory-owned housing, and enjoy virtually all the amenities provided their working colleagues. In addition, through a system known as *dingti*, they can get jobs for their children as they themselves leave the workforce.

The 1984 reforms sought to improve the abysmally low productivity of the industrial workforce by introducing incentives. The tenure system would be phased out and new workers hired on limited-term contracts, renewable depending on performance. The standardized wage scale based exclusively on seniority was to be replaced by one based on productivity.

To change their relationship with customers, enterprises were given new authority to determine their products' prices. The reform document described a "chaotic" system of prices, in which variation in quality of goods was ignored, the prices of producer goods—raw materials and semi-processed goods—were artificially depressed, and the state absorbed the difference between the price that urban residents paid for food and housing and the actual cost of these items.

Creating order out of this chaos would inevitably be painful for city dwellers, so the decision was made to implement price reform piecemeal rather than all at once. Increases in living costs were to be partially offset by wage increases and special subsidies. Price reform was a highly sensitive issue, for it could cause inflation, and inflation, the government knew, would trigger a strong reaction among city dwellers.

Reform of the urban economy was launched in earnest in the spring of 1985 and proceeded with some success for three years. The inflationary effects began to be felt in 1988 and retrenchment measures were implemented in the fall of that year. When concern over urban inflation (among other issues) brought hundreds of thousands out into the streets in protest during the spring of 1989, reform of the urban economy was put on hold. It was revived again in 1992, but the old reform program was ill-suited to the new circumstances.

When the urban reforms were announced in 1984, it was noted that about a third of China's hundred thousand state-owned industrial enterprises were operating at a loss; by the early 1990s that number had nearly doubled. Under these conditions, the idea of replacing subsidies with bank loans was impossible, for the banks had all but exhausted available credit and the state was once again in the business of subsidizing losses. Government support for state-owned enterprises amounted to nearly $50 billion in 1994, including, in addition to outright subsidies, "stability and unity loans," tax waivers, and supplementary payments to workers—a figure equivalent to half of China's total national budget. Looking beyond the enterprises' profit and loss statements the picture was even grimmer. One-third of the output of state-owned enterprises in 1994 remained unsold at year's end. In addition, those enterprises were very slow in settling their financial obligations among themselves. This so-called triangular debt among enterprises in the state sector amounted to an additional $70 billion by early 1995. Nor did the situation improve in 1996. During the first quarter of that year losses in state-owned enterprises exceeded profits for the first time; indeed, total net losses exceeded the entire equity of China's banks. Looking at industrial profits for 1996 as a whole, collective, private, and joint-venture enterprises accounted for 99 percent of total profits, state-owned enterprises only for a tiny 1 percent.

A major reason for the unprofitability of China's state-owned enterprises is their burden of payroll and benefits. Enterprises are, on average, about 20 percent overstaffed, yet because the tenure system is still in effect for workers hired before the reforms began, it is very difficult to downsize the workforce. Nationwide, enterprises are responsible for the pensions of some eighteen million individuals, and the number is growing. The cost of health coverage for workers and retirees is also mounting sharply. With no health-insurance plans, enterprises are effectively self-insured, covering the medical costs of their employees as they are incurred; when the cost of medical care was very low, this was not onerous, but as the costs have increased, enterprises are limiting the coverage they are prepared to offer. Lastly, housing is an additional financial burden, which is only increasing as housing stock ages and prices rise.

China's central government has acknowledged for some time that the state sector is in crisis. The current level of government financial support needed to keep state-sector enterprises afloat is untenable even in the short term. A logical, if drastic, solution is to allow the least successful state-owned enterprises to go out of business. With this in mind, and after extensive debate, the National People's Congress passed a bankruptcy law in early 1989. Yet implementing that law would send hundreds of thousands of workers onto the streets unemployed and angry, and the government regards this as equally untenable.

A number of proposals have been advanced to resolve this dilemma. One that gained some popularity in the early 1990s was that of creating "enterprise groups," in which a marriage would be arranged between a profitable, well-managed state-owned enterprise and an unprofitable, ill-managed one, the theory being that the successful one would, with its better management and new ideas, pull the unsuccessful enterprise up by its bootstraps. In practice, the unsuccessful enterprise often served as a sea anchor on its more successful partner, thereby multiplying the effects of its failure.

Another solution is divestiture: the state sells its interest in the enterprise to the employees or to outsiders in the form of equity shares, the enterprise moves from the state to the collective sector, and its employees shoulder the burdens once borne by the government. A variation on this idea is to get a foreign investor to buy out some or all of the assets of an unsuccessful state-owned enterprise. But determining the value of state-owned assets has been problematical for many potential investors. Some enterprises are in such bad shape that their real-estate holdings turn out to be their only asset of any value.

For the worst-off enterprises, bankruptcy is the only realistic alternative. A plan was announced in late 1994, designed to avoid some of the potential danger involved in putting state firms out of business, that would apply the bankruptcy law experimentally to enterprises in eighteen cities, cities which were to get central-government funds to assist in worker outplacement and to establish municipal social-security systems giving retirement support for those put out of work. Even with these built-in safeguards, the bankruptcy program is still filled with political risk for local politicians. It is also highly unpopular among those who continue to believe that a large and vibrant state sector is the sine qua non of a socialist economy.

However the immediate crisis is addressed, over the longer term a solution must be found for lightening the onerous burden of the benefits package. Creating a government-funded retirement program is a high priority. To date, plans for one call for its being based on worker contributions and managed by local governments. But if the plan is to succeed, a large infusion of government funds will be needed up front, since contributions from the current workforce will not begin to cover the cost of even the existing pensions.

Plans are also afoot to change the housing system. A first step has been to raise rents on factory-owned housing at least to a level that covers construction and maintenance costs. Although rents are still remarkably low, the current average urban household expenditure on housing is nearly ten times what it was a decade ago. Secondly, enterprises have begun to sell off their housing stock to residents. This was not at first easy, for the prices were high and the quality low. There was little incentive for tenants paying low monthly rents to increase their out-of-pocket expenses and also take responsibility for maintaining their decrepit quarters. As a property market begins to be created in China's cities, however, the possibility of getting in on the ground floor of what might be lucrative real-estate investments is sweetening the deal in the minds of many tenants. And thirdly, the number of new employees entitled to the full package of benefits has been reduced. Many of those newly employed in the state sector are hired on fixed-term contracts with limited access to benefits.

In the case of some foreign joint ventures, the state-owned enterprises have been split into two independent corporations, one a manufacturing concern, the other a service corporation providing employee benefits. A portion of the production company's profits is earmarked as a contribution to the service company, but the service company must find cost-reduction strategies and increase employee contributions to bring its operations into some approximation of fiscal balance.

The official figure for unemployment in the urban sector of China's economy is a modest 2.9 percent. The majority of unemployed are young people who have yet to start full-time work. (Indeed, the Chinese term for the unemployed—*daiye*—means "awaiting employment" and reflects the composition of the group.) Finding employment for young people entering the workforce—some twenty million annually—is a major task for the government. Nonetheless, were these the only urban residents whose livelihoods were at risk, China's leaders would have relatively little to worry about, particularly given the growth rate of the urban economy.

The official figure, however, is a far from perfect guide to the employment status of the urban workforce. First, it omits workers who have been put on furlough rather than having been laid off from state-owned enterprises, which, as we have seen, are significantly overstaffed. Meeting the monthly wage bill is a major problem for many state-owned enterprises that are also trying to turn a profit at year's end; by the end of 1996 some 8 percent of the state-sector workforce, or fourteen million workers, had been placed on unpaid furloughs, or on reduced hours and reduced pay.

Second, the official unemployment figures do not mention the approximately 100 million floaters in the urban workforce. Those temporary city residents who do find work are employed only on a temporary basis, many of them work only intermittently, and millions are, in effect, unemployed. Because their legal residence is the rural communities from which they come, they are officially not city residents and have no claim on housing, health care, education, or social services. They have, in effect, slipped through the cracks of what was once a very tight system of social control. These floaters, living just beyond the long arm of the law, are able to flout birth-control regulations and may be major contributors to the increasing amount of urban crime. They are a current headache and a potential catastrophe for urban officials.

In an effort to control the influx of floaters and to offset the costs of genuine city residents, the Beijing government announced in late 1994 that it was instituting a new licensing system for floaters: job applicants were to be charged $5,600 for a work license. A firm seeking to hire floaters could cover the cost of a license, but then the rate would double to $11,200. These figures are so far out of line with anyone's ability or any firm's willingness to pay that one wonders how the regulation can possibly be enforced.

News reports from Beijing in the tumultuous spring of 1989 during the demonstrations in Tiananmen Square were often misleading: it was not, despite the general opinion in the West, a desire for democracy that brought demonstrators out. The students, the first to demonstrate, had very specific issues in mind: they were dissatisfied with the low quality of their university education and the crowded conditions of their dormitories and wanted them changed; workers and professionals who later joined the protests shifted their focus to the broader issues of corruption and inflation, particularly sensitive and long-standing issues in the Chinese political context.

Immediately following the Japanese surrender in 1945, the Chinese Communists gained public support by pointing to runaway inflation in the economy and rampant corruption in the political system, both of which they blamed on the Nationalist government, which, they argued, appeared powerless to control either. The Communists promised to put in place a scrupulously honest regime that would master the problem of inflation, and they did just that upon taking power in 1949. That regime was hopelessly mired in corruption by the early 1990s, and after three decades of nearly stable prices, inflation reappeared, the unwelcome consequence of the economic reforms and recent rapid economic growth.

The average rate of inflation during the first three decades of the People's Republic was just under 2 percent; retail prices rose only about 65 percent in thirty years. In 1988, however, the retail price index increased by 18.5 percent, and even more for urban residents, and it continued to mount through early 1989. City dwellers found this decline in buying power and real wages alarming. Their alarm turned to anger as they realized that the government officials were not only incapable of resolving the problem, but also insulating themselves from its effects through rampant corruption. It was this alarm and anger that brought them out in unprecedented numbers onto the streets of eighty cities in China in opposition to the government.

The retrenchment measures the government had put in place to slow economic growth and curb inflation in late 1988 were redoubled after the demonstrations had been put down in early June 1989. As a result, the overall inflation rate was reduced from 17.8 percent in 1989 to just a little over 2 percent in 1990. It began to rise again in 1993 and reached a new high of 24.2 percent in 1994 (35 percent in the urban economy). Once again, the government took steps to bring inflation under control, and by late 1995 the rate had been reduced to 14.8 percent.

Until 1995, the inflation rate in China's cities consistently exceeded the rate for the economy as a whole by several percentage points. Food expenditures account for a high proportion of urban household budgets, and food prices in urban markets increased 32 percent in 1994—partly because of the effort to bring the prices paid to rural producers closer to market levels and partly because of bad weather during the growing season.

The government has had difficulty in meeting the targets it sets each year for bringing inflation under control because it is unwilling or unable to address the underlying causes. It solves its cash-flow problems by increasing the money supply, it uses up bank credit to shore up the teetering state sector, and it cannot control local government speculation in property schemes. It seems to harbor the hope that periodic wage increases will anesthetize the public to the effects of inflation.

Yet, for all of the problems, China's cities are infinitely more interesting and pleasant places to live than they were fifteen years ago. Foodstuffs, once available only in limited quantity, low quality, and no variety, are now on the market in abundance, high quality, and great variety. (A sign of this progress was a slump in the cabbage market at the beginning of the 1994–95 winter. Chinese city dwellers had always bought great quantities of cabbage in the late fall for use during the winter when no fresh vegetables would be available, and they stored it in every possible cranny in their cramped living quarters; then, day after winter day, they would pull out a head, peel off the decayed outer leaves, and boil up yet another monotonous meal. Today, with fresh vegetables available throughout the winter, cabbage growers have no market for their once essential product.) Consumer goods of all kinds are abundantly available in China's cities, domestic goods are also plentiful, much of them produced, as we have seen, in factories owned by the armed forces, and more and more imported merchandise is also to be seen in city shops and department stores. Retailing has emerged as an area of joint-venture interest, and several large Hong Kong and Japanese retailers have flourishing outlets in China's largest cities.

Twenty years ago China's city streets virtually closed down when the sun set: store fronts were boarded, crowds dispersed, and the sidewalks were only dimly lit. Today street life extends well into the night hours. Neon lights and illuminated storefronts beckon. Restaurants and fast-food outlets are abundant and their clientele numerous. Films, mostly domestically produced, attract large audiences, as do discos and karaoke bars. For all of these improvements, though, Chinese city life is not easy. Housing is still inadequate, most apartment buildings are old and in disrepair, and most urban families still live in cramped quarters and must share bathroom and kitchen facilities with their neighbors. A major push to construct new housing has increased and improved the housing stock, and per capita living space in China's cities has doubled over the last fifteen years, but people still have less than one hundred square feet, on average, of living space.

China's urban population has increased sixfold over the last forty years, and this does not include the additional 100 million floaters. Shanghai's population per square mile, for example, is a third higher than that of New York City. The construction of urban infrastructure—roads, bridges, public transportation, sewers, water supply systems, and the like—has lagged far behind the population growth, and getting from place to place, whether by bicycle, public transportation, automobile, or on foot, is most often slow. Moreover, air and water quality are seriously deficient in virtually all Chinese cities.

Add to these difficulties the insecurities brought on by unemployment, underemployment, and inflation and the lack of confidence of most urban Chinese in the capability of their government officials, and you have the potentially explosive mix that China's leaders must seek to defuse. Any failure to do so is virtually certain to give rise once again to politically destabilizing demonstrations like those that shook the government in 1989.

# —VIII—

# The Centrifugal Forces
# of Regionalism

Over the past few years, the authority of the Party and the national government it controls has significantly weakened, while provincial and local governments have become more assertive in advancing their interests, often at odds with those of the central government and of other localities. Will the central authority of the Chinese state collapse in the near term? Will the country break up into independent political and economic entities competing with one another for scarce resources?

In chapter I we saw the differences in economic opportunity that obtain among three very broad categories of provinces—those along the coast, those in the center of the country, and those in the west. While the provinces and regions in each category have much in common, it is highly unlikely, were China to break apart into regional fragments, that these three would constitute the resulting pieces, for important interests are not shared among the provinces and regions in each. This is perhaps most obvious in the case of the coastal provinces, which compete for foreign investment and, in several instances, are closely linked with the economies of their principal foreign partners.

The anthropologist G. William Skinner, in a close study of the economic geography of nineteenth-century China, concluded that it was useful to consider China not as a single economic system but as divided into nine "macroregions." (Skinner's macroregions are shown on the map.) These macroregions are defined by their river basins and by the mountain ranges that serve as barriers to commerce and trade. While economic activity within each region was intense, there was relatively little economic activity across the macroregional borders. The geographical features that divided macroregions are of course still in place, but much has changed in the Chinese economy over the course of the century and more since the period to which Skinner's data refers. Communications links have expanded. Railroads, air routes, and highways now connect places that were once isolated, and the economy is much more unified. Through the strenuous efforts of the Nationalist government in the years leading up to World War II and, later and more successfully, of the Communist government after 1949, the economy was centralized and came to be managed under a single, unified plan. And when the centralized and planned economy was subsequently decentralized once again, the units to which economic decision making was relegated were political, not physiographic or economic.

To gauge the realities of China's economic regions today, one would have to subject the contemporary scene to the same careful scrutiny that Skinner applied to economic interactions of a century ago. Short of this, we can speculate about the outcome of such a study. It would surely reveal additional macroregions: the far west is one, given the importance of the natural resources being explored there. A second might result from dividing North China into coastal and hinterlands regions. Study of the economic activity within the latter and of its links to the Lower Yangzi region might suggest a redrawing of macroregional boundaries in central China. But apart from these adjustments, Skinner's macroregions still co-

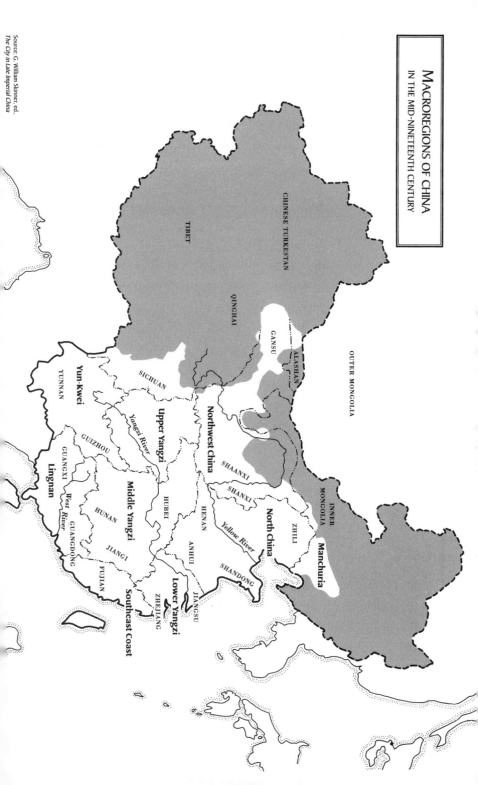

MACROREGIONS OF CHINA
IN THE MID-NINETEENTH CENTURY

CHINESE TURKESTAN

TIBET

QINGHAI

GANSU

ALASHAN

OUTER MONGOLIA

YUNNAN

Yun-Kwei

SICHUAN

Upper Yangzi

Northwest China

INNER MONGOLIA

Manchuria

GUIZHOU

Yangzi River

SHAANXI

ZHILI

Lingnan

GUANGXI

West River

HUNAN

Middle Yangzi

HUBEI

SHANXI

HENAN

Yellow River

North China

GUANGDONG

JIANGI

ANHUI

SHANDONG

FUJIAN

Southeast Coast

ZHEJIANG

Lower Yangzi

JIANGSU

here today, despite the many changes wrought by political integration, economic development, and technological modernization. Were China's central government to fail and a breakup occur, at least some of the resulting pieces would closely resemble these macroregions.

Chinese politicians have a strong preference for ad hoc arrangements that are negotiated case by case over formal arrangements applied uniformly. This preference is well illustrated by the messy web of relationships that link center and region in the Chinese political system.

The American federal system was created by local governments coming together and, after careful negotiation, surrendering certain powers to the newly created central government. The Constitution provides that all powers not specifically surrendered to the federal government remain in the hands of the states.

The Chinese system, by contrast, still contains elements of the traditional division of authority between center and regions, in which provincial and local officials were supposed to serve as agents of the central government. The carefully crafted arrangement put in place to ensure that these agents did not become advocates of local interests in competition with the interests of the throne broke down when the throne was weak, threatened, and in need of the assistance of local authorities to suppress the Taiping rebels in the middle of the nineteenth century. Thereafter China experienced nearly a century of fragmentation; local interests became strong and entrenched and the central government had little or no power over them, finding that the best it could do was to negotiate among local warlords for their cooperation in projects benefiting the nation as a whole.

In the current relationship between center and region in China, there are echoes of both mandarins and warlords. The central government would like to think of provincial leaders as their agents, but very often it finds itself negotiating for their cooperation. Their relationship is the end result of a period of centralized decision-making authority and a subsequent one of intentional decentralization. The Chinese Communist Party and the Red Army worked closely together to unify the country after a century and more of war, civil war, and revolution. Military and civilian authorities shared in running the territories they had captured and then, as the new government was established in Beijing, handed over control to civilian authorities in the central and provincial governments.

Military regional commanders remained actively involved in Party and government affairs, however, and eventually they became entrenched in the affairs of the territories under their command. To break up their strong regional identities, and to stop them from forming stable long-term local interests, the Party periodically reassigned commanders.

Once having succeeded in reasserting control after a century of regional fragmentation, the Party began to see the disadvantages of a highly centralized political system. It was impractical and inefficient to try to manage an economy as large and diverse as China's from a single command post, and Mao was mistrustful of the bureaucracy that was being created to do this management. Finally, he believed in the "mass line"—the idea that policy should reflect both central interests and local initiative—and that decisions were best made at the level where they were most likely to express local initiative. So beginning in the mid-1950s the center began to devolve decision-making authority to local officials, selected for their loyalty to the interests of the central government, among other qualities. This was seldom accomplished by means of uniform provisions applying equally to all provinces or to all cities but rather on case-by-case negotiations, the outcome of which reflected the relative clout of the parties involved.

One of the Party-state's most important levers in controlling local officials is of course the power of appointment, and provincial officials are to some degree agents of the center. On the other hand, they are most likely to be effective if they have the confidence of the local community. It used to be the case that almost all of them were outsiders brought in by and thus beholden to the center. More recently, after a long history of loyal but ineffective appointees, Beijing has been tending to appoint to important provincial and municipal posts officials with strong local affinities.

The power to levy taxes, the second lever the center uses to control local government, expresses a very concrete aspect of the center-region relationship—who determines the local budget and how the revenue for that budget is generated.

In the American fiscal system, the power to tax and the revenue generated from the tax are assigned, depending on what is being taxed, to different jurisdictions. Personal and corporate income, for example, is taxed by the federal government, by state governments, and by some cities. The sales of many goods are taxed by state and local governments, but certain items, such as alcohol, tobacco, and gasoline, by the federal government. Personal and real property is taxed by county, town, and city governments. Customs duties are collected by the federal government. (The table compares tax revenue by source for the American federal and the Chinese central government.) Towns and counties must draw up expenditure budgets, the size of which is determined by their projected tax revenues. They are generally precluded from deficit spending, though they may borrow money for capital projects. The federal government, though, is permitted to spend more than it takes in in a given year, and, exercising that option, it has accumulated a national debt of $5 trillion. There are, in addition, transfers of funds from the federal government to state and local governments that can amount to as much as a quarter of expenditures for the latter.

### Tax Revenue by Source, United States and China, 1993
(in percents)

| Source | United States | China |
|---|---|---|
| Individual income tax | 69 | 1 |
| Corporate income tax | 17 | 89 |
| Customs duties | 2 | 7 |
| Agricultural tax | 0 | 2 |
| Construction tax | 0 | 1 |
| Excise tax | 7 | 0 |
| Estate/gift tax | 2 | 0 |
| Other taxes | 3 | 0 |

*(Sources: China Statistical Yearbook 1994 and American Almanac 1994–95)*

Prior to the economic reforms of the 1970s, China's Party-state operated on the assumption that all government revenues were its to distribute. Most revenue derived from state-owned enterprises. Corporate income was subject to taxation, and, in addition, as we have seen, the government recouped corporate profits from state-owned enterprises in the form of transfer payments. Besides industrial and commercial taxes, the government had the revenues from customs duties on imported goods, a tax on salt, and an agricultural tax. Neither property nor personal income was subject to taxation.

Although Beijing controlled the distribution of all tax revenue, it relied on local governments to collect the revenues, and until 1994 there was no central tax-collection agency. Local authorities collected taxes and corporate profits, then forwarded on to the central government a pre-agreed proportion of this revenue, retaining what was needed to cover their approved annual budget. The proportion forwarded to Beijing was subject to annual renegotiation, each province and municipality had its own negotiated rate, and these varied widely. For many years the city of Guangzhou, for example, contributed only 10 percent of its municipal revenues to central coffers, while Shanghai during the same period was routinely turning over 90 percent.

Expenditure budgets for governments at all levels were determined in a highly centralized fashion, with the budget at each level being set by the level just above it: the center set budgets for provinces and the directly administered cities; provincial authorities set budgets for their counties and cities. While some effort was made to balance revenues and expenditures at the national level, nothing related provincial, county, or city expenditures to the revenues generated in that jurisdiction. Rather, wealthy areas were expected to spend less than they took in, and Beijing used a portion of the surplus to cover the deficit in poorer areas, which routinely spent more than they could raise.

In reforming the economy, the central government looked for new sources of tax revenue, as is shown in the table. In addition, the government began a scheme, known as "eating from separate kitchens," under which the provinces turned over a proportion of their revenues that was fixed for five years so as to allow them much-needed long-term planning; they could set their own budgets, but on the understanding that the central government would no longer cover their over-budget expenditures.

Uniformity was the goal, but in practice many different arrangements were put in place under the rubric of "eating from separate kitchens." Sixteen of China's twenty-seven provinces and regions agreed to having title to some state-owned enterprises shifted from the central government to them. Beijing got the tax revenue from its enterprises, while tax revenue from the provincial enterprises went to provincial governments. Other arrangements were made with other localities: Guangdong and Fujian Provinces agreed to lump-sum transfer payments, to remain unchanged for five years;

### Chinese Government Revenue by Source, 1978 and 1995
(in billion yuan)

|                                       | 1978  | 1995  |
|---------------------------------------|-------|-------|
| Taxes:                                |       |       |
| Industrial and commercial             | 45.1  | 458.9 |
| Tariffs                               | 2.9   | 29.2  |
| Agricultural tax                      | 2.8   | 27.8  |
| Salt tax                              | 1.1   | 0.0   |
| Other tax revenues                    | 0.0   | 87.9  |
| Revenue from enterprises              | 57.2  | 0.0   |
| Subsidies to loss-making enterprises  | 0.0   | −32.8 |
| Development levies                    | 0.0   | 1.7   |
| Other revenues                        | 3.0   | 51.5  |
| Total                                 | 112.1 | 624.2 |

*(Sources: China Statistical Yearbook 1996 and*
*World Bank, Revenue Mobilization and Tax Policy, 1990)*

Jiangsu Province was assessed a percentage of its total revenue, fixed for five years; Beijing, Tianjin, and Shanghai were assessed percentages that were to be renegotiated annually, as in the past. The eight poorest provinces and regions, where revenues did not cover expenditures, were assigned fixed subsidies, to increase annually by 10 percent for five years.

Total budgetary revenue increased steadily thereafter, but an unintended consequence of "eating from separate kitchens" was that the central government's share of the revenue shrank from nearly 60 percent in 1978 to close to 40 percent by 1993. In transferring title to state-owned enterprises, the central government had kept control of strategic but not necessarily profitable factories. As its revenues declined, it shifted entire categories of expenditure from the national budget to local ones, which put local governments in a bind: their revenues were fixed, but now they had to take on new expenditures. To solve this problem, they relied increasingly on extra-budgetary funds—every imaginable kind of fee, fine, levy, toll, assessment, commission, and tariff. At the beginning of the reform period, extra-budgetary funds amounted to no more than 20 percent of regular tax revenues, but by 1993 they had increased to more than 100 percent of regular tax revenues and were a particularly sore point with the people.

A second round of tax reform was put into effect on 1 January 1994. The economy was then growing with unprecedented speed, but tax revenue as a proportion of output was declining. (Whereas tax revenue amounted to about a third of the total output value of the economy in 1979, it had declined to about 15 percent by 1992.) Moreover, state enterprises were draining resources from the central government rather than contributing substantially to its resources, as they had been doing a decade earlier. The new reform created, for the first time, a central-government tax-collection agency with local branches. The reform set as a goal that 80 percent of all tax revenue would be collected by central-government agents and only the remaining 20 percent by local collectors, which, if successful, would reverse the situation in which most revenue was retained by the provinces. Under the new arrangement, the central government would get the lion's share of tax revenues and provide grants to the local governments where needed to cover their expenditure budgets. The scheme of distinguishing central from local government ownership of state-sector enterprises is to be universalized, with all enterprises paying both national and local corporate income taxes. A problem may well arise from the fact that those who staff the tax bureaus, though they report to the central government, are local residents with, we might assume, local interests at heart.

.    .    .

As we have seen, Mao's egalitarian ideal had expressed a kind of Robin Hood approach to China's provinces, with the central government taking funds from the wealthier provinces and cities and redistributing them to the poorer ones. His idea was that only when regional inequalities had been reduced could China move forward—slowly, but equally. But Deng Xiaoping rejected this egalitarian approach to development, believing that it kept the best-endowed regions from realizing their potential and made for unacceptably slow growth. He justified his new approach with what we often call trickle-down economics, arguing that letting regions with the greatest potential develop rapidly would eventually benefit the poorer regions as well. Using an analogy, he described the special economic zones along the coast as pivotal points of two fans, the one extending out into the world economy, the other extending westward into the hinterlands. Capital, technology, and new markets would be drawn to the coastal cities along the ribs of the outward-extended fan and, in turn, would spread into China's interior along the ribs of the inward-extended fan.

There are many Chinese who are not persuaded by Deng's argument. Either they consider the trickle-down too slow or they dispute that there is one. China's experience during the past several decades suggests to them that a kind of center-periphery relationship is emerging, in which poorer provinces serve as suppliers of raw material, semifinished products, and labor power for the economic centers, which, awash in foreign capital and advanced technology, reap all the profits.

To counter these trends, China's interior provinces are actively courting foreign investors with bargain rates on real estate and labor and at the same time vociferously opposing any favoritism allowed to the coastal zones in the form of tax breaks for potential investors, arguing that only if they have comparable leeway can they compete effectively. In the meantime, they are learning to turn the successes of the coastal enclaves to their own advantage, becoming major investors themselves in enterprises and property located in the coastal zones.

Having grown accustomed to a greater degree of autonomy, the provinces now tend to resist any effort by the central government to recoup its control of local affairs. The center, for its part, believes that China's economy is overheated and wants to hold down its growth rate. Many of the issues that pit regions against the center arise from this conflict of interests.

Bank credit is an example. The central government became concerned in mid-1993 that local governments were authorizing too many loans for highly speculative projects, limiting the amount of credit available for less lucrative but vitally needed infrastructure projects and, it was thought, contributing to the high inflation rate. Acting on this concern, the central bank ordered local banks to call in their most speculative loans. But six months later, Vice Premier Zhu Rongji, who had temporarily taken charge of the central bank, admitted that the order had been only modestly successful in freeing up local credit for worthwhile purposes.

Similarly, the central government wants to be able to control and direct the flow of foreign investment, while the provinces want the freedom to attract foreign investors and the authority to cut deals with them. The center sets restrictions with respect to the size and nature of investments that may be locally approved; the provincial governments then set about calculating how to circumvent these restrictions.

Yet another source of conflict between center and region is what in the United States would be called unfunded mandates. Like our own federal government, China's central government has had a habit of enacting laws and regulations that require local government action but provide no funds to cover the costs. For example, the central government, wanting to improve the quality of air and water, has a full set of environmental laws and regulations but gives little or no financial support to local governments to cover the cost of enforcing them. Similarly, it is actively engaged in a program to reduce the size of the Chinese population but vests responsibility for implementing this program with local governments and provides no funding to offset the costs involved. In education, too, the central government enacts programs for expansion and improvement, but it relies on the local governments for the funds to carry out this mandate.

Provinces and regions frequently find themselves competing with one another for the resources, benefits, and exemptions distributed by the central government, for foreign investors, and for opportunities to engage in lucrative foreign trading deals. To better their positions, they try to maximize their ability to make independent decisions, and, to promote their local interests, they rival one another in lobbying the central government and currying favor with its officials.

Occasionally competition among regions has taken the form of protectionism. Some years ago, state-owned department stores in Shandong Province, for example, launched an informal "Buy Shandong" campaign, agreeing to exclude merchandise from other provinces and to limit the stock in their stores to goods produced in Shandong. Similarly, when officials in Hunan Province concluded that they were on the losing end of an economic competition with neighboring Guangdong Province, where factories were buying goods from Hunan suppliers at low (regulated) prices and making finished products that they sold at high (unregulated) prices, they closed Hunan's border with Guangdong and stopped the flow of goods in both directions. Only when the central government intervened was the border reopened and cross-border trade resumed. (It was perhaps this episode that Nicholas Kristof had in mind when, in *The New York Times*, he wrote an article sketching out three scenarios for "China in the Year 2000" in one of which economic cross-border competition between Hunan and Hubei Provinces erupts into a civil war that an impotent central government cannot bring under control.)

There are other issues that set provinces and regions at odds with one another. Water and air pollution seldom affect only the immediate area in which the pollution occurs; provinces or regions responsible for enforcing environmental regulations find their efforts undermined by neighboring regions that are unwilling to undertake or are less responsible for enforcement. Similarly, major public-works projects like the Three Gorges Dam or a proposed South to North Water Diversion Project have consequences that benefit one region while harming another. (In the case of the latter, for example, the northern provinces will have more water, but the central-south provinces not only get no extra water but must bear the cost of the land taken out of cultivation for the right-of-way.)

Finally, with a newly mobile population, the movement of workers is a source of conflict. More than 100 million people have left their original jurisdictions for distant cities. Is it the responsibility of the cities or the rural communities from which they came to bring this population under control? A Wild West variant on this problem concerns the so-called Gold Lords, who staked out illegal mining claims in China's hinterlands, hired migrant rural workers as miners, and defended their claims against rival claimants (and local authorities) with massive arsenals. Here again, region is pitted against region: Is it the responsibility of Qinghai (where many of the claims are located) to control this "attractive nuisance" or of the regions from which the prospectors come to give them jobs and control their movement?

The means at the disposal of a province or a region for asserting and defending its interests are varied. The mildest form is the time-honored technique of persuasion through debate, jawboning, or lobbying. Local officials who think their interests are being threatened by the central government or by their neighbors will try to argue the case as persuasively as they can with the best-connected representative they can find. The central government seems to operate most comfortably by treating each case as sui generis and is least at ease when trying to enforce uniform regulations uniformly, which means that a region or province can quite easily make the case for being treated as one among many exceptions to a given rule or regulation.

If this argument falls on deaf ears, local authorities can resort to the next means at their disposal for asserting their interests; given the nature of China's political system, this tactic—passive resistance—is perhaps the most effective. Paying lip service to the interests of the central government or of neighbors yet actively pursuing one's own plan is usually a highly effective way to stymie rivals. Bureaucratic practice is replete with methods for appearing to conform while actually failing to do so.

If all else fails, active resistance is possible, but this third level of asserting one's interests is a dangerous strategy because of the possibility of violent retaliation. Whether setting forth new local regulations, encouraging local practices that directly contravene central directives, failing to collect or forward tax revenues due the central authorities, or closing one's borders to cross-border trade, a province must carefully calculate the capabilities and intentions of its opponent. Active resistance against China's central authorities has only been tried two or three times since 1949, and it was always unsuccessful, but that was when the central authorities were strong, unified, and credible.

For some years after the 1949 revolution, China's central Party and government enjoyed great credibility, central and regional interests were seen as united, and the united interests were contained in and explained by an ideology to which many were deeply

committed. But much, if not all, of the credibility of the Party-
state has now been lost, as a result in part of disastrously mistaken
policies, bloated egos, pervasive corruption, and the collapse of
ideology and its replacement with a shallow, self-seeking materialism. In the absence of credibility, China's central authorities
have had to secure compliance with their directives by manipu-
lation, persuasion, or coercion.

One method they use to further the cause of local compliance
is to minimize the differences between central and local interests.
An example of this strategy is the shift of policy after Deng's
inspection trip to the Shenzhen special economic zone in February
1993, where retrenchment policies adopted in 1988 to slow economic growth and cap inflation had been very unpopular, but
where a new policy of encouraging market reform won the immediate approval—and compliance—of all but a handful of local
authorities. Still, local interests are diverse, not uniform, and
bringing central policy into conformity with the interests of one
region inevitably raises difficulties with the interests of other
regions.

A second strategy that the center uses to secure compliance
from local governments is to bargain, since it holds a limited but
significant number of chips that it can use in the game with local
authorities: items that benefit the individual official like appointments and promotions, and items that benefit the constituency like
tax waivers or public-works projects. The process is akin to the
pork-barrel politics with which Americans are familiar, though it
is compliance and not votes that is the operative currency in the
Chinese case. It is because of the advantages that it gets from
bargaining that the center is so reluctant to formalize, regularize,
or "federalize" its policies vis-à-vis local governments.

Where compromise and bargaining fail, the center can always
appoint or dismiss local officials. This power is somewhat limited
since effective local officials need the confidence of their com-

munities as well as that of the center: the center can replace a
rebellious official, but his replacement will be a success only if
he gains his constituency's cooperation. As we have seen, the center appoints people with strong local ties more and more frequently, but this undermines its leverage.

As a final resort, local compliance can, in theory, be secured
through coercion as it has been in the past. The center has a
nominal monopoly on the instruments of coercion—that is, the
People's Liberation Army and the People's Armed Police. In practice, however, it would take a very flagrant example of a local
government's flouting central authority to induce the center to send
in troops. And then there is the question of whether the armed
forces would obey such an order. Certainly there are reasons for
military commanders to think twice before carrying it out. First,
there is the question of where a commander's loyalties lie. Despite
the Party's best efforts, the Army itself suffers from regional divisions, and one can imagine situations in which a regional military commander would see his interests aligned with those of the
region where he is stationed and not with those in distant Beijing.
He would also reflect on the negative consequences for the armed
forces of its having obeyed the orders of the elders in Beijing in
1989. In short, there are reasons for the Army to doubt the wisdom
of acting as the coercive arm of a tottering political authority.

Were it to do so, as I believe it well might, it would do so to
end an interregional conflict threatening civil war or if it perceived
that central authority had collapsed, as in the former Soviet Union
in 1991. But intervening under these circumstances, it would see
itself as a substitute for the paralyzed Party-state, not as its agent.

Given the divergence of interests between the central government
and local governments in China and the relative weakness of the
former, it is very likely that more and more decentralized political
and economic systems will emerge. Given their rivalries and their

growing ties with foreign economies, China's macroregions will act with greater and greater independence in determining the direction of their development. The central government will probably be unable to amass the authority, the bargaining chips, or the coercion to reassert its power in the near term.

# ―IX―

# The Challenge of Environmental Degradation

The dark side of a high standard of living in the modern style is its adverse effect on the environment. With every improvement—greater mobility, a more varied diet, more living space, and more abundant personal possessions—attendant costs must be borne by the environment. Given the huge size of China's population, the success of its rapid economic development in raising the living standard has posed a particularly ominous threat of environmental degradation. Coping with this threat is one of the most serious problems confronting China and, because China's environment is also our environment, the rest of the world as well.

The Chinese state in traditional times worked hard to preserve a delicate balance between human needs and natural resources. The central government took responsibility for mobilizing the labor needed to build and maintain a system of flood control and irrigation works, as well as a network of inland waterways. Generations of Chinese peasants perfected a system of farming that made maximal use of limited land and, by means of intensive recycling practices, preserved its fertility. There was very little profligacy in the Chinese people's use of natural resources.

That delicate balance has been destroyed in modern times, and for several reasons. The first of these was a very rapid growth in the Chinese population during the eighteenth century. As we have seen, China's population remained stable at between 50 and 100 million people for nearly sixteen centuries; then, in the early years of the Qing dynasty in the late seventeenth century, it began to grow rapidly, multiplying by a factor of five within two hundred years. Although new crops and techniques increased agricultural productivity, the fivefold increase in population was accompanied by an increase in the amount of land under cultivation of only 25 percent. The delicate balance of human needs and natural resources was destroyed.

A second factor contributing to the breakdown of this balance was industrialization. The Chinese had sat out the industrial revolution that swept Europe and the United States in the early nineteenth century, indeed were almost wholly ignorant of its products until Western powers used modern weaponry to force China to open its doors to trade. Weapons factories became the entering wedge of industrialization in China, and by the last years of the nineteenth century the Chinese government had reluctantly and belatedly decided to emulate the West with full-scale industrialization.

A third factor was that China's industrialization was achieved under socialist auspices. Capitalist industrialization can hardly be said to have proceeded without environmental damage, but as we have all seen in the past few years in Eastern Europe and Russia, socialist industrialization seems to have been especially pernicious in its effects on the environment. For one thing, with the land and its resources publicly owned, no one takes responsibility for the land or represents its interests. For another, water and energy are supplied to consumers at no cost or at a heavily subsidized cost, and there is no incentive to conserve their use. Worse, the deficiencies in the quantity and quality of land, air, and water are escalating rather than improving.

China has a serious shortage of arable land. As we have seen in chapter 6, this shortage is daily exacerbated when land is taken out of cultivation and used for factories, roads, railroad rights-of-way, housing, and other accoutrements of rural industrialization and economic development. Scarce farmland is also lost as the unintended consequence of deforestation. Wood and plant stalks supply about four-fifths of the energy used for cooking and heating in the countryside, and this has resulted in the deforestation of nearly 300 million acres of land over the last forty years, which in turn adversely affects adjacent farmland. In the absence of forest windbreaks, some 16 million acres have been lost to desertification since 1949 and another 40 million acres are at risk. The cutting of trees also greatly increases water runoff, soil erosion, and siltation of riverbeds, raising the water level and augmenting the devastation caused by floods.

Air pollution is an especially serious problem in China, even according to Chinese standards, which are not as stringent as Western ones. The air in 90 percent of China's cities does not meet Chinese government clean-air standards. Beijing air is, on average, sixteen times more polluted than New York City air, and the city of Benxi, near Shenyang in Liaoning Province, periodically disappears from view on satellite maps because of the overlay of polluted air, the quality of which is second only to that of Milan, which has the dubious distinction of being the world's most polluted city.

The principal cause of air pollution in China is the burning of soft coal, which accounts for three-quarters of the energy used. Two-thirds of China's factories are contributing to air pollution in this way, and their outdated and inefficient equipment means they are using excessive quantities of the polluting fuel. China's industrial plant currently uses 5 times the amount of energy per dollar of gross national product (GNP) as Japan's and 2.5 times the United States'. But dust carried on prevailing winds from the desert regions of the northwest also contributes to urban air pollution, particularly in China's northern cities. Until recently, automobile exhaust was not a significant contributor to urban air pollution, but that is likely to change in the near future. There are currently only about 7 million automobiles on China's streets and roads—a tiny fraction of the 144 million automobiles registered in the United States—since the Chinese rely instead on bicycles and buses as their principal means of urban transportation. But in the fall of 1994 the government decided to make the automobile industry a primary force in the next stage of economic development, and an annual production target of 3 million new automobiles has been set for 2000 (three-fifths of the current annual American production). Foreign manufacturers actively compete to participate in the joint ventures that will help China meet this target.

The decision to develop the automobile industry has sparked a lively debate in China. Government planners have published specifications for a small, fuel-efficient, and low-polluting "family car" of the future. But promoting such a car as the principal means of transportation carries with it a multitude of undesirable consequences. A quarter of a billion automobiles would pollute the air, require paving over still more acres of scarce farmland, exhaust the country's oil reserves, and render China's already congested cities unnavigable. Moreover, automobile engineers are skeptical that the features called for in the specifications can be achieved in a car that is supposed to cost no more than ten thousand dollars.

China, currently the world's fourth-largest source of greenhouse gases (producing about 10 percent of the total), has a rate of economic development that translates into an increase of about 6 percent per year in energy consumption. At that rate China will exceed the United States, which is currently the largest producer of greenhouse gases, by the turn of the century and reach three times the current U.S. level of production by 2025.

Industrialization and a higher living standard are ordinarily accompanied by an increase in water consumption. Indeed, the consumption of tap water in China's cities has increased fivefold over the last fifteen years. (Water consumption in Beijing amounts to some 500 billion gallons per year.) Water being supplied free of charge to urban residents, there is no incentive to conserve it. Yet the water supply in China is neither adequate nor evenly distributed. Southern China, with about one-third of the arable land, has three-quarters of the water supply, while northern China has a serious water deficit. More than half of China's cities currently have a water shortage.

Unless new sources of water are located or stringent conservation measures adopted, experts estimate that Beijing will be short by up to 250 billion gallons a year by 2010. A highly controversial solution to this problem is the proposed South to North Water Diversion Project, plans for which include an 850-mile aqueduct to move water from the Han River, in Hubei Province, to reservoirs near Beijing and Tianjin. The cost of the project was initially estimated at $5 billion and would take six years to complete.

Not only is the water supply inadequate, but the quality of water is rapidly deteriorating. In 1995 factories and cities in China discharged 37.3 billion tons of sewage and industrial wastes into waterways and coastal waters. More than a quarter of the nation's freshwater supply is polluted, and 90 percent of the water flowing through its major cities is impotable.

This discouraging situation has developed not because of a lack of agencies, laws, or regulations. On the contrary, China has a reasonably complete set of environmental protection laws and regulations and a fully articulated structure of government offices devoted to environmental matters.

The problem of environmental pollution was first addressed in 1973 at a national conference on the subject—five years before the economic reforms began. Six years later the National People's Congress passed an Environmental Protection Law, and five years after that, in 1984, a National Environmental Protection Agency (NEPA) was formed. Revisions to the Environmental Protection Law, which were adopted by the National People's Congress in 1989, require environmental impact studies for all major construction projects and impose stiff fines for violating the pollution limits. Undeniably these conferences, new agencies, and new laws have had positive results. China is currently spending close to 1 percent of GNP, or $6.5 billion, on environmental protection annually. This puts it within, if at the low end of, the international average expenditure as a percentage of GNP, which stands between 1 and 2 percent.

Research and training in environmental sciences have developed quickly at universities and research institutes, and these institutions are well connected with professional equivalents outside of China. As is the case in other fields of academic endeavor, the hard science in these institutions is of reasonably high quality, while social science lags behind.

One specific result of this research effort is a new, clean-burning coal compound that is being introduced into China's cities to replace the highly polluting soft coal. There are other examples: in conjunction with its bid to be the site of the summer Olympic games in 2000, the city of Beijing took steps to reduce air pollution by replacing coal with natural gas as a household and industrial fuel, cutting coal use to 15 percent of its earlier level and cutting particulate matter in the air by 50 percent; and both coal and water have been placed on the price-reform agenda, which will encourage conservation of their use.

Environmental issues are difficult to resolve in any political setting. Correcting one source of environmental degradation can often give rise to new and potentially more dangerous sources of pollution; action that benefits the environment in one region may have detrimental effects in a neighboring region. But environmental issues seem particularly difficult to resolve in the Chinese political system, where as we have discussed a clash of interests between the central government and regional authorities often ends in deadlock and inaction. The decision to build a dam on the Yangzi River at the site of the Three Gorges gives us a useful example.

The scenic Three Gorges are located on the Yangzi River between the cities of Chongqing and Wuhan. Damming the Yangzi at the Three Gorges was initially proposed by Sun Yat-sen in 1923, but revolution, war, and civil war intervened, and the idea was shelved. The project was revived again under the aegis of Mao Zedong in the mid-1950s, then buried in the chaos of the Cultural Revolution. In 1979, the project was revived yet again. As it has taken shape in our time, it has three objectives, each of which, taken alone, dictates a set of specifications and benefits a particular geographical region.

The first objective, to control flooding along the lower reaches of the Yangzi, is best served with a high dam, though it might be equally well accomplished by a series of smaller dams on the river's tributaries, and it benefits exclusively those living downriver from the dam. The second objective, to generate electrical power, a highly desirable clean alternative to coal, also requires a high dam; the higher the dam, the more hydroelectric power can be generated. Given China's electrical grid and the topography of the area upriver, most of the power generated at the dam will go to those living downriver from the Three Gorges. The third objective, to improve navigation by deepening the river channel behind the dam in order to allow ships of up to ten thousand tons of displacement to get upstream as far as Chongqing, would benefit exclusively the communities upriver from the dam. (In fact, there is some possibility that downstream navigation would become more difficult, given the reduction in flow.) Navigation enhancement also imposes some very specific restrictions on the design of the dam.

So obviously several major issues, over which opinion was deeply divided, had to be resolved before work on the dam could begin. The first was the question of whether to build a single dam or a series of smaller dams. Only a single, high dam would raise the water level and improve navigation, but hydroelectric power generation and flood control could both be accomplished with smaller, safer, less costly, and technologically simpler dams. A second, highly controversial issue was the height of the dam and its effect on the people now living in areas that would be inundated by the reservoir behind it. A 650-foot-high dam, with the capacity to produce twenty-five thousand megawatts of electrical power, would displace, by conservative estimates, more than 1.4 million people; a 450-foot dam would produce six thousand megawatts and displace about 250,000 people. A third set of issues concerned the cost and financing of the project. Estimates proved extraordinarily difficult, given the disagreements over objectives and varying sets of specifications. And it seemed almost impossible to do a cost-benefit analysis, since the cost bases for navigation, power generation, and flood damage are each different from the other. Moreover, the project is expected to take more than a decade to complete, during which time price reform will affect virtually every item in the budget, and future inflation rates are difficult to predict. So project costs are a moving target. These factors help to explain why published estimates of the cost of the Three Gorges project vary by a factor of eight.

The current financing plan is based on an official budget of $11.5 billion, a figure that falls well below the median cost estimate. It calls for funding half the project from government revenues (a national tax on electrical power and profits from power generated at the Gezhouba Dam, downstream from the Three Gorges site). An additional 7.5 percent of the cost is to be covered by the sale of power produced at the dam once the first stage of the project is completed. The State Development Bank is to be tapped for loans covering a further 21 percent of the project cost, and an additional 4.5 percent is to come from loans extended by foreign providers of equipment. This still leaves a shortfall of nearly 20 percent of the money needed to cover a low estimate of the total cost. The World Bank has indicated its unwillingness to consider loan applications for it, which the Chinese have in any case been reluctant to seek, not wanting to deal with the required environmental impact studies.

Perhaps the most serious technological issue at stake in the dam project is finding a solution for the problem of siltation. Although silt carried by the Yangzi River is only a little more than a third of that carried by the Yellow River, it nonetheless amounts to some 500 million tons a year. Controlling the silt to protect the dam structure and to keep the upriver channel clear poses unprecedented technical problems, while predicting the effect on the eroded downstream riverbed caused by a reduction in silt poses still more.

As originally conceived, the project had another seemingly insurmountable technological problem. Initial plans called for hydroelectric generators with a capacity of one thousand megawatts, but the largest generators produced in China have a capacity of three hundred megawatts, the largest outside China seven hundred megawatts. Past experience suggests that generator-capacity technology has advanced at a rate of approximately one hundred megawatts a decade. At that rate it will be well into the next century before big enough generators will be available for the Three Gorges.

It is no surprise that China's political system is so deeply divided—indeed, at loggerheads—over the Three Gorges project. There are not only sharp disagreements among several regions but apparently irreconcilable divisions among central government agencies. Within the Ministry of Water Resources and Electric Power, a recent merger of two ministries, the section responsible for water resources favors the dam, arguing that it is the most effective solution to the problem of flood control, while the section concerned with electrical power opposes the project on the grounds that a series of smaller dams is a less expensive, technologically more feasible, and more reliable way to increase the country's electric power supply. The Ministry of Communication and its Yangzi River Transport Bureau oppose the large dam on the grounds that its effect on the navigability of the river downstream of the dam is highly unpredictable and its very long construction period will disrupt existing river traffic. A third agency, the Yangzi River Planning Office, established in the mid-1950s to develop an overall plan for the Yangzi River basin, consistently advocated the high dam, primarily because of its positive effect on flood control.

Depending on the dimensions of the final plan, local governments along the Yangzi River differ substantially with respect to the costs they will bear and the benefits they will enjoy. The municipality of Chongqing is an enthusiastic booster of the project, because it hopes to be able to expand its port facilities to receive bigger ships. The city government has very specific dam heights in mind: a water level of 588 feet at the dam will raise the river such that ships of ten thousand tons can reach Chongqing; if the water level is lower than this, only smaller ships will reach the new port, and if it is higher, large ships will reach a largely flooded Chongqing.

The provincial government of Sichuan has a mixed response. Expanding the port capacity of Chongqing will greatly assist Sichuan by strengthening its links to China's rapidly developing coastal provinces, but on the other hand, it will not benefit from flood control. Moreover, the power grid is such that relatively little of the new power will benefit Sichuan. Yet one of the greatest costs and most vexing problems—that of resettling the people displaced by the reservoir—falls exclusively to Sichuan provincial authorities, a most unwelcome burden.

Similarly, the township and municipal governments in the areas to be flooded are divided in their views. Some towns along the river will be eliminated entirely; others must abandon riverfront property and rebuild above the new water level. Project funds are budgeted to compensate those displaced by the reservoir, a portion going to resettled people, and a larger portion to the local governments responsible for building new homes and creating new job opportunities. The current allocation is 30 percent to individuals and 70 percent to local governments, which they may well take as a windfall. For example, the town of Wanxian, asked to draw up a relocation budget, came up with a figure of $2.9 billion. The central authorities were stunned, having budgeted only $3.5 billion for *all* relocation expenses.

The governments of Hubei and Hunan Provinces are the most enthusiastic in support of the Three Gorges project, for they are in a win-win position, being the principal beneficiaries of flood control of the dam as well as of increased power generation, while none of their residents will be displaced by the reservoir. There is less enthusiasm downriver. Jiangxi, Jiangsu, Anhui, and Shanghai will benefit from flood control and power generation, but the river channel will erode in unpredictable ways with the newly silt-free water flowing over the dam; farmland may flood, and river ports become inaccessible.

Given a virtual gridlock of conflicting interests, it is surprising that the project was ever launched. But having been launched, it is highly possible that the gridlock will keep it from being completed. That construction started in June 1993 was largely because Premier Li Peng adopted the project and exerted strong pressure to get it under way. As minister of Electric Power in the early 1980s, he was on record as having opposed it, but then he came to see it as a monument to his personal accomplishments. Using his authority as head of government, he mobilized the various agencies supporting the project, overrode the central agencies opposed to it, and engineered a compromise in the project's scope that satisfied at least some of the conflicting objectives.

Thus in March 1992, the National People's Congress considered a proposal to build, at an estimated cost of $10 billion, a dam of just over 600 feet in height with a reservoir level of 570 feet. The generating capacity of the power plant would be eighteen thousand megawatts, utilizing twenty-six seven-hundred-megawatt generators. The proposal estimated that 1.13 million people would be displaced by the reservoir and that the project would take sixteen years to complete. Responsibility for supervising the project was vested in a newly established Three Gorges Construction Committee chaired by Li Peng. Although the proposition passed the legislature with an overwhelming majority, the level of opposition was unprecedented: of the 2,600-odd delegates, 166 voted against the project and 664 abstained.

Although ground has been broken and the project has been under way since the fall of 1993, many doubt it will be completed as planned. Each succeeding cost estimate is significantly larger than the last. Financing has yet to be fully put in place. The technological problems are still unsolved. Local opposition takes the very effective form of foot-dragging, and corruption eats away at the funds for relocation of refugees. Environmental issues continue to plague the project. On the positive side of the ledger is that, at least over the short run, eighteen thousand megawatts of hydroelectric power will provide a clean-burning substitute for soft coal. But the negative side of the ledger also contains entries: many fish species are threatened with extinction because of the slower flow above the dam, and the upriver journey of river sturgeon to spawn will be thwarted. Archaeologists have reminded the Chinese government and the world that the site of the second "cradle" of Chinese civilization, as important as that in the Yellow River basin, will be inundated. Finally, were this very large dam to fail for any reason, the downstream disaster is difficult to calculate.

The factor most damaging to the prospects for completion of the project is not the environmental calculus but the fact that its leading proponent and chairman of its Construction Committee, Li Peng, is now China's least popular politician—whose political career is most unlikely to thrive in the wake of the death of his mentor, Deng Xiaoping.

Conflicts of interest over the Three Gorges Dam are exemplary of the broader problem that has, to date, kept China's environmental protection from being more effective: the conflict of priorities between environmental protection and economic development. When push comes to shove, the latter always takes precedence over the former, as it does in many circumstances around the world.

First, there is insufficient funding for environmental concerns at the national level. Qu Geping, for many years head of the National Environmental Protection Agency and currently chair of a National People's Congress committee on environmental protection, has argued that China has a double burden: not only to reduce the damage currently being done to the environment, but, like Russia and Eastern Europe, to clean up the damage caused by past excesses and omissions. To accomplish both, he estimates that at least ten times the level of current expenditure is needed: Instead of spending 1 percent of GNP, China should spend 10 percent, or $69 billion, a year—a figure corresponding to nearly 85 percent of the current total national expenditure budget.

As is clear in the case of the Three Gorges Dam, the conflict between economic development and environmental protection is worked out in the grid of China's political system, where local and national interests are often at odds. NEPA directives and regulations travel down the vertical paths of the grid and are thwarted at the horizontal local level, where it is represented by the provincial, municipal, or county Environmental Protection Bureaus (EPBs). These bureaus, like other central-government agencies at the local level, report not only to Beijing but also to the local government. When it is a question of developing the local economy by building a new factory, local authorities pressure the head of the local EPB to waive regulations so as to get the factory built as expeditiously and cheaply as possible.

The conflict of priorities is exacerbated by the fact that most of the central-government regulations take the form of unfunded mandates, and as a result, virtually the entire cost of compliance with them must be covered by local budgets. The local government that is in compliance thus suffers a double blow: construction is prevented or delayed on factories that might bring it income while poisoning the local air and water, and the local government not only loses the tax revenue the factories would have generated but must also pay for the EPB officials who stand in the way.

Newly built collective enterprises are by no means the only source of water and air pollution, of course. State-owned enterprises, many of them built when there was no thought given to their detrimental ecological effects, are also serious polluters. And given the other fiscal problems plaguing China's state sector, they are in no position to cover the cost of upgrading their equipment.

There is yet another reason that rapid economic development always wins over environmental protection in China. In other countries, active and engaged grassroots movements have helped to build public consciousness about environmental concerns. Until very recently there has been no such movement in China. The state is hypersensitive about groups that might become nuclei for political opposition, and this has made forming a "green movement" virtually impossible. But news of one grassroots protest movement reached the Western press in 1993. A township-owned chemical factory in remote Gansu Province was polluting a local stream so seriously that peasants wading in the stream to fish were getting blisters on their legs. When the factory operators and township authorities ignored the protests, the residents descended on the factory, drove its operators out, and shut it down. There are other examples like this one, but they are isolated episodes and show no signs yet of a national movement that will significantly affect the actions of local governments.

International pressure on China to do more with respect to the environment elicits a response heard elsewhere in the developing world. Concern for the environment, this argument runs, is a pastime taken up late in life by wealthy nations, which themselves achieved economic development with little or no attention to its environmental consequences. Given this, why should poorer countries be held to new and higher standards in their economic development than the developed nations were in years past? If the West believes that developing nations should be held to these high new standards, then it should help to pay for the very expensive process of doing so. China held this position when, in agreeing to take part in the 1991 Montreal Protocols on reducing the release of chlorofluorocarbons, it made its participation contingent on its being granted access to foreign aid and technology to assist in the reduction.

The fact of the matter is we all inhabit the same planet. Chinese people are the first to suffer from the poisoning of China's air and water, but ultimately we all suffer. The first line of responsibility for China's extraordinarily serious environmental problems is, of course, the Chinese state, but in the end the responsibility is international. Until the Chinese state has struck a balance between the conflicting priorities of economic development and environmental concern, however, international assistance is of little use.

# One Billion Plus:
# Controlling Population Growth

For most Chinese, China's population is the country's greatest problem and one that the Chinese government has acknowledged for more than twenty-five years. At the beginning of the reform period, it initiated a series of programs and regulations designed to slow population growth. The one-child policy, as these are collectively known, is almost universally unpopular. In the cities it is accepted as a necessary evil; in the countryside it has met with widespread resistance. This resistance is triggered in part by a traditional preference for male children, but also by the fact that the incentives and penalties of the one-child policy run directly counter to those of the household-responsibility system. The one-child policy tries to limit population growth by rewarding families with a single child and penalizing larger ones, but the household-responsibility system in effect rewards large families by giving them a high income, and in practice, the incentives to have a large family are significantly stronger than the penalties for exceeding the single-child limit.

The birth-control program is yet another good example of the problems in the power grid of China's political system. The central government has come up with a program it wants implemented everywhere, but it must rely on local authorities—indeed, government at the very lowest level of the political system—to enforce it. And, like pollution control, the birth-control program is an unfunded mandate. Since the program is both highly unpopular and unfunded, local governments have either modified, delayed, or thwarted it.

Alarmed by local noncompliance, evidence of which surfaces in each national census, the central government pressures the localities by imposing specific limits and quotas. Under the gun to meet these, local authorities resort to enforced abortions and sterilizations, practices that of course further alienate their constituencies, already disaffected by other grievances, and anger the central authorities, who denounce such draconian measures as illegitimate local violations of a legitimate central policy.

The birth-control program is in sharp contrast to the economic-reform program, the thrust of which is to remove the government from the daily lives of its citizens. The government makes fewer and fewer decisions for the Chinese people, who less and less often find the government looking over their shoulders to monitor their political correctness. But the birth-control program has inserted the government into their lives in an unprecedented way, involving it in their most intimate decisions. This imposition of political authority angers many people outside China, who regard the one-child policy as an invasion of the most private aspect of an individual's life and a violation of a fundamental human right. Many who hold this view are also unequivocally opposed to abortion. But with their own conception of national sovereignty, individual rights, and the overwhelming magnitude of their population problem, Chinese authorities find this criticism impossible to fathom.

In March 1995 China's population passed 1.2 billion people. At the current rate, we can expect that each year about 18 million children will be born in China and about 6 million Chinese will die, for a net increase of about 12 million. With that net growth, the Chinese population will pass 1.3 billion by the turn of the century and 1.5 billion in about 2015. At that point, there will be three times as many people in China as there were at the founding of the People's Republic in 1949: the population will have trebled in sixty-five years' time.

Demographers use three figures when discussing change in the size of a population. The first is the *birthrate*, usually expressed in births per thousand people in the population as a whole. China's birthrate in 1995 was 17.1 per thousand. The second figure is the *population growth rate*, the birthrate less the death rate. The death rate in 1994 having been 6.6 per thousand, the population growth rate was 10.5 per thousand. Expressing that figure in a percentage (as is most frequently done), the 1995 population growth rate was 1.05 percent. The third figure is the *fertility rate*, the average number of children born to women of childbearing age. China's fertility rate is currently 2.3. The rate significantly differs for the urban and rural populations: the urban rate being 1.3, while the rural fertility rate is 2.8. In practical terms, this means that, whereas most city families have a single child, most rural ones have three.

### Population Growth, United States and China

|  | *United States* | *China* |
|---|---|---|
| Population 1995 | 262 million | 1.2 billion |
| Birthrate | 16.3/1,000 | 17.1/1,000 |
| Mortality rate | 8.6/1,000 | 6.6/1,000 |
| Net migration rate | 3.8/1,000 | 0/1,000 |
| Population growth rate | 1.15% | 1.05% |
| Fertility rate | 2.1 | 2.3 |
| Life expectancy | 75.7 years | 70.0 years |
| Median age | 33.4 years | 25.0 years |

*(Sources: China Statistical Yearbook 1996 and American Almanac 1994–95)*

To bring its population problem under control, the Chinese government has set a target birthrate of thirteen per thousand, which the one-child policy, as it has been modified in practice over time, is designed to achieve. One obstacle is an unusually large number of women of childbearing age (between the ages of fifteen and forty-nine)—currently more than 300 million, or roughly one-quarter of China's total population.

Success in limiting births will exacerbate another social problem in China. With fewer young people, the median age will rise, accelerating the already rapid "graying" of China. In the 1990 census, the retired-age population numbered 117 million, or just over 10 percent of the population; by 2050 it is estimated that there will be more than 400 million retirees—more than 25 percent of the population. Whereas today there is one retired person for every four people of working age, by 2050 that ratio will be very close to one to one. (The problem in the United States is comparable, though the figures are somewhat smaller: our retired-age population is currently 12 percent of the total; that figure will grow to 20 percent by 2050.)

Attempts to limit China's population growth were slow in coming, largely because of Mao Zedong's views on the subject. It was his opinion that a large population was a national asset: he thought of every person added as two more hands whose work would contribute to national development and defense. For the first twenty years of the People's Republic, no effort was made to restrict births, and the birthrate was well over thirty per thousand (except during the years of recovery from the Great Leap Forward).

Zhou Enlai took a different view. He came to believe that controlling population growth was a prerequisite to economic development, and he was responsible for initiating China's first national program to limit births in 1971, the goal being to reduce the birthrate to twenty per thousand by 1980. In practice, Zhou's program amounted to a two-child policy. The campaign's slogan was "late, sparse, and few." Couples were encouraged to delay marrying until their late twenties, to space their children at least four years apart, and to limit themselves to two children. The campaign was a success. Although by no means every family was limiting itself to two children, the birthrate in 1980, at eighteen per thousand, had been reduced by a third in a ten-year period.

Despite this success, projections drawn up in 1978 suggested that the Chinese population would pass the 1 billion mark in 1980 and would reach 1.4 billion by 2000. Deng Xiaoping and his reformist colleagues shared Zhou's view that economic development could not proceed unless population growth were controlled, but they were alarmed by these projections and concluded that Zhou's gradualist approach to the population problem was insufficient. Out of their alarm was born the one-child policy.

As just shown, the goals of the one-child policy are significantly closer to being realized in China's cities than in the countryside. There are a number of reasons for this success, some of them attributable to the policy, others having little to do with it. Urban couples are more removed from the influence of tradition and less likely to feel pressure from parents and relatives to produce large families and male heirs. Moreover, as we have seen, the cities are extraordinarily crowded and living space very limited, so city residents experience the problems of a large population every day, whereas those problems seem rather remote to people in the less crowded countryside. Urban couples are generally better educated, and worldwide there is a correlation between the level of education (particularly that of women) and the decision to limit births. Finally, in most cases both urban parents work outside the house, and, because childbearing disrupts the woman's career, it is more likely to be delayed and limited. Child care is also more expensive and somewhat more difficult to arrange in the city than it is in the countryside, where grandparents are near at hand.

The one-child policy has proved much more difficult to implement in the countryside, where tradition is still quite strong and favors male children. The birth of a son is cause for celebration; the birth of a daughter is only a "small happiness." In part, this is simple gender bias: a son carries on the family line, a daughter does not. But in part, it is based on an economic reality: when a daughter is married, she leaves her parents' home and becomes a member of her husband's family, contributing to her in-laws' family exchequer, not to her parents', while a son is responsible for his parents as they retire and age. In the absence of a public pension scheme, giving birth to a son means providing for one's retirement security.

As we have seen, the incentives of the household-responsibility system undermine efforts to enforce the one-child policy in the countryside, since they reward large families: increasing the "hand-to-mouth ratio"—that is, the number of a household's able-bodied workers in relation to the number to be fed—gives one a direct increase in household income. At the moment, increased productivity is winning out over decreased fertility.

In the early years of American travel to China, after President Nixon first went in 1972, a visit to a commune was an obligatory event on every tourist's itinerary. Directing the tour group into the production team's office, local officials would point with pride to a complicated chart on the office wall: a very public display of information on the menstrual cycles, birth-control practices, and pregnancy records of every woman in the team. When the tour guide translated the explanation, foreigners would be aghast—a reaction that, in turn, perplexed the officials. For the birth-control program, from its inception, made a public issue of what, to most foreigners, is a very private matter.

Yet the results of having done this are impressive. Today in China, information about contraception and contraceptive devices is widespread, and the Chinese government estimates that close to 85 percent of the sexually active population practices some form of contraception. Still, abortion is a common form of limiting fertility. Recent figures show that eleven million abortions are performed annually, or one for every two live births. This is higher than the rate in the United States, which is one for every three live births, but lower than that in Russia and parts of Eastern Europe, where it is not uncommon to find rates of one abortion for each live birth.

To encourage compliance with the one-child policy, the government is prepared to offer an array of incentives. In Guangan County, in Sichuan Province, in the early 1990s, these included subsidies. Although a subsidy comes to no more than a dollar a month, this constitutes a 3 percent increase in the average household income there. There is also access to a pension plan, additional land in the household's farming contract, a reduction in the grain tax, and, finally, tuition assistance for a one-child family. This package seems well structured to appeal to the needs and interests of young rural couples, but in general, incentives packages like these are not enough to persuade the parents of a girl not to try once more for a boy.

When carrots fail, sticks are applied. Monetary fines are the most widespread form of penalty for noncompliance, the minimum fine being on average about four hundred dollars, or the equivalent of a year's income for the offending household. When the income exceeds four hundred dollars, the fine is usually 1.5 times the annual income, but even these substantial fines are often insufficient, since the income and family security a son will provide his parents over their lifetimes far exceed even the stiffest current fine. Many farming households consider noncompliance and payment of the fine as a wise investment in the family's future.

Frustrated by the failure of incentives and penalties to reduce reproduction, local officials often use coercion, especially when their superiors assign birth quotas and hold them personally responsible for keeping them. Coercion ordinarily begins with verbal harassment of noncomplying couples: women are urged to undergo sterilization, and pregnant ones are urged to have an abortion. Those who resist are threatened. One recent account describes the work of a tough-minded local family-planning official, identified as "Mrs. Liao," who marched into a remote rural community in south-central China, lined up the village women, singled out those with the most children, and told them that, unless they reported to the local clinic for sterilization, their houses would be blown up. "Mrs. Liao" is not alone: there is fairly widespread evidence of the destruction of personal property in retaliation against those who ignore the one-child policy.

In extreme cases, women have been physically restrained and forced to undergo abortions or sterilizations against their will, though I have not found reliable evidence on which to base an estimate of how frequently this occurs. There is reason to believe that it is not common. Forcing a surgical procedure on an unwilling constituent may satisfy a superior and avoid a fine, but the local official must live with the consequences, and given conditions in most rural communities, the last thing he is interested in is further alienating his constituents. Also, these atrocities attract unwelcome international attention, for forced abortions are repugnant not only to those for whom abortion under any circumstances is wrong but also to human-rights activists, even when they might favor abortion when undertaken as a free choice.

In order to avoid alienating both the rural population and the international community, China's population-planning authorities have relaxed the one-child policy where resistance is greatest. In fact, the policy has had loopholes from the outset. Ethnic minorities have always been exempt, on the theory that it was important to preserve their continuity and because the areas inhabited by most ethnic minorities are China's least densely populated. Today approximately half of the rural population is subject to a relaxed policy that, in practice, permits one child where that child is a boy, two children where the first child is a girl, and no third births. In a 1994 survey of couples of childbearing age, 63 percent had a single child. Somewhat more than 25 percent had a second child, and only the remaining 10 percent had three or more children.

As with many unpopular policies, for every method of enforcement the central and local governments have put in place, those determined to violate the policy have thought up a way to avoid compliance. The most straightforward of these is simply to pay the fine for over-quota births, treating the expenditure as an investment in the family's future.

Since the object, in the case of many families, is to produce a male heir, what is done in the unwelcome event of a "small happiness"—the conception or birth of a female? As sonograms have become more widely available, they have increasingly been used to identify the gender of fetuses. When a female is identified, many women choose to have an abortion. This use of sonograms has recently been outlawed, but enforcing this new law will be difficult. Sonogram equipment, now manufactured in China, is widely available, and there is money to be made in offering the service.

Once a female child is born, the simplest method to avoid having her count against the family's quota of children is not to record her birth. The gradual relaxation of social control associated with the reforms and the possibility of going away from home to give birth have made it easier to conceal births from those charged with limiting their number. The widespread incidence of this practice was revealed in the 1990 census, generally regarded as the most thorough one ever conducted in China, when officials assured citizens that no retroactive penalties would be imposed on unregistered births. The census showed the Chinese population to stand at 1.13 billion, a figure that exceeded projections by some 13 million. Part of the discrepancy can be accounted for by statistical flaws in the projections, but most of it was due to the number of female children whose births had gone unrecorded.

Other methods of avoidance are more serious. Some parents decide to put girl babies up for adoption or, worse, to abandon them. The vast majority of children available for adoption in China or being raised in orphanages there are girls, or boys with handicaps. There are also stories of female infanticide, some involving medical practitioners. When girl babies' lives are terminated at birth, the deliveries are recorded as stillbirths. Other stories describe instances where infanticide is committed by parents or family members desperate to avoid having the child count against the family's one- or two-child limit, though the Chinese press emphasizes that infanticide is against the law in China and that cases are prosecuted wherever they are detected.

The cumulative effect of all these methods of avoidance is a marked skewing of the gender ratio among Chinese children. Whereas the worldwide ratio of male to female births is 106 males for every 100 females, the ratio in China is currently 111 males for every 100 females. Newspaper accounts describe the plight of unmarried Chinese men unable to find a spouse because of the shortage of unmarried women; the 1990 census showed three unmarried males for every two unmarried females. Among China's small but growing number of divorced people, the gender ratio is two males for each female. While some suggest that the one-child policy is responsible, it is actually too recent to have had this effect. The gender ratio for the cohort now of marriageable age is very close to the worldwide norm.

When all other methods of avoidance fail, rural Chinese now have a new option that they are choosing with increasing frequency: they can leave home and migrate to a city. While most floating workers are single males, there is also a significant number of couples who have found a way to avoid the sharp eyes and draconian penalties of the redoubtable "Mrs. Liao" and her family-planning colleagues. Floating workers are in something of a limbo so far as China's system of social control is concerned, having severed ties with rural officials and not yet been picked up by urban ones, who are reluctant to legitimate their presence in the city. Many rural couples take advantage of this to pursue their quest for a son.

From the perspective of the central government, the one-child policy has the potential for solving China's most pressing problem. But from the perspective of local officials, the situation looks somewhat different. The one-child policy, even in its relaxed form, is highly unpopular among the rural population. To the extent that these officials align themselves with the central government and enforce the policy, they alienate themselves from their constituents; when they must resort to coercion, that alienation only deepens. And because they need to secure the compliance of their constituents on many other issues besides birth control, they are reluctant to align themselves too closely with the central government's policy.

This is all the more true because they are less well qualified than their predecessors to enforce an unpopular policy. There was a substantial turnover of local officials in the 1980s, during the course of which older officeholders retired and were replaced by younger, less experienced ones, and the number of women holding public office in rural communities also declined. Some of the most effective family-planning workers at the local level had been older women, now retired, whose younger, male successors find it hard to take their place.

Economic reform in the countryside has also altered the function of local officials. Today they are significantly less pervasive a presence than were the production-team and brigade leaders they replaced. As the private realm has expanded greatly everywhere in China over the last twenty years, the government's ability to control individual behavior has declined.

Confronted with this decline in efficacy and in order to ensure stringent enforcement at the local level, the central government has taken to making local officials personally responsible for the success of the family-planning program by docking salaries or fining them for over-quota births. While some officials respond positively to this pressure to resort to coercion, others avoid the problem by making false statistical reports to their superiors.

A final problem is that the one-child policy is such an expensive unfunded mandate. Although the state claims that nearly $1 billion is spent annually on implementation of the birth-control program, virtually all that money comes from local governments, which, already pressed to meet other financial obligations, find themselves paradoxically funding the birth-control program exclusively from fines levied against those who violate it.

Family-planning policy in China since the early 1970s has been based on the premise that economic growth cannot occur until population growth has been brought under control. Others argue that the reverse is true: population growth can only be brought under control when economic growth has occurred. The experience of other developing countries has shown that two factors associated with economic development—urbanization and education—both result in decreased fertility, and observers mark that this is true in China as well, that is, in Chinese cities. Along this line of reasoning, revisionists argue that the one-child policy has not significantly changed the population growth rate in China and that a more relaxed policy would have achieved about the same results and avoided the widespread anger and disaffection brought on by the attempt to enforce a much more stringent program.

The one-child policy touches very sensitive nerves among foreign, particularly American, observers. Any policy that interferes with personal decisions regarding childbearing is for some a violation of human rights, for others not only a violation of human rights but also a sin. Still others find the one-child policy acceptable but are disturbed by enforcement measures that violate human rights. In the fall of 1994 the Chinese government released its newly drafted Maternal and Infantile Health Care Law, initially publicized as a "eugenics law," since it addressed the problem of the ten million people in China with birth defects that, in the words of the law, "could have been prevented." The new law called for sterilizing the mentally ill and aborting the fetuses of those suffering from hereditary diseases or abnormalities. The Chinese government seemed genuinely surprised and nonplussed by the storm of criticism from abroad, and its response was not to repeal the law, but to avoid using the term "eugenics" when discussing it and to emphasize the provisions for ensuring informed consent on the part of those affected by it.

The Chinese claim that concern over reproductive rights, like certain environmental issues, is a luxury of the rich and less populous nations of the world and contend that the magnitude of China's population problem is such that honoring individual rights with respect to reproduction endangers the rights of the society as a whole. Extraordinary measures are necessary for China to continue to feed and clothe its population, they claim while deploring the excesses that they consider unintended consequences of their policy. It remains to be seen whether that policy will succeed in reducing the size of the rural Chinese family or whether, in trying to do so, it will dangerously undermine the already tenuous authority of local governments, in which case the state may be obliged to resort to the slower but in the long term equally effective strategies of urbanization and expanded educational opportunities.

# Human Rights
# and the Rule of Law

From the American perspective, the single most significant obstacle to better U.S.–China relations is the Chinese government's systematic violation of its citizens' human rights, but almost
as important is the absence of a fully articulated set of laws and,
more fundamentally, of the concept of the rule of law. It is with
human rights and our devotion to the rule of law that many of us
are least willing to make concessions for cultural differences. We
believe not only that our position on these issues is correct, but
that it is the *only* correct position and thus should be universally
accepted.

Yet it is true that the cultural differences in this area are great.
The American political system—and to a great degree the Western
political tradition of the modern nation-state—is rooted in the concept of the rule of law, by which we mean that the law stands
above individual officeholders as a neutral arbiter to which disputes are referred and on the basis of which they are resolved. All
citizens are equal before the law and everyone, regardless of position or status, is subject to it. But China's political system is
rooted in the concept of the rule of men (in recent years expanded
in a limited way to include some women), and the individual of-

ficeholder stands above the law and serves as the arbiter to whom disputes are referred. These diametrically opposed concepts derive from diametrically opposed ideas about the significance of the individual. The primacy of the individual, and his or her rights and freedoms, based on philosophical traditions that go from classical Greek thought through the European Enlightenment, is the firm basis of the American economy and political system, and our legal system is designed to protect it. But the concept on which Chinese culture is based is the primacy of the family and the society, and the emphasis in that tradition is on individual obligations, not rights or freedoms. The individual has obligations to the family, and the family has obligations to society. The ruler's task is to ensure that these obligations are fulfilled.

There is a school of Chinese philosophy that supports the necessity of a fully articulated legal system. Han Fei, whose ideas were taken up by the first Qin emperor in the third century B.C., asserted the principle that people are inherently evil; therefore, good behavior could be elicited only by means of carefully drafted laws backed by generous rewards and stringent punishments. Emperor Qin Shi used these ideas, later known under the name of "legalism," during his brief but repressive rule, the most important accomplishment of which was the first unification of the Chinese state. But because of his brutality, legalism was discredited, and subsequent rulers looked to the very different views of Confucius as the basis for their state ideology.

Confucius, who predated Han Fei by two centuries, began with an opposite presumption about human nature. Believing that human nature is fundamentally good, he argued that good behavior was most effectively elicited by means of the ruler's example. Confucius's concept of a web of human relationships, which we examined in chapter II, involved mutual responsibilities: the subordinate was obliged to obey, the superior to provide a moral example, and if all went well, laws, rewards, and penalties would be superfluous.

In describing the cycle of dynastic growth and decline, I have touched on the so-called right to rebel. There were, in fact, circumstances under which the obligation to obey was suspended: when the ruler failed to provide the moral example that it was his obligation to embody, an official had a duty to remonstrate, but this was not a kind of embryonic freedom of speech, for the emphasis was on not the official's freedom to disagree, but rather his *obligation* to disagree. Carrying out this obligation might prove fatal, but the obligation stood, nonetheless. Moreover the right to rebel was only granted ex post facto to the successful rebel. The unsuccessful rebel was guilty of treason.

The system that emerged under the Confucian order was not devoid of written law. Although there was little in the way of written civil law, there were criminal and administrative codes, regulations for the conduct of criminal investigations and the administration of justice. Nonetheless, the performance of the ruler or official, not the written code, was the critical element in the successful functioning of the political system.

Scholars have noted analogies between the political system constructed by the Chinese Communist Party under Mao Zedong and the Confucian political system that preceded it: Marxism-Leninism and the Confucian canon, the Party cadre and the scholar-official, the core leader and the emperor. Yet the legal system as it operated under Mao Zedong only faintly resembled its Confucian antecedent. Like the Confucian past, there was no rule of law under Mao, but unlike the Confucian past, there was essentially no law at all under Mao.

When the Chinese Communists did make some effort to introduce new legal codes, as in many other areas of life in China in the 1950s the Soviet Union was their model. The legal system was made up of three institutions: a Ministry of Public Security, which was responsible for police work; a "procuracy" at each level of government, which investigated and prosecuted crime and reported to the Supreme People's Procuracy; and courts at each level of government, headed by the Supreme People's Court, which heard and decided cases and set punishments.

Despite this formal apparatus, the major political movements of the 1950s and 1960s—in which millions of landlords, bureaucrats, dissenters, intellectuals, and, finally, Party officials were stripped of status, wealth, and power and sentenced to long periods of hard labor or even to death—took place without reference either to laws or to the system, which focused most of its attention on criminal cases. Civil disputes were most often resolved within the units where the conflicting parties worked, disputes between work units by the administrative agency to which both reported or, more informally, by Party members within the contending units.

Mao believed in ideological principles, not laws. Ideological principles gave rise to a "line" of correct thinking, which in turn was translated into specific policies, each of which had implementing regulations. The regulations tended to be vague and subject to broad interpretation. And even ideological principles were subject to change. Late in life, Mao began to manipulate his ideology to serve his own purposes. At that point, the only reliable guide to action became the Chairman's gnomic "latest instruction."

Mao rejected the idea that the law is universally applicable, borrowing from Marx and Engels the idea that law is a tool that one social class uses to oppress another: in years past, the landlord class had used Chinese law to oppress the peasantry; in a capitalist society, the bourgeoisie used the law to oppress the proletariat; but in socialist China, the law would be used to overthrow and suppress the landlords and bourgeoisie.

By the late 1950s, these enemy classes had effectively been eliminated or rendered powerless—though not through the force of law—at which point Mao's concept of class became more fluid. He abandoned the categories "proletariat" and "bourgeoisie"— categories that had plausible roots in the workplace—and in their place began to use broad categories that he called "the people" and "enemies of the people." The people were those who followed the current line; enemies were those who opposed it. One set of rules (which he chose to call "democracy") was to apply among the people, who, he said, constituted the vast majority of the population; another (which he termed "dictatorship") applied to the small minority that made up the enemies of the people.

In the years leading up to and during the Cultural Revolution, Mao resumed the use of class labels, talking of a renewed class struggle, but this time the line between "bourgeoisie" and "proletariat" was just as fluid as the line between the "people" and their "enemies." In both instances, the defining criteria were attitudes toward ideological principles, not economic or social relationships.

Three elements of this largely lawless system remain in post-Mao China. The first is the crime of counterrevolution, which, until its abandonment in 1997, served as the basis for the prosecution of political crimes. In practice, the ambiguous term "counterrevolution" was up to the Party to define, and the definition could also be changed ex post facto. The demonstrations in Tiananmen Square in 1976 that marked the beginning of the end of the reign of the Gang of Four were initially branded counterrevolutionary, and participants were prosecuted accordingly. After their fall was complete, a "reversal of verdicts" came, and first the 1976 demonstrators, and subsequently a whole host of those persecuted during the Cultural Revolution, were rehabilitated on the basis of a new set of definitions of "revolution" and "counterrevolution."

Today there is talk of another "reversal of verdicts," this time to clear the names of those who demonstrated in Tiananmen Square in 1989. A few cautious voices even suggested that it is time to eliminate once and for all the crime of counterrevolution from the statute books. At its meeting in March 1997 the National People's Congress considered legislation eliminating counterrevolution as a crime and substituting for it the crime of endangering state security. While the new language is more up-to-date, it retains its ominous ambiguity.

A second carryover from the Maoist era is the concept of thought reform. Hundreds of thousands of people branded as counterrevolutionaries were executed, and many millions more were subjected to what, in its most extreme form, was "brainwashing"; its much more common form was "reform through labor" or "reform through education." The principle behind the concept was that counterrevolution was a mistaken pattern of thought that could be changed, most effectively by indoctrination and persuasion, accompanied by a stiff regimen of physical labor. In extreme cases, persuasion was accompanied by isolation and torture.

The third surviving Maoist element, also present in its Confucian antecedent, was the absence of a presumption of innocence. The criminal who was brought to trial was presumed guilty, which wherever possible should have been established by means of a confession. Because any profession of innocence was likely to be taken as a mistake with counterrevolutionary implications, defendants who refused to confess to the crime of which they were accused were often subjected to all the tools of thought reform I have described. Once brought to trial the defendant was routinely granted access to a defense lawyer, whose function was not to establish the defendant's innocence, but to offer evidence in mitigation at the time of sentencing. As noted earlier, the 1997 revisions to the criminal procedures law are a step in the direction of establishing the presumption of innocence and giving defense lawyers an active role in criminal trials.

The initial impetus to establish a system of laws during the reform era arose from China's rapidly expanding interaction with the world economy. Foreign firms that wanted to invest in or trade with China were reluctant to do so without laws in place that would regulate these transactions and protect all parties' interests. So the first new laws defined the terms on the basis of which joint ventures would be formed and trade conducted. Since then, the reforms themselves have created new circumstances that require regulation and adjudication, in response to which many new laws have been written and adopted by the National People's Congress.

China's legal profession has grown at an extraordinary rate. Starting from a base of only about 3,000 lawyers at the beginning of the reform era, the government has set as a goal a legal profession numbering 150,000 by the end of the century. Law schools and law departments have proliferated, though their number is insufficient to meet the need. It is estimated that even if the government reaches its goal, only about half of the lawyers will have completed a formal legal education. But even more important than their expanding numbers is the emerging sense of independent professionalism among Chinese lawyers, who, in the past, saw themselves as no more than minor government bureaucrats.

Legal reform proceeded smoothly and without interruption during the 1980s. Unlike other aspects of reform that periodically threatened to undermine the Party's monopoly on political power, legal reform was a nonthreatening way to create the appearance of moving toward a more modern, less arbitrary political system. But the goal was always to create a *system of laws*, never to establish the *rule of law*, a distinction that became fully evident at the end of the decade in the Party's handling of the Tiananmen demonstration in 1989. A small group of retired leaders, feeling that their backs were to the wall, set aside laws, regulations, procedures, and regularly appointed officials in order arbitrarily to impose their disastrously misguided solution.

The need for a genuine rule of law in China has become more urgent as political corruption has increased in this decade. Corruption is pervasive throughout China's political system, and periodic efforts to attack it founder because those assigned to the task are themselves the worst offenders. The problem appears unsolvable until the law takes the place of the arbitrary official.

The events in Tiananmen Square on the night of 3 June 1989 served as a wake-up call for many thoughtful people in China. They also brought about a radical shift in American public opinion about China. Ever since Richard Nixon's visit to China in 1972, Americans seemed to suspend judgment on the subject of Chinese politics and many of those who called attention to the violation of human rights in the Soviet Union and Eastern Europe appeared to ignore comparable violations in the People's Republic of China. But this dual standard suffered a fatal blow when tanks rumbled down the streets of Beijing.

Serious misunderstandings arise when Americans and Chinese sit down to talk about human rights. Not only are there very different assumptions that the two sides bring to the table, but very different definitions of the term "human rights" and what it encompasses. Where Americans emphasize China's failure to guarantee political and civil rights, the Chinese emphasize the American failure to acknowledge Chinese accomplishments in guaranteeing its citizens' economic and social rights.

A comprehensive definition of human rights would include economic, social, political, and civil categories. *Economic* rights protect the individual's access to sustenance and participation in the workforce. *Social* rights guarantee access to goods and services provided by the state, such as education, social security, health care, and the like. *Political* rights guarantee the individual's ability to participate in the political process. *Civil* rights protect the individual from illegitimate interference by other individuals or by the state. And it is true that an assessment of the protection of human rights in all four of these categories reveals both positive and negative results in China. Paradoxically, economic reforms have expanded human rights in some areas but restricted them in others.

The Chinese point with pride to the accomplishments of the Chinese state in extending the right of sustenance to the entire Chinese population. They claim that with the exception of the period immediately following the Great Leap Forward, when many starved to death and hunger was widespread in much of the country, China has managed to avoid the devastating famines of the past. Output of food has increased, the distribution system has improved, and public-works projects have reduced the devastating effects of natural disasters. Yet economic reform has both advanced the right to sustenance and jeopardized its future: it enhanced agricultural productivity but failed to limit population growth and reduced the amount of land under cultivation.

Prior to the initiation of economic reforms, China's planned economy provided universal employment, and though many people in both the rural and urban sectors were underemployed, they were all guaranteed right of access to the workforce. The creation of a labor market and a gradual loosening of controls over the flow of workers from job to job, place to place, and even sector to sector has given China's workers new freedom, but employment is no longer universal. Rural production-team leaders are no longer at their posts finding some kind of work for everyone. When the fiscal crisis in the state sector is seriously addressed, many workers once guaranteed jobs will find themselves unemployed. If current trends persist, unemployment rates among women will be significantly higher than those among men.

With respect to social rights, the achievements of the Chinese government during its first forty years in power are impressive. In 1949, fewer than half of China's elementary-school-age children were enrolled in school; forty years later it was 97 percent. Access to medical care has also substantially improved. In 1949 there was one doctor for every 1,500 people and one hospital bed for every 7,000 people; by 1989 the figures had increased to one doctor for every 650 people and one hospital bed for every 430 people. Similarly, by 1989 about one in every five members of the workforce had access to some form of state-provided retirement plan.

The economic reforms have had mixed effects on the state's ability to guarantee these social rights, particularly to rural citizens. The household-responsibility system has led to an increase in the number of children leaving school before graduation, since the system's incentives encourage parents to make their children work in the fields or local factories as soon as they are old enough.

Public health officials took justifiable pride in China's rural health care delivery system. "Barefoot doctors"—young workers with only rudimentary medical training—were deployed in brigades and teams throughout the commune system to give basic care in a well-organized referral system of commune clinics and county hospitals. But over the last ten years, barefoot doctors have all but disappeared from the Chinese countryside. Disparaged for their lack of formal training, substantially underpaid, and attracted by many more lucrative employment opportunities, a large number of them left their posts. It has been hard to replace them, and there are consequent gaps in the once quite complete rural system.

As for social security, the shrinking of the state sector has reduced the proportion of workers with access to state-funded pensions. Planning is under way to create a system funded directly by the government rather than by individual state-owned enterprises, with workers matching the government funds with a percentage of their wages. Until this system is fully operative, the vast majority of Chinese workers will have no access to regular income upon retirement.

The record with respect to political rights is somewhat different. Here, although the right to participate in politics is widespread, that participation is, generally speaking, devoid of significance.

Elections are regularly held for executive and legislative posts, but, until recently, never with more than a single candidate for each post, a candidate selected and vetted by the Party. A little-publicized component of the political reforms of the 1980s, the democratization of local politics, has eventuated in having several candidates run for certain offices, and it is by no means always the Party-endorsed candidate who wins. So the reforms have made political participation more meaningful, if only locally.

Civil rights are the subject that Americans debate about most, and the debate is sometimes difficult for Chinese to understand. Asked whether their lives are subject to more or less government interference than they were fifteen years ago, the majority of Chinese would likely respond that they are significantly freer. They can speak freely and critically about political issues, read and hear a reasonably broad range of information and opinions, and make decisions about their place of residence, careers, and leisure that were formerly made for them. But this expansion of civil rights is less the intended consequence of Party or government policy than the unintended consequence of the weakening of Party and government influence. An exception are the debates within the Party-state about expanding freedom of information. In this debate, it is assumed by both sides that unorthodox ideas are imported, not domestic, commodities. A campaign against "spiritual pollution" was launched in 1983, and there have been sporadic rumblings since about "bourgeois liberalism." Arguing against the conservatives who advocate closing off China from undesirable foreign influences, Deng and his like-minded colleagues used an analogy: to allow fresh air into a room, one must open the windows; along with the fresh air, flies and mosquitoes may come in, but that is not enough to justify closing the windows.

As the debate goes on, however, technology has intervened. The introduction of the fax machine, the satellite dish, and on-line information services increases exponentially the information, ideas, and images available to the Chinese public. The proliferation of these new sources of information far outstrips the government's ability to monitor and control them. In fact, when a regulation was passed banning personal ownership of satellite dishes, it was revealed that the single largest supplier of the dishes was military-owned factories, and the regulation remains on the books, unenforced.

American human rights organizations and the U.S. Congress have been interested less in the rapid expansion of civil rights for the majority of Chinese people than in the very serious violation of a small minority's civil rights, the individuals who have been imprisoned or sentenced to reform through labor for their dissident political or religious views. As many as twenty million people, it is estimated, are incarcerated in Chinese prisons and labor reform camps, but I have seen no reliable estimate of the fraction who are imprisoned for political crimes. Accounts of those who have survived prolonged incarceration in the labor reform camps tell us that prisoners are often treated with extraordinary harshness, deprived of regular contact with their families and friends, and only under very unusual circumstances released and allowed to return to their normal lives when their sentences expire.

Wei Jingsheng, the most highly publicized political prisoner in China, was jailed in 1979 for his views on the need to democratize the Chinese political system. He was released in September 1993, six months before his fifteen-year sentence expired, in what many took to be a transparent ploy to help China secure the 2000 summer Olympics, and six months thereafter was rearrested in 1994, accused of illicit contact with foreign visitors and reporters. Wei has experienced particularly harsh treatment for at least two reasons: first, he is a worker, not an intellectual or a student, and the government considers disaffected workers a greater threat to political stability than it does disaffected intellectuals or students; second, what he wrote and said seems to have aroused the personal animosity of Deng Xiaoping. As a result, his case was always dealt with at the very highest levels of the government system, and favorable treatment was accorded him only with the greatest reluctance.

International human rights organizations have been very effective in compiling information on China's prisoners of conscience, tracking their cases, and putting pressure on the government to improve their treatment in prison, to give them medical attention when needed, and even, in some cases, to release them prior to the expiration of their sentences. Based in part on the information gathered by these organizations, the U.S. government has espoused particular cases, too, sometimes with positive results, in other instances less successfully.

There are several points on which it is worth reflecting as we consider what Americans can do to bring about an improvement in China's human rights record. The first has to do with our assumptions about the universality of our views on law and human rights, our notion that they are appropriate standards for all societies to adopt, regardless of their possible disjunction with other traditions and other cultures. The second point is often raised in Chinese rejoinders to American complaints about their human rights violations. In looking at conditions in another country, Americans often measure real conditions abroad against an idealized vision of conditions at home, and thus seem blind to violations of human rights in their own society at the same time that they ferret out evidence of violations elsewhere.

A third point to bear in mind is that in asking China's leaders to allow dissidents freedom of movement and expression we are asking them to do the very thing they are least likely now to do willingly. China's leaders understand the Party's weaknesses and are well aware of the many sources of dissatisfaction within Chinese society. As they often say, political instability threatens the nation's continued economic development; more, it threatens their own power, position, and perquisites. Under these circumstances, they would regard giving free rein to dissidents as an act of national betrayal and political suicide.

The importance Chinese attach to the question of sovereignty is a fourth point worth touching on. The Chinese interpret the history of their interaction with the outside world during the nineteenth century as a long series of painful episodes of national humiliation in which foreign powers constantly trampled on China's sovereignty. "Ours will no longer be a nation subject to insult and humiliation. We have stood up" were the words Mao chose to mark the founding of the People's Republic of China in 1949. Over a half century, the Chinese government has been especially sensitive to incursions on its sovereignty, and it regards foreign comment on its handling of the civil and political rights of its citizens as a serious infringement. The position is not irrational: imagine the reactions of the American government were the Chinese to make continued American investment in joint ventures contingent on Congress's strengthening affirmative action programs, for example.

Another point has to do with tactics. We often seem to forget that when we deal with Chinese officialdom we need to do so in a way that minimizes the potential for their losing face. This is problematic, for very often U.S. government actions are effective in the American political context only if they are carried out in a high-profile and public manner. Two examples—the one successful, the other much less so—serve to illustrate this point. The American Embassy in Beijing served as a safe haven for the well-known dissident astrophysicist Fang Lizhi and his wife for several months when they sought refuge there in the immediate aftermath of the Tiananmen massacre. Through quiet, protracted, and skillful negotiations, James Lilley, then American ambassador, secured permission from the Chinese authorities for Fang and his wife to leave China unharmed. He was successful in doing so because he gave the authorities a face-saving stratagem: Fang had suffered a mild heart irregularity, and when told of this, the authorities could describe his release for treatment abroad as a humanitarian gesture on their part, not a caving in to foreign pressure. But considerably less successful, because carried out in the glare of full press coverage, was former Secretary of State Warren Christopher's visit to Beijing in March 1994. The Chinese foreign minister could not afford to appear as though he had given ground to the United States—particularly because the entire National People's Congress was then assembled in Beijing. Christopher, likewise, had to take a tough position in order to reassure those in the United States who were arguing against renewal of China's most-favored-nation status. No progress whatever was made during the visit.

The most consistently successful efforts on behalf of Chinese religious and political dissidents are private, not public. They are the work of an American, John Kamm, who has taken up with the Chinese authorities the causes of dozens of dissidents on a case-by-case basis. He is effective because he understands the importance of working slowly and quietly with his interlocutors to get the Chinese to agree without their losing face.

The final point has to do with linking human rights with access to the American market. Frustrated by a lack of leverage in dealing with the Chinese government, members of Congress have seized on China's most-favored-nation status as one of the few tools available to secure compliance with demands related to human rights, and the administration has responded with an argument about the number of American jobs that would be lost were China to retaliate by cutting back its imports from the United States. It also argued—and was joined in making the argument by the Hong Kong governor—that withdrawing China's most-favored-nation status would adversely affect the Hong Kong economy at a critical time in its preparation for a transfer of sovereignty.

A more significant argument, I believe, is that using trade sanctions to promote greater attention to human rights is counterproductive. Trade sanctions cannot be crafted in such a way as to hurt those in the Party-state responsible for the violation of the civil rights of dissidents and cannot avoid penalizing the very sectors of Chinese society that are most receptive to the ideas we want to promote. Sanctions will also reduce contact with the outside world, through which some Chinese citizens have begun to become familiar with the rights of citizens in other countries and, armed with this new knowledge, to press their own government to guarantee them the same rights. Restricting that contact will reverse this process and delay the political liberalization that is already under way and that has significantly expanded the freedoms enjoyed by most Chinese citizens.

# Intellectual Freedom
# and Chinese Education

In American culture, the term "intellectual" carries several connotations along with its standard meaning of someone who devotes himself to the life of the mind, who thinks about thinking. The other connotations are frequently uncomplimentary. Intellectuals are seen as iconoclasts. They question orthodoxy. They are assumed to be liberals—in the political sense, but more often in the sense of seeing both sides of an issue and being reluctant to come down firmly on one side or the other, spending a lot of time saying "on the one hand . . . and on the other hand." Finally, "intellectual" may often be a term of disapproval. Americans have a long tradition of anti-intellectualism, intellectual historians point out. Pointy-headed intellectuals are absentminded and hopelessly impractical, isolating themselves in ivory towers from the real world rather than offering practical solutions to real-world problems.

Yet American culture takes intellectual *freedom* very seriously indeed, the freedom that individuals—not just intellectuals—have to think, say, write, publish, and teach whatever they choose. American law offers safeguards for intellectual freedom as well as for what is called "intellectual property." Moreover, American schools and universities with their tenure systems protect teachers and professors from political reprisals against what they publish or what they teach in the classroom.

Chinese intellectuals are aware of this Western—indeed peculiarly American—concept of the intellectual but know it to be very different from the concept of the intellectual in the Chinese tradition: an individual who had mastered a particular canon. Mastery was confirmed by passing an examination set by the imperial government, and, once credentialed, the intellectual might contribute to the canon by modifying it incrementally with interpretations or commentaries. But it was not his role to be openly critical or iconoclastic. Tradition and authority were to be respected, not assaulted. The goal of intellectual life was not to retreat from the world and engage in reflection but to enter public life, ideally in an official position. Public service was the intellectual's obligation. Once in office, he was obliged to serve as a moral and ethical example to those whom he governed and to hold not only himself, but also his colleagues, his superiors, and even his emperor to the highest standards of conduct, and to criticize them when they failed to uphold these standards. Carrying out this latter obligation might cost him his job or even his life, but even under these circumstances the obligation held.

Chinese intellectuals first became acquainted with the American concept of intellectual life in the late nineteenth century. American missionary organizations set up schools and colleges in China in which many young Chinese students were educated; some of them came to the United States, continued in colleges and universities here, and then returned to China.

The moment most frequently associated with the abandonment of the old image of the Chinese intellectual and the adoption of a new, Westernized image is the May Fourth Movement in 1919, when a protest against Japanese incursions on Chinese sovereignty at the end of World War I gave rise to a movement that marked the emergence of a new nationalism in China and the acceptance by many young Chinese intellectuals of the obligation to take a politically active and iconoclastic stance against traditional culture. Mao Zedong was a part of the May Fourth generation, but he also separated himself from its intellectuals; though for a brief period as a young man he lived and worked on the fringes of their group at Beijing University, he was never fully accepted by them, presumably because they took him for something of a hick. When they began to explore the ideas of Marx and Lenin, Mao became committed to these ideas far more fervently and faithfully than they.

He came to hold a highly contradictory view of intellectuals, perhaps because he had been bruised by this failure to be accepted in the inner circle of radical young intellectuals, perhaps because he scorned its liberal tendency to equivocate in commitment to a new political orthodoxy. Whatever the reason, despite the fact that Mao *was* an intellectual—he read, he wrote, he thought, he occasionally composed poetry—he was deeply mistrustful of intellectuals and made them the target of political attack on several occasions, the anti-rightist campaign in the mid-1950s and the Cultural Revolution in the mid-1960s being the most sweeping among them.

The notion of intellectual freedom—that special protection must be given to a person's right to expound his own point of view—is totally foreign to Mao's thinking. Mao's quite different goal was to develop a new intellectual community that would be, in his words, "both red and expert." He was looking for people who were absolutely dependable in their political orthodoxy but at the same time scientifically and technologically adept.

Chinese official attitudes toward intellectuals have changed since Mao's death. Deng Xiaoping's own record in this respect was far from admirable. He was deeply involved in the campaigns of the late 1950s during which many Chinese intellectuals were imprisoned or denigrated, yet he and some of his like-minded colleagues assigned a high priority to China's becoming fully modern and realized that this could not happen without the active cooperation of China's intellectuals. In part because he thought they had too favorable an attitude toward the intellectual community, Mao tarred them all with the same brush, and Deng and his colleagues suffered the same terrible fate as intellectuals did, both victims, during the Cultural Revolution.

Shortly after Deng returned to power in 1977, he lent his support to a remarkable burst of public expression of dissident views. Democracy Wall, near the center of Beijing, became a place where a vigorous debate on China's recent past and its future course was permitted. It was here that Wei Jingsheng posted a manifesto critical of Deng for having failed to add democracy to his "four modernizations" (of agriculture, industry, science and technology, and the armed forces) as the critically needed "fifth modernization." But this support for intellectual freedom was highly instrumental and very short-lived. Deng used the dissidents and their views to help him displace Hua Guofeng, Mao's designated successor, but once that was accomplished and his position was secure, he first moved the wall to a distant part of the capital and then closed it down entirely. Wei Jingsheng was arrested on a technical charge of having given state secrets to a foreign reporter and sentenced to jail.

Intellectuals in China today have recovered a measure of the status they lost during the Maoist era and are respected because of the contribution they can make to their country's effort to modernize. They are allowed a measure of latitude with respect to the ideas they propound, but this absolutely does not extend into the realm of political ideas. Intellectuals have not recaptured the preeminent position their forebears enjoyed in traditional society, for in today's China that position is already occupied—by the entrepreneur.

China's schools have a total enrollment of nearly 300 million students. Schooling begins with prekindergarten nursery schools, widely available in China's cities, less so in the countryside. Elementary school begins with six-year-olds in kindergarten and extends through six grades. Neighborhood schools are the rule, though there are "key schools" in most cities where some or all of the places are filled by competitive examination. Elementary education is close to universal.

### School Enrollment in China and the United States

|  | China | United States |
|---|---|---|
| Percent enrolled in primary school | 98 | 99 |
| Percent enrolled in middle school | 89 | 98 |
| Percent enrolled in high school | 42 | 90 |
| Percent enrolled in college or university | 4 | 40 |
| Number enrolled in graduate school | 145 thousand | 2.1 million |

Secondary education begins with lower middle schools, grades seven through nine, admission into which is by examination. About four out of five elementary-school students continue on to lower middle school. Students are assigned to a class of about fifty, which stays together for all their courses during the three years. Admission to upper middle schools, grades ten through twelve, is again based on examinations; depending on these and on their preferences, students are assigned to either academic or vocational high schools. Two out of five lower-middle-school students go on to upper middle school on average, though the figure is much higher in the cities than it is in the countryside.

Expanding the availability of China's postsecondary education has been a priority since the economic reforms began. Nonetheless, there are fewer than three million places in colleges and universities for the close to seventy million young people of college age. Most of the colleges and universities are four-year institutions, with students admitted on the basis of a national competitive examination taken the summer after their high school graduation. Entering students are assigned a major field of study and take courses only in the relevant department; professional education in law, business, and medicine is offered at this level. Beginning in 1982 university departments were also accredited to admit graduate students. There are now just under 150,000 students enrolled in graduate programs leading to an M.A. or a Ph.D. degree.

Given the wide range of available adult education opportunities, one in six adults is enrolled in part-time schooling, correspondence courses, or television classes, a quarter of them in elementary literacy programs, most of the rest in secondary school courses. Only a small number of college-level courses are available.

Expenditure for education is 15 percent of total government spending in both China and the United States. But as a fraction of gross national product, China's expenditures on education are less than half those of the United States and below those of many developing countries.

---

### Educational Financing in China and the United States

|                                                        | China | United States |
| ------------------------------------------------------ | ----- | ------------- |
| Amount spent on education, 1995                        | $13B  | $503B         |
| Average percentage increase, 1985–95                   | 15    | 5             |
| Average percentage increase, 1985–95, after inflation  | 6     | 1             |
| As percentage of total government expenditures         | 15    | 15            |
| As percentage of GNP, 1995                             | 2     | 7             |
| Per-student, 1995                                      | $64   | $7,600        |

*(Sources: China Statistical Yearbook 1996 and American Almanac 1994–95)*

---

Primary and secondary schools are tuition-free for urban residents, being financed by the municipal governments or, in some instances, by large state-owned enterprises. Parents must pay only for books and school supplies. Schools in the countryside charge tuition, since their school budgets are met principally through tuition receipts, with only supplementary funds coming from the local governments.

Universities are operated by the central government and by provincial and municipal governments. Funding for national "key schools" comes directly from the budget of the State Education Commission, for other colleges and universities from the government that operates them. Government funding no longer supports the operating costs of postsecondary institutions, which have been encouraged to devise other income-producing strategies.

Until 1992 university education was given at no cost to the student; since then students have been charged a tuition that varies by school and discipline, the average today being approximately $250 a year. Tuition is lower in those disciplines to which the government is interested in attracting students; teachers colleges, for example, charge nothing at all. Scholarships are given out on a system based on financial need and academic achievement. Universities generate additional income by admitting students who failed the national qualifying examination but whose families will pay a special high tuition for their postsecondary education.

In addition to the usual forms of academic funding, most colleges and universities have established collective enterprises, which run the gamut from small factories to consulting companies, and some schools lease out space on their already overcrowded campuses for shops and restaurants.

The most recent education act passed by the National People's Congress allows for the establishment of private schools at all levels. A few are now in operation, most of them built with funds contributed by overseas Chinese. High tuitions are charged at these schools—figures as high as three thousand dollars per academic year are not uncommon.

The substantial American influence on education in China is in part due to the many Americans who taught in and ran missionary schools in China, and it is also the result of the work of John Dewey, the American educator and pragmatic philosopher who spent two years lecturing in China in the early 1920s and supervised the work of Chinese graduate students who became influential educators in their own country. Despite this extensive influence, one of the fundamental principles of American education—the community-based school system—was never adopted in China. Looking to Japanese and later Russian examples, Chinese educators advocated the adoption of a uniform curriculum for the entire country.

The current version of that national curriculum is fairly restrictive at the primary and secondary levels, allowing for very little local innovation. It stresses basic skills and gives short shrift to the arts and humanities. Arts training for gifted students is available in after-school programs or in special schools. English-language instruction is now almost universal in lower middle schools, and at the primary level for students at the best urban schools. Methods of instruction rely heavily on rote memorization and in-class recitation. Cross-cultural studies have shown that these methods produce, as might be expected, students with excellent memory skills but weak creative and analytical skills.

The curriculum at universities and colleges, also set by the national government, allows for more local flexibility. Because students take courses only in their major department, a college education in China is highly specialized, and the idea of a liberal arts education, or even of imposing requirements designed to expose the student to a wider range of subject matter, is absent.

Mastery of an accepted body of knowledge, and not the development of critical intellectual skills, is the goal of most of China's university educators.

Many positive changes have been made in Chinese education since the reform period began. During the Maoist years, primary and secondary instruction was heavily larded with political lessons: ideological maxims figured prominently in language texts; problems in mathematics required students to quantify and calculate the landlord's exploitation of his peasants, say. Periods of physical labor were integrated with periods of study at all levels, with a view to ensuring that intellectual lessons were not divorced from the realities of the workplace.

With the education reforms came a depoliticization of instructional materials and the end of almost all the work-study programs. Reformers believed that the earlier efforts to universalize primary education and expand the number of middle schools, notably in the countryside, had gone too rapidly and that the quality of instruction had deteriorated. They consolidated some schools, closed others, dismissed inadequately prepared teachers, and expanded and professionalized teacher-training programs. They also increased the number of vocational secondary schools. At the outset of the reform period, only one in twelve high schools offered a vocational curriculum, while the other eleven, with their equivalent of a college preparatory curriculum, were doing a disservice to their students, only a tiny handful of whom could be accommodated in universities. Building new vocational high schools and introducing a vocational curriculum in existing high schools have nearly equalized the number of vocational and academic high schools today.

Postsecondary education was the level hardest hit by the Cultural Revolution, during which schools at all levels were closed down. University enrollment peaked at close to a million students in 1960, but ten years later only 48,000 students were enrolled, so expanding university education was a first priority in the reform period. In 1977 there were 625,000 spaces in colleges and universities for a college-age population of close to 70 million; in the two decades since, spaces in colleges and universities have quadrupled, and postsecondary adult education programs have trebled, for a total capacity of close to 4 million students today. Despite this, only 4 percent of college-age young people are enrolled in school.

As colleges and universities had reopened in the later stages of the Cultural Revolution, admission had been based almost exclusively on a kind of affirmative-action program for the politically correct. Class background and political attitude alone counted in making admissions decisions. Schools became populated by students, many of whom, in the words of one college instructor, "would have been happier somewhere else." One of the very first acts of the reform period was to reinstitute the national college entrance examination as of 1977 and to open it to a broad age range. As it is currently administered, the entrance examination is offered once each year, in the July following a student's high school graduation. Those who fail it can take it again, but not after they reach the age of twenty-two.

Because of Mao's mistrust of intellectuals, worker-peasant-soldier instructors were introduced into college classrooms during the 1970s, for their experience and background were considered fitting for monitors of the academic faculty, to ensure that the faculty presented ideologically correct material and to supplement excessively abstract lessons with real-world information. When political priorities changed, though it proved easy to change the composition of the student body, it was very difficult to change the faculty. Like all government employees, faculty members, including the political monitors, were virtually impossible to fire. Even today, one encounters departments in Chinese universities where the faculty outnumbers the students and where a small handful of qualified instructors carry the full course load while their less competent colleagues have no teaching responsibilities at all. Paying these nonfunctional faculty members drains the already straitened university budgets.

During the Cultural Revolution, China was almost completely cut off from contact with the outside world, which had a deleterious effect on the academic community, whose members not only could not do research in China but were allowed virtually no communication at all with their colleagues abroad. Libraries received neither books nor journals from abroad. Scientists lost touch with what their colleagues were doing in laboratories outside China.

The academic community immediately took advantage of the open policy that accompanied the reforms. Scholars were encouraged to travel abroad, "sister school" relationships were established with American colleges and universities, foreign professors and teachers were invited to China for short- and long-term teaching assignments, and Chinese students enrolled in American graduate and professional schools, even a few as undergraduates. Asked during his 1979 visit to the United States whether he was worried about a brain drain, Deng was nonchalant. He would send twice as many students and scholars to the United States as were needed in China, he said. Then, when only half of them came home, China would still be adequately served. Today more than 125,000 Chinese are studying abroad, about half of them in the United States, where they constitute the largest national group among the international students at colleges and universities.

The most pressing issue facing China's schools is their inadequate funding. With expenditures on education totaling only 2 percent of gross national product, China lags behind the world average of 5 percent, and many developing countries outspend it on their schools.

More money for primary and secondary education would help to attract and keep teachers. Since teachers' pay and prestige are both very low, it is hard now to attract anyone into the profession, much less highly qualified people. University applicants who find themselves in a teachers college will do almost anything to avoid the fate of a classroom career: entire graduating classes of teachers colleges have failed to report to their assigned schools, going into the infinitely more promising private sector instead. To counteract this, some teachers colleges have withheld the diplomas of their graduating seniors, handing them over only after they actually show up and begin their first teaching assignments.

Universities, too, suffer from a shortage of funds. The austerity of university budgets restricts the scholarship funds available for those to whom the newly instituted tuitions are an insurmountable obstacle. But the most important shortfall is in adequate space. Although they have expanded rapidly, China's colleges and universities can still turn out only 600,000 graduates each year, which means that less than 1 percent of the Chinese population has a college education (as compared to 22 percent in the United States), a wholly inadequate number to support the development to which China aspires.

Like their school colleagues, university teachers suffer from low pay and low status. Efforts have been made to ameliorate this situation, especially to encourage foreign-educated intellectuals to return to classrooms and laboratories in China, but many faculty have to take a second job to make ends meet. This has an immediate adverse affect on the quality of research and instruction, of course, and similarly, the time and energy that faculty and administrators spend devising new moneymaking schemes to augment inadequate budgets are time and energy not spent on educational tasks.

A second issue facing China's educators is the high dropout rate from rural schools, and the consequent high rate of illiteracy, especially among young women. The reasons are economic: it costs money to send a child to school, and while the child is enrolled the family does not get what the child would earn in the workforce. Rural people in China do not see that investment in education will yield a return. In addition, as we have seen, an unintended consequence of the economic-incentive structure in the household-responsibility system is to encourage parents to end their children's education early; the economic rewards for doing so seem both more immediate and more tangible than those that accrue when the child is educated through a high school diploma, since a high school education is not yet considered useful preparation for work on the farm or in the local factory. Government-supported, tuition-free rural schools would encourage families to keep their children in school, and as the rural economy develops and higher skills are required, perceptions about the value of a high school education may change. But eliminating the financial gain from putting teenagers into the workforce instead of the classroom is a difficult problem to solve.

## Gender Differences in Educational Attainment in China

|  | Percentage of total population age 15 and over | Percentage of male population | Percentage of female population |
|---|---|---|---|
| Illiterate | 22 | 12 | 32 |
| Primary school | 34 | 35 | 34 |
| Middle school | 30 | 36 | 24 |
| High school | 8 | 11 | 7 |
| Technical school | 2 | 2 | 2 |
| Junior college | 1 | 2 | 0.7 |
| University | 0.7 | 0.9 | 0.4 |

*(Source: China Statistical Yearbook 1995)*

Access to education is very limited for those with physical or learning disabilities. This is particularly true at the higher levels, from which the physically disabled are generally excluded. Presuming that the limited number of spaces at the college level should be reserved for the able and fit, applicants are screened by physical as well as academic examinations.

A third issue facing Chinese educators is the spread of excessive competition and examination-based education. The root of the problem is the paucity of spaces in comparison with the size of the applicant pool, which makes college entrance extraordinarily competitive, a tone that has spread downward through the whole system. It was the national college entrance examination that gave rise to a system of examinations at every level. The result of this hierarchy of examinations is to make students intensely competitive in the classrooms and to limit what is taught there to the material students will need to master in order to clear their next academic hurdle.

All of this adversely affects students' motivation once they are at college. As in other highly competitive systems—Japan's is an example—they know that a bright future is guaranteed them regardless of their performance in the classroom. But many university students in China find the quality of their college experience far below the high expectations generated by the competition that they have successfully survived. Classes are large, the curriculum is unimaginative, and the level of instruction is often disappointingly low. Moreover, housing and food are generally far worse than in their own homes. Students are housed eight to a room that is barely adequate for two in an American dormitory. Three times a day, they carry bowls to a canteen too small to have tables and chairs and must consume their unpalatable food on the run.

The dissatisfactions generated by campus life give rise to academic apathy and periodic outbursts of student protest. It was very concrete complaints about university life, not abstract demands for democracy, that brought students onto the streets of China's cities in the protest demonstrations that began in the mid-1980s and culminated at Tiananmen Square in June 1989.

Finally, although Deng seemed sanguine in 1979 about the possibility of so many Chinese young people staying abroad after finishing their education, the problem is in fact much more serious than he was willing to allow. Since 1979 some two hundred thousand Chinese students and scholars have gone abroad for further education, and of that number, only about seventy-five thousand have chosen to return. In the mid-1980s, a series of incentives was put in place to encourage them to do so, but these were only modestly successful, and the problem was seriously aggravated by the Tiananmen massacre, after which many Chinese studying abroad took public stands against their government that made it dangerous for them to return. Foreign governments relaxed immigration regulations to take account of their situation. Although many Chinese intellectuals living abroad have gone home in recent years, they are attracted by business opportunities, not by academic careers. The brain drain has been slowed, but Chinese colleges and universities have yet to feel the effect.

It is as good a time to be an intellectual in China as it has been since the People's Republic was founded nearly fifty years ago, for the country is enjoying greater intellectual freedom than at any time since the May Fourth Movement in the 1920s. But unfortunately, just when the restrictions on intellectual life have been somewhat relaxed, many intellectuals find themselves wishing they were entrepreneurs.

To say that intellectual freedom has increased is not to say that the Chinese are free from all restrictions with respect to what they write, say, or teach; public expression of unorthodox political ideas is still unacceptable. Yet dissident intellectuals concern the regime less than dissident workers or dissident unemployed, and the most serious repressions have been exerted against those like Wei Jingsheng and Han Dongfang—workers whom the government believes can organize fellow workers in opposition to Party and government authority. This assessment of relative threats to the regime seems well founded. Chinese intellectuals have inherited a disdain for, and thus an inability to collaborate with, the country's working population, and although their protests in 1989 were joined by workers and even government officials in eighty cities, the students and intellectuals who initiated the movement were reluctant to ally themselves with workers and actively resisted taking their movement to the rural workforce.

Dissident intellectuals everywhere have a morbid tendency to fragment their efforts, and this is true in China. Those who occupied Tiananmen Square impressed observers with their ability to organize themselves, to distribute food, information, and medical care, and to use telephone, fax, and the foreign and domestic press to spread word of their protests to other cities in China and to the outside world. And after the massacre a spontaneous and highly effective underground railway sprang into being along which numerous dissidents were spirited out of harm's way. But on the other hand, neither the dissidents who escaped China nor those who remained could organize an opposition to the Chinese Communist Party. A significant amount of money was collected in America and Europe in support of their work, conferences were held, and publications distributed. Nonetheless, individuals and groups found their differences greater than their common ground.

If Chinese intellectuals could outgrow their fractious tendencies and their disdain for the working classes, they might be able to join hands with the huge numbers of other people in China who have reason for discontent. Were this to occur, the regime would be obliged to take them very seriously indeed.

# Artistic Freedom and China's Contemporary Culture

In China today, artists like intellectuals are enjoying more latitude than they have experienced for a half century. The dead
hands of political didacticism and socialist puritanism do not rest
as heavily on the arts as they did, though there are still boundaries
that artists cannot cross. The cultural scene is vibrant, diverse,
and cosmopolitan, as Chinese artists take advantage of their new-
found liberties to produce works that are beautiful or bizarre, crass
or transcendent, esoteric or merely sensational.

Traditional Chinese culture was in many respects as rigid as its
socialist successor. As iconoclasm was frowned on in the intellectual world, so it was also in the arts. Aspiring artists were trained
to study models of calligraphy and painting and then to duplicate
them flawlessly; only after they had mastered this skill was subtle
innovation or refinement of the tradition deemed appropriate.
Forms and styles in art changed very slowly, and looking at the
tradition as a whole, one is impressed more with its continuities
than with its changes.

Among the many ideas they borrowed from their Russian men-
tors, the Chinese Communist Party brought socialist realism to the

arts in China. Many artists and writers were attracted to the Communists' base area in Yan'an, in the northwest, during the 1930s; they looked to the Communists as an honest and patriotic alternative to the corrupt and ineffectual Nationalist Party and supported the anti-Japanese war effort under Communist leadership. In 1942 at a "forum" on art and literature, Mao introduced some of these men and women to the Party's political line on the arts —a line that remained in force until his death thirty-five years later.

According to Mao, art and literature exist to persuade and to teach—appreciation of art for its own sake is unacceptable—and the central ideological lesson to be conveyed is the superiority of the worker and peasant who serve the revolution through their labor. Art, literature, and the performing arts should depict exemplary figures to serve as either models or counter-models for the rest of society. The audience for the arts, in Mao's view, is made up of working people; and because they are simple, uneducated, and uncultivated, art must be uncomplicated and straightforward. Heroes and heroines should be glorified, villains debased. Acting styles in theater and film should be broad and melodramatic. Mao singled out for criticism what he called "middle characters," who simply complicate the message—those who have doubts, good characters who have flaws, and villains with redeeming features.

Taking their cues from these instructions, painters painted larger-than-life perfectly modeled, ruddy-complexioned workers strategically posed in front of factories and power plants. Writers wrote novels and short stories in which oppressive landlords are shamed into subjection by honest, good-hearted, and hardworking peasants. Playwrights composed plays about corrupt, degenerate Nationalist Party members who sold their country to sadistic Japanese agents, only to be defeated in the end by burly Communist patriots. Music, dance, and film followed suit. Given that the work of foreign artists met virtually none of Mao's criteria, contact with the international art world was severed early on.

The Great Proletarian Cultural Revolution aimed to draw the strings of the straitjacket even more tightly. A lingering fondness for traditional Chinese culture was to be eliminated by encouraging young people to break, tear, or deface any remnants of the tradition that had managed to survive. The Yan'an rules for art and literature were scrapped and new regulations drawn up. Writers and artists were now suspect and not considered trustworthy to convey the ideological lessons of the day. It was no longer enough that art and literature be *for* working people, they must be *by* working people as well.

In much the same way that Mao had found himself on the fringes of the Beijing intellectual community in the May Fourth era, his third wife, Jiang Qing, an actress in B-grade Shanghai films, had found herself on the fringes of the Yan'an artistic community in the 1940s. And it was Jiang Qing who took on an unofficial position as commissar of arts when the Cultural Revolution began. Her mission was to ensure that the rigid didacticism of the 1940s was reasserted, with a glorified Mao as the focal point of every work of art. She brought the performing arts to heel, insisting that every theater, dance company, and film studio restrict itself to productions of five model works based on inspirational tales from the revolution. Jiang Qing's control of the cultural world remained firm until, as a member of the infamous Gang of Four, she suffered her downfall in 1976.

Since the end of the Cultural Revolution and the beginning of the reform period, diverse currents have influenced China's culture, both popular and high. By far the most important among these has been the influence of Western art forms, with which Chinese artists have become reacquainted after long isolation. But a revisiting of the Chinese artistic tradition has also been important, both inspired and facilitated by extensive new archaeological finds over the last fifteen years and their exhibition in impressive new museums that use advanced techniques for preservation and display, many of them introduced with advice and assistance from abroad. A third current, which is felt particularly in popular culture, comes from the Chinese diaspora. Popular culture in Taiwan and Hong Kong exerts a powerful influence on music, television, and pulp fiction on the mainland, and the influence of the overseas Chinese community elsewhere is beginning to be felt. A fourth, somewhat unexpected current can be seen in a new use of the styles and forms of socialist realism. The plodding images of the recent past are put to diverse, often surprising uses, sometimes whimsical, sometimes critical.

China's two premier music conservatories—in Beijing and Shanghai—had extensive experience training students in performing, composing, and instrument making in both the Chinese and Western classical traditions. But during the Cultural Revolution, the faculty at these conservatories were humiliated, beaten, and confined, a plight movingly depicted in Isaac Stern's film *From Mao to Mozart*, released in the United States in the early 1980s, which describes the violinist's first visit to the conservatories and introduced Western audiences to several extraordinarily talented young performers, many of whom later had successful careers on the international concert stage.

Musicians have figured prominently among the Chinese scholars at American schools in the past decade or two. All the major American conservatories have enrolled large numbers of Chinese students, and their Chinese graduates are beginning to appear regularly in opera companies, orchestras, and recital series. The well-known cellist Yo-yo Ma (born in Paris and trained in the United States) has been active in introducing young Chinese musicians to concert audiences in the United States.

Chinese classical music has also been revived in recent years, though not with quite the same gusto. China's major conservatories offer training on Chinese instruments and in the Chinese repertoire, but concert and recital opportunities are somewhat more limited than are those for Western music. The Beijing and other opera companies are once again offering the rigorous training required to perform the highly stylized, complex classics of traditional Chinese opera, but few young people are taking the time to acquire it. Chinese opera audiences are most often made up of at least as many curious foreign tourists as appreciative local aficionados.

Chinese composers have been liberated from the political constraints of socialist realism, but much of their creative work is being done outside China. Jin Xiang's opera *Savage Land*, based on a play by the popular modern Chinese playwright Cao Yu, was well received in a Kennedy Center production in 1993; Tan Dun, a composer currently living in New York City, is experimenting with syntheses of traditional Chinese sounds and contemporary Western musical forms. Their voluntary exile has to do less with political constraints—though the official press occasionally rumbles about "inaccessible" music—than with the lack of financial support and appreciative audiences at home.

No such problems exist for the composers and performers of popular music, whose audiences and the revenues they generate are vast. Some critics deplore what they consider a baneful and ubiquitous influence of American popular music: if Chinese popular music is subject to this influence, much of it comes indirectly, via Hong Kong and Taiwan. In any case, the popular songs and MTV videos produced in China give an initial impression of being politically engaged and dissident. But in fact the lyrics and general tone are marked by an apolitical—or, perhaps better, post-political—cynicism, well expressed in the title of a hit song some years back by the Taiwanese female vocalist Su Rui: "Follow Your Feelings."

Rock musicians are subject to more political constraint because their audiences number in the tens of thousands. Crowds of that magnitude, particularly when young, are inevitably disturbing to the peace of mind of municipal authorities. One of China's best-known rock stars, Cui Jian, who was peripherally involved in the events leading up to the Tiananmen massacre, has often had difficulty booking space and securing permits for his concerts, though he claims his music is "cultural," not political.

Some years ago, the pop music scene was invaded by a bizarre phenomenon. An enterprising musician resurrected the fervid if tedious songs of the Cultural Revolution—"The East Is Red," "Socialism Is Good," "Without the Communist Party, No New China"—and repackaged them in new arrangements backed by a synthesizer's soft-rock beat. The cassettes were wildly successful. The fad was over before the authorities had decided whether this was homage or sacrilege.

Performing-arts companies were among the first of China's state-owned enterprises to be introduced to market reform. The introduction was brutal: their state subsidies were cut from 100 percent of their operating budgets to 30 percent. Despite their unique character, these companies malfunction just like factories in the state sector. They are responsible not only for paying a large, tenured staff, but also for giving them housing and health care and for meeting the pension payments of their retirees. The reduction in state subsidies could not have come at a worse time, for the audience for theater, opera, ballet, and dance, which had been steadily shrinking, declined sharply at the beginning of the reform period, as Chinese bought television sets in record numbers and the film industry increased production. Although theater companies continue to exist in China's major cities, they are having a difficult time remaining solvent. To supplement box-office receipts, they engage in every imaginable form of for-profit activity: they run restaurants and karaoke bars, they dub translations for foreign films, they make television commercials and feature films; and then, time permitting, they produce plays.

One can still find "politically correct" potboilers on the Chinese stage—plays about the economic development of the new Pudong region of Shanghai, for example. One director suggests that a potboiler or two each season pleases the local cultural bureau and gives the company leeway for the contemporary dramas in which they and their audiences are really interested.

Two recent hits give a sense of what serious playwrights are creating for the Chinese stage. The Beijing Art Theater mounted a highly successful production of Guo Shixing's *Bird Men* in 1994. Set in a Beijing park, the play depicts the conversations of three men who meet periodically to engage in a unique urban pastime for Chinese men: walking their caged birds. *Miss Stay-at-Home*, produced by the Shanghai Art Theater, focuses on what, for Chinese audiences, is the fascinating experience of those who go abroad, in this case from the perspective of those left behind. A man and woman meet and, discovering that each has a spouse working in the United States, keep each other company and fall in love. Both plays featured a naturalistic acting style that contrasts sharply with the overdrawn manners of earlier Chinese stage and film actors that are still encountered today. And the Shanghai production was innovative in its use of an unusual cabaret format. Both productions attracted large audiences over extended runs.

The best-publicized of a number of joint productions with foreign directors, plays, and actors was Arthur Miller's Beijing production of *Death of a Salesman*. A more recent, highly popular, and significantly more complex joint production took place in Beijing in 1996 when the China National Beijing Opera and the New York Greek Drama Company collaborated in mounting Euripides's

*Bacchae*, with spoken parts in Chinese, singing in Greek. The production was directed by Chen Shizheng, a Beijing native living in New York City.

A great many novels and short stories are published in China today, but, as in every country, lowbrow fiction attracts the largest audience by far. Among the most successful writers of popular novels is Wang Shuo, who writes in a highly colloquial, breezy style—atypical of most contemporary Chinese fiction—and critics compare him to Jacqueline Suzanne and Danielle Steel. Like their works, Wang's books appear regularly and reach a wide audience of devoted readers. But reading his work in a very different way, other critics compare it to the cynical satires of Evelyn Waugh.

Jealous of the financial success of writers like Wang Shuo, Jia Ping'ao, a serious novelist, turned his hand to writing lucrative trash. His novel *Fei Du* (The abandoned capital) was a *succès fou*. It was described by one reviewer as a "steamy sex fest," but much of the steam it generates depends heavily on the reader's imagination. Periodically, when the action becomes most intense, the author resorts to a novel device for titillating his reader: "Here the author has omitted 368 characters," the text reads. In its official version, the novel sold well over a half million copies; several industrious printers sold at least another million pirated copies.

A third example of contemporary popular fiction relies, as does *Miss Stay-at-Home*, on the interest generated by people who live abroad. *Beijing Man in New York*, which originally appeared in serial form in the *Beijing Evening News*, is an extended soap-opera-like treatment of the complicated lives of Chinese transplanted to New York City that capitalized on the sudden popularity of television soaps—some imports, some domestic. One of the most popular domestic soap operas, a fifty-five-episode series called *Kewang* (Yearning) attracted a huge following, despite stilted acting and a plotline so filled with "family values" that it won the endorsement of the Ministry of Culture.

Three trends mark the rapid changes occurring in the visual arts in China. Some artists have returned to traditional images and media but reworked them. The restrictions against innovation having been set aside, traditional forms are radically modified by these contemporary hands. Another trend looks to modern Western art. Since contact with European and American artists and their work has been restored, some Chinese have carefully perused the stages through which Western art has moved over the last half century to find out what they have missed, while others move directly to contemporary media and forms. As with music, theater, and film, these contemporary and foreign styles of art are known to only a very small public in China. It is mainly abroad that these artists find viewers and a market, and many have become expatriates for that reason. A third trend is a revisiting of the socialist realist tradition. Artists take the larger-than-life images of the past and, in paintings reminiscent of American pop art, of Andy Warhol or Roy Lichtenstein, juxtapose them incongruously with icons of the commercial world today, thus expressing the disjunction between current lifestyles and those of the very recent past.

Like the Cultural Revolution songs reset to a rock beat, these last paintings coincided with a broad wave of Mao nostalgia that swept across China's popular culture in 1993, just as the Party-state was grappling with the sensitive issue of how to mark the centenary of the Chairman's birth. Mao badges were pulled out of the bottoms of drawers and worn and sold on city streets; plastic-encased Mao amulets were hung from rearview mirrors in automobiles, buses, and taxis, and a Cultural Revolution theme restaurant opened in Beijing that was supposed to recapture the chaotic ambience and bad cooking of the 1960s. In one light, the phenomenon was simply a fad. But for some, superstition also played a part. If asked why they were displaying the Mao amulet in their taxis, drivers would cite accidents in which only those who had no amulets were injured. Others—many serious artists among them—used Mao's image as a vehicle for political protest under a perfect cover: it was hard to object to the display of the image, and who could really tell whether it was intended to honor or to mock?

Many people in China have a genuine nostalgia for the Maoist era, and it has lingered long after the fad has passed. It will be a long while before the men in power in China will feel able to undertake a thoroughgoing public reassessment of the former Chairman, since to do so would jeopardize the very foundations on which the power of the Party rests. As a result, much about Mao's professional and personal life is not known in China. (The partial reassessment that took place shortly after the fall of the Gang of Four in 1976 concluded that Mao was "60 percent correct and 40 percent incorrect," meaning, really, that he was 100 percent correct for the first 60 percent of his career and 100 percent incorrect for the last 40 percent.) But for all the privations people suffered during the Mao period, they thought it had its virtues as well, at least in retrospect. Rather like older Americans who look back on an earlier, simpler, clearer, and better time, so there are Chinese who find some of these same virtues in the China of the 1950s and 1960s, when, they think, values were crystal clear, the government was honest, and life was predictable. All of that is appealing today, when self-enrichment is the chief value, the government is corrupt, and change is ubiquitous.

Thanks to the bridge across languages provided by subtitles, Chinese film is the popular cultural activity most accessible to audiences outside China. Paradoxically, the movies that have been most successful in capturing international awards and attracting international audiences are least successful in the Chinese market and least acceptable to the Chinese authorities.

China's twenty-two film studios produced, in 1993, more than 150 officially approved feature films, the vast majority of which were historical epics revisiting great moments in the Chinese Communist Revolution and glorifying its heroes and accomplishments. They play to large audiences, though not as large as they were when television was duller and less accessible. The leading film school in China, the Beijing Film Academy, was closed down during the Cultural Revolution but reopened in 1977. The students of film direction in the fifth class to graduate after its reopening, who left the school in 1982, are referred to as the Fifth Generation of Chinese filmmakers, and it is these filmmakers whose work is best known to moviegoers outside China: Zhang Yimou, Chen Kaige, and Tian Zhuangzhuang.

Some Fifth Generation films veil their criticisms of the recent past by the use of symbols; others are more direct. Zhang Yimou's *Ju Dou* and *Raise the Red Lantern*—both set in the early years of this century, both featuring a spectacular use of color and imagery—are critical of the old order. In *Ju Dou*, the heroine is married against her will to the much older owner of a cloth-dyeing factory, and she falls in love with his young assistant. In *Raise the Red Lantern*, the heroine is forced to become one of several concubines in the house of a wealthy landowner. Although the oppressors in both cases are part of the old order that the Communist regime overthrew in 1949, both films can be read as commentaries on contemporary Chinese society.

Setting a film in the more recent past is a dangerous game for Chinese filmmakers. Chen Kaige's *Farewell My Concubine* portrays two actors who join a Beijing opera troupe as young apprentices in the 1930s, follows their lives through the end of the Cultural Revolution, and concludes with the suicide of one of them. The film was unacceptable to the authorities not so much because of its characters (one of whom is homosexual) as because the suicide takes place after the "bad old days" are over and the current period of reform has begun.

Much more mundane lives are explored in Zhang Yimou's *To Live* and Tian Zhuangzhuang's *Blue Kite*. *To Live* portrays a young man who, having lost his family fortune at the gambling tables of the old society, becomes a puppeteer and lives with his young family on the margins of the new society. The central character in *Blue Kite* is a boy born in 1953, just as word of Stalin's death is being broadcast in his parents' neighborhood. The two films depict most powerfully the lives of Chinese city dwellers in the 1950s and 1960s. In both cases, families are buffeted by events and movements over which they have no control, while being only dimly aware of their substance. Because neither film distinguishes clearly between the officially accepted "good" era that ended in 1958 and the "bad" period that extended from the Great Leap Forward through the Cultural Revolution, they were banned from screens in China.

An exception to the critical stance assumed by Fifth Generation filmmakers is Zhang Yimou's *The Story of Qiu Ju*. Here the heroine's husband, a farmer, is injured when he is kicked in the groin by a village official. The film depicts her numerous trips to seek redress from officials at ever-higher levels of the rural bureaucracy. Apart from the violent act that sets the plot in motion, government and Party officials are treated rather sympathetically in the film. (From a technical standpoint, *The Story of Qiu Ju* is intriguing because of Zhang Yimou's use of nonactors for all but a handful of roles.)

But Fifth Generation films—those that have not been banned —are not especially popular with Chinese audiences, who find them too slow paced, rather obscure in their symbolism, and occasionally too critical. Most recent films by Fifth Generation directors are foreign co-productions and rely on screening abroad to recoup their investment.

A group of younger filmmakers—sometimes called the Sixth Generation—tend to express the cynical nihilism of the youth culture: Zhuang Yan's *Beijing Bastards* and Wu Wenguang's *My Time in the Red Guards* have both been banned. Chinese filmmakers in Hong Kong and Taiwan make films that are very different from the mainland ones, and Hong Kong movie people are a wild lot, churning out a hundred or more movies a year, most of them martial-arts action films. One of the more interesting Hong Kong filmmakers is Tsui Hark (Xu Ke), who combines the conventions of kung fu films with those of farce and Beijing opera to retell modern Chinese history. By contrast, Taiwan films are rather staid, except for those of Ang Lee, who was trained in the United States and whose films attract an unexpectedly large American audience. Ang Lee concentrates on family relationships, and his humor is situational rather than visual. His *Wedding Banquet*, though produced by a government-owned film company, was hardly the usual Taiwan fare: its hero is a young, gay Taiwanese professional in New York City. When it won a prize at the Berlin Film Festival, the Taiwan government warmly acknowledged Ang Lee and the film despite its unorthodox plotline. Their reaction contrasts sharply with the mainland authorities' stiff-lipped response to the Cannes Film Festival's award of the Palme d'or to Chen Kaige's *Farewell My Concubine*.

As I have said, the political straitjacket in which Chinese arts are confined has loosened in recent years, but the arbitrariness of what is acceptable and what is forbidden makes for an incongruous, often unpredictable cultural mélange. The government censors' puritanism appears to have been relaxed, and the sex, violence, and nihilism of contemporary popular music, film, and literature are largely ignored. For example, only when sales of Jia Ping'ao's

*Fei Du* approached a million copies did the Party-state get around to banning it. It is also acceptable to be critical of the past, notably if the criticism is directed against events prior to 1949 or during the excesses of the Cultural Revolution.

What triggers censors' attention and disapproval is any criticism of the Party-state and its policies prior to 1957 and after 1977. They are particularly sensitive to any mention of the events at Tiananmen Square in 1989. Foreign books and foreign films are almost always a cause for concern. Until very recently, Chinese distributors imported few films and publishers translated few foreign books. With the important exception of *The Sound of Music* —which seems to have been seen at least once by every living person in mainland China—most available foreign films are cheap B-grade movies: the criteria for what gets imported concern cost more than salaciousness or political incorrectness. As Chinese audiences become better informed about international culture, the demand for foreign films rises, and it is to satisfy this demand that the burgeoning industry of pirated video cassettes has sprung up, to the distress of all those in other nations who have agreed to protect intellectual property rights.

As standards of acceptability have relaxed, many of the government and Party control mechanisms of the arts have fallen into disarray, though in certain areas they still function. For example, virtually all performance spaces are owned by the state and all major performing-arts companies depend on state funds for at least part of their budget. Local bureaus representing the Ministry of Culture must review and approve the repertoire of all performing-arts companies and all art exhibits. Most gallery and museum space is state-owned and managed, and exhibitions are subject to government monitoring. The major film studios are government-owned; their films are screened and, if necessary, censored before public release.

The situation is very different with respect to the printed word and television. Prior to the reforms, Party officials reviewed virtually everything before it was published; that they no longer do so is partly the result of rapid growth in the publishing industry. Official statistics for 1978 and 1993 show a fivefold increase in the number of newspapers during that time, a sixfold increase in the number of books, and a sevenfold increase in the number of magazines, and these figures do not include the burgeoning unofficial publications. The government used to control book publishing by issuing book numbers to state-owned publishing houses, without which no book could be published. Publishers have taken to selling their unused book numbers, at a profit of course, to private publishers and printers who turn out great quantities of books, many of which the authorities find unacceptable.

Like the publishing industry, television has become more difficult to control. Television stations now number more than 800, and the number is growing 15 percent per year. The number of television sets has doubled over the last decade and now stands at close to 300 million. The government owns all television stations and monitors the content of their broadcasts, but with the proliferation of stations, most of them locally managed, the diversity of programming has increased significantly. The old, stultifying diet of official news and didactic documentaries has given way to soaps, MTV, and even talk shows (with a built-in fourteen-second delay to allow for screening callers' comments before they hit the airwaves). In addition, satellite dishes and cable connections bring a range of foreign programs to Chinese viewers.

Television coverage of the events in Tiananmen Square in 1989 is an interesting case in point. The extensive international coverage of these events was the result of a coincidence. Foreign reporters, cameramen, and satellite hookups were all in place for the visit of Mikhail Gorbachev to Beijing in May. While his visit was given a share of coverage, most of the reporters were riveted on the demonstrators and their hunger strike, and so these images reached television viewers all over the world.

The extensive Chinese television coverage of the early stages of the demonstrations and occupation of the square was generally sympathetic to the demonstrators. Students and workers in cities across China learned of the events in Beijing through the official media, and they acted on what they saw, heard, and read by going out into their own city streets. Only after the declaration of martial law in late May was domestic television coverage reined in and closely scrutinized. Even then, television reporters were able to signal their opinions by means of dress, body language, and facial expression. And once official television ceased to be an effective means of communication between demonstrators and their out-of-town sympathizers, the fax machine took its place.

The images of what actually occurred on the streets of Beijing on 3 and 4 June were seen by viewers outside China and by the few Chinese who had access to foreign television broadcasts in hotels and offices, while the events were described and ana-lyzed on Voice of America and the British Broadcasting Corpora-tion's shortwave radio transmissions. But Chinese television did not cover the events, and the Party-state could make up its own story, which, devised with carefully edited footage, told of student demonstrators as perpetrators of violence and innocent soldiers as victims of their aggression. Broadcast over and over again in the aftermath of the massacre, this account persuaded many in China that the students had erred, that the People's Liberation Army had saved the day, and that the foreign press was manufacturing other versions to smear the reputation of the Chinese army, state, and Party.

This recasting of news would be difficult or impossible to bring off today, given the proliferation of uncontrolled and uncontrolla-ble media within China and between the Chinese people and the

outside world—satellite dishes and cable connections, fax machines, and, since 1994, international on-line information services.
Realizing the potential dangers of free access to the information
superhighway, the Chinese government issued new regulations
on Internet use in February 1996. Modeled after laws in effect
in Singapore, the new measures aim to provide censored access.
There are currently three ports monitored by the Ministry of Posts
and Telecommunications—in Beijing, Shanghai, and Jinan. While
it may be possible for the government to monitor the Internet at
its current level of 50–100 thousand, as volume increases and
"hackers" become more adept, the system is very likely to break
down.

It is certainly no easier to assess China's contemporary culture
than it would be to assess the state of the arts in our own country.
For every Chinese critic who waxes enthusiastic, there is another
who deplores what has been lost. One group of critics finds *Fei
Du* a new Chinese classic in the tradition of *The Dream of the Red
Chamber*, while another dismisses it as the limited sexual fantasies
of a small-town literary wanna-be. There are architects who laud
the glass and steel structures that now dominate Beijing, and others who deplore the loss of the courtyard houses these new buildings displaced. Foreign critics praise the works of Chinese
painters, and wealthy patrons collect their work, but the Chinese
public avoids them. What is one person's gold is dross for another.
   One can say, however, that for better or for worse the cultural
scene is the part of Chinese society that most closely approximates
the non-Chinese world. There is a freedom to explore and experiment, to enjoy or reject, that never existed in China before and
that does not yet exist in other parts of Chinese society even today.

# Hong Kong:
# Beyond 1997

How the Chinese government handles the aftermath of the transfer of sovereignty in Hong Kong is a matter of great moment. This vibrant financial center, which supplies nearly two-thirds of China's foreign direct investment, could become a stagnant urban backwater. Also, effectively administering Hong Kong would demonstrate to the people of Taiwan the viability of the "one country, two systems" formula under which China proposes eventually to reunify with its renegade province, while a failure to maintain Hong Kong's political, economic, and social systems intact will confirm the expectations of many skeptics on Taiwan.

The British Crown Colony of Hong Kong was formed on the basis of three treaties between Britain and the Qing dynasty government of China. The Treaty of Nanjing was signed in 1842 at the conclusion of the First Opium War, fought when the Chinese imperial government tried to exclude British opium from China. By its terms, the Chinese government ceded in perpetuity the island of Hong Kong to Great Britain. Foreign Secretary Lord Palmerston was not pleased with the work of his envoy, Charles Elliot, who negotiated the treaty, and described Hong Kong (accurately, it happens) as "a barren island with hardly a house upon it." Eighteen years later, at the conclusion of the Arrow War in 1860, the First Convention of Beijing ceded more territory to Britain, including Stonecutter's Island and the peninsula of Kowloon as far north as present-day Boundary Street. Hong Kong's territory today includes a third parcel of land several times the size of the earlier ceded land: the New Territories, the subject of the Second Convention of Beijing, signed on 1 July 1898. The terms of this agreement were different: rather than ceding the land outright, China leased this additional land to the British government for ninety-nine years, a lease that expired on 30 June 1997.

Taken together, the three parcels—a large peninsula at the mouth of the Pearl River on the South China Sea and a number of islands surrounding the peninsula—amount to about 419 square miles, making it roughly one-third the size of Rhode Island.

The colony got off to a slow start. Ten years after it was first established as a base for British naval and military operations in East Asia, fewer than two thousand foreigners and a little more than thirty thousand Chinese lived there. As a commercial center it was eclipsed by Guangzhou, and, by the early twentieth century, Shanghai outpaced it as a manufacturing and financial center.

On the eve of World War II, Hong Kong's population had grown to close to a million. When the Japanese occupied Hong Kong in 1941, the foreign population was imprisoned, and many Hong Kong Chinese fled for Macao, which remained neutral under Portuguese control. By the end of the war, only about six hundred thousand people were living in Hong Kong, but the number grew swiftly, as civil war between Nationalist and Communist forces swept southward through the Chinese mainland, and quadrupled in less than five years. Many of Hong Kong's new residents were businessmen and their families from Guangzhou and Shanghai, who, fleeing from the prospect of life under Communist rule, brought their skills and capital to Hong Kong.

After the founding of the People's Republic in 1949, Chinese citizens continued to enter Hong Kong, a few legally and many, many more illegally. Most came from neighboring Guangdong Province, and many risked their lives in making their escape. A large proportion of Hong Kong's current population of about six million are people who chose not to be citizens of the People's Republic of China.

The economy of Hong Kong has undergone several transformations over the last fifty years. Through the 1950s, its principal economic raison d'être was commerce—as a free port and as China's principal economic window to the outside world—and then in the 1960s it began to industrialize. The process began with the manufacture of low-end consumer goods and gradually shifted into appliances and electronics. In the early 1970s, when Hong Kong's labor and real-estate costs rose, manufacturers moved to other East Asian countries that were cheaper, and the Hong Kong economy shifted to money and banking; the city became, after Tokyo, East Asia's second financial center.

Following the inauguration of reforms in China and its opening up to the world economy, Hong Kong's focus shifted once again to manufacturing. This time, however, while the companies are owned and managed by Hong Kong residents, the factories are located across the border in Guangdong Province, in the newly opened special economic zone of Shenzhen or elsewhere. Today, more than two million workers in Guangdong are employed in Hong Kong–owned businesses and factories.

When Prime Minister Margaret Thatcher, flush from the British victory over Argentina in the Falkland Islands in 1982, visited Beijing, she had been urged to raise the issue of the future of Hong Kong with her hosts. Hong Kong businessmen, concerned over the status of their holdings once the lease on the New Territories expired in 1997, wanted to know whether the Chinese intended to renew the lease.

The existing arrangement had always worked to the benefit of the Communist government. When local leftist zealots had attempted to take advantage of the chaos of the Cultural Revolution to overthrow the Hong Kong government, Mao and his colleagues had reined them in to preserve the symbiotic relationship. By 1982, Hong Kong was providing 40 percent of China's foreign exchange and was China's largest trading partner. Hong Kong firms were investing in joint ventures in Shenzhen and Guangdong and gave every indication they would continue to do so. Hong Kong issues were occasionally discussed by the Foreign Ministry and the British ambassador in Beijing, but day-to-day relations between China and the Hong Kong government were carried on by the former's unofficial emissary in the territory, the head of Xinhua, the New China News Agency.

Thatcher did indeed raise the issue of Hong Kong during her meeting with Deng Xiaoping. She reminded him rather starchily that the British always honored their treaties and expected other nations to follow suit. Making her remarks in this setting and framing them as she did, Thatcher succeeded in touching simultaneously two raw nerves: China's view of its sovereignty and the matter of "face." Questioning China's right to govern its own territory was bad enough, but she did this in a public way such that failure to respond would entail China's loss of face. Deng reminded Thatcher that the treaties to which she referred were signed under duress by a Chinese government no longer in power. He said that Hong Kong, being Chinese territory, must be returned to Chinese sovereignty and that he hoped he lived long enough to visit the city after that occurred. He came within five months of realizing his hope.

Had Thatcher made her point in different terms and another

setting, the Chinese side might have considered renewing the New Territories lease. But that was now out of the question, and the British side concluded that the ceded territories alone—Hong Kong Island, Stonecutter's Island, and the tip of Kowloon—did not constitute an economically viable entity. Some arrangement for the transfer of sovereignty to China would have to be negotiated.

The negotiations, involving seventeen sessions over three years, resulted in the Joint Declaration on the Question of Hong Kong, signed in December 1985. The declaration set up three new bodies: a Basic Law Drafting Committee, made up of Hong Kong and PRC citizens, to draw up a constitution under which Hong Kong would be governed after 1997 as the Hong Kong Special Administrative Region (SAR); a Basic Law Consultative Committee, made up of Hong Kong citizens and charged with assessing Hong Kong public opinion with respect to the provisions of the Basic Law; and a Sino-British Joint Liaison Group, responsible for ongoing negotiations with respect to questions that might arise between the two sides during what the British called the "run-up" to 1997.

Several aspects of these negotiations—not all of them perfectly clear at the time—came to be very significant as the transfer of sovereignty approached. One was a conflict over the premises of negotiations. The Chinese position was based on an offer the government had first extended to Taiwan in 1981 and then to Hong Kong in 1983: to leave their economic and political systems intact for fifty years after the transfer of sovereignty. The Chinese understood this to mean that no change would be made to Hong Kong's economic and political systems *as they existed at the time of the signing of the agreement, in 1985,* while the British position presumed that it could legitimately make alterations in Hong Kong's governance, as it saw fit, prior to the transfer of sovereignty in 1997 and that China's offer meant it would make no change to the economic and political systems of Hong Kong *as they existed at the time of the transfer of sovereignty in 1997.*

During the negotiations, both sides used the "through train" as a metaphor for the transition. Visitors to China in the 1970s will recall the ritual of boarding a train at the Kowloon station to go to mainland China and traveling on it to Lowu, a town on the border. One got off the train at Lowu, walked across a bridge spanning the border, and, after going through customs formalities, boarded the Chinese train on the other side at the Shenzhen station. For frequent travelers, it was a great moment when a through train was inaugurated that allowed passengers to board in Kowloon, cross the border on the train, and disembark in Guangzhou. In the context of the negotiations, the through train meant that every effort would be made to ensure that the city's political system in the time just before the transfer of sovereignty would fit as closely as possible with the political system to be inaugurated after it. If the track was properly laid and the train properly built, the shift of sovereignty would require no one to disembark.

One final aspect of the negotiations proved significant: the people of Hong Kong were not represented in them, though the British side had pressed at the outset for three-way negotiations among representatives of the governments of China, Britain, and Hong Kong. The Chinese rejected the idea, insisting on bilateral negotiations between Britain and China, since the Hong Kong government, they argued, reported ultimately to the British government, and the people of Hong Kong, being Chinese, were adequately represented by the Chinese government. But if the people of Hong Kong had been represented by their own delegates, they would certainly have made a strong case for maintaining the status quo. Polls taken in Hong Kong in the early 1980s showed that an overwhelming majority favored a continuing British presence in the territory and opposed a transfer of sovereignty to China—not surprising, given the substantial number of Hong Kong citizens who had fled Communist rule in China.

These views began to change, however, in the years immediately following the signing of the Joint Declaration. Hong Kong residents observed the rapid reform and growth in the Chinese economy and its extensive new links to the world economy. Many of them took advantage of this to establish business ties across the border. By 1989 more than 2,000 factories in Guangdong were wholly or partially owned by Hong Kong interests. Adding in subcontracting agreements between Hong Kong and Guangdong firms, it was estimated that Hong Kong–related enterprises accounted for more than a million jobs in southern China. As Hong Kong business interests became linked with those of China, people began to have a personal stake in a smooth working relationship among Beijing, London, and Hong Kong. And as political reforms began to alter somewhat the character of the Chinese government, making it seem slightly less repugnant, widespread skepticism about the future was superseded by cautious optimism.

The massacre in Beijing in June 1989 was a major turning point however, not only in public attitudes in Hong Kong but also in the relations among Beijing, Hong Kong, and London. The news from Beijing on 4 June had a devastating effect on public confidence in Hong Kong, anger and fear politicizing a large segment of a population famous for its lack of interest in politics. Millions of Hong Kong residents poured into the city streets to express their outrage. Thousands contributed in various ways to support the democracy movement and to aid its fugitives by means of a hastily constructed underground railway to safe havens in Europe and the United States.

Several political groups were founded in Hong Kong in 1989 that have subsequently evolved into formal political parties. Martin Lee and Szeto Wah are the two most prominent among the many individuals who stepped forward at this time, motivated by concern that, without an effective political voice, Hong Kong citizens faced as precarious a future as did the advocates of good government in China itself.

A comparable shift of attitude occurred in Beijing. The image of Hong Kong as an apolitical golden goose faded, and in its place Chinese authorities saw a hotbed of pro-democratic dissent and a potential threat to their own stability. The situation seemed dangerously out of control when not only the editor of a PRC-supported newspaper in Hong Kong but even Beijing's chief spokesman in the colony, Xu Jiatun, spoke out against their government's actions.

The British position shifted as well: Britain joined the many other nations that responded to the Beijing massacre with economic and political sanctions. The future of Hong Kong looked significantly less secure than it had during the negotiation of the Joint Declaration. With London's concurrence, the Hong Kong government announced a $17 billion proposal to develop a new airport and expand harbor facilities, a measure designed to stimulate the economy, hard hit by the sudden interruption in China's economic interaction with the outside world, and to bolster the confidence of the Hong Kong population in Britain's intention to take positive actions on its behalf in the time remaining under British sovereignty.

At the same time, the Hong Kong government pushed forward with plans, based on a study conducted in 1987, to democratize the territory's political system. It proposed to enlarge the functions of elected local councils and to expand the number of elected positions on the fifty-seven-member Legislative Council. With this decision, the through train was dropped as a metaphor for the transition, and in its place came talk of making Hong Kong "indigestible"—as democratic as possible in the time remaining so that, when the Chinese took control in 1997, undoing the changes would cause them the maximum possible international embarrassment.

The election for seats on the Legislative Council, held in September 1991, marked the debut of political parties in Hong Kong.

The United Democrats, under Martin Lee and Szeto Wah, took sixteen of the eighteen contested seats; the other two went to the Liberal Democratic Federation, a pro-business alliance; the pro-China Hong Kong Democratic Federation failed to capture a single seat. Despite the flurry of interest generated by the election, in a now all too familiar pattern, voter turnout was very low—only 32 percent of those eligible to participate. Observers describe the Hong Kong electorate as "interested spectators" who have an active interest in political issues and take the time to keep themselves well informed but are reluctant to participate.

At this point, the differences in understanding the terms of the Joint Declaration began to emerge, for Beijing took a dim view of these developments in Hong Kong. The Chinese side, registering its disapproval, reminded Hong Kong and London that it had committed itself to preserving the political and economic status quo as of 1985. The British side, noting that it retained sovereignty over Hong Kong through 1997, reaffirmed its right to do to the form of government of the territory what it saw fit. The Chinese therefore stalled in negotiations over every issue that arose between the two sides, the most important being capitalization for the new airport.

Christopher Patten, appointed governor of Hong Kong in May 1992, replaced David Wilson, who had served in the post since 1987. Wilson, like many of his predecessors, had been well prepared for his job and knew the Chinese, but after Tiananmen, understanding and sensitivity were regarded by Westerners as inappropriate, and Wilson was deemed too ready to yield to the Chinese side when negotiating the many disputed issues that were obstacles to a good relationship. Patten, by contrast, was neither a Sinophile nor a Sinologue but a highly successful politician who had been head of the Conservative Party and had recently suffered an embarrassing electoral defeat in his bid to retain a seat in Parliament.

Patten's mandate was to take a strong stand with the Chinese and to proceed at full speed with democratizing the Hong Kong government. It was a mandate that was not likely to endear him to his Chinese collocutors. He began his term with a series of extensive conversations with people in Hong Kong probing for their views on whether and how the government should be restructured in the five years remaining. Five months after taking office, he presented proposals for political reform to the Legislative Council, based, he said, on the opinions he had gathered; they called for an accelerated expansion of representative government that would double the size of the electorate, make local governing bodies elective rather than appointive, increase the number of elected seats on the Legislative Council, and shift the balance of power from the governor and his Executive Council to the now fully representative Legislative Council.

The Chinese response to Patten's proposals was unrelentingly negative. Although Patten claimed to have hewed very closely to the letter of the newly adopted Basic Law, Beijing took the position that the proposals were fundamentally at odds with it. Were the Legislative Council and reconstituted government to adopt the Patten proposals, they said, the authority of that government would be terminated when sovereignty was transferred. There was no question now of a through train.

Reaction to the proposals in Hong Kong was mixed. At first they were supported by a strong majority, but two factors caused that support to diminish: First, the proposals were out of sync with the electorate's reluctance to participate. The political activism stirred up by reactions to the Beijing massacre was relatively short-lived, and although sizable crowds turned out to mark the anniversary of the event each year, for most of the rest of the year the Hong

Kong public was more comfortable being an interested spectator
than an active political participant. Second, the Hong Kong business community, reacting to Beijing's opposition, was cool; with
more and more Hong Kong firms dependent on links with the
mainland, China found it easier to disengage the business community from support for democratization.

Before putting his proposals to a vote in the Legislative Council,
Patten agreed to discuss them with China. After seventeen rounds
of negotiations and no progress, Patten submitted his proposals to
the Legislative Council in two batches, one in December 1993,
the second in July 1994. The first and relatively noncontroversial
batch passed easily; the second and more difficult one passed
thirty-two to twenty-four. With this, China stiffened its position.
They refused to recognize the legitimacy of the democratically
elected Legislative Council created by the reforms and replaced
it with a legislature chosen by a 400-member Selection Committee.

In December 1996 the Committee made the British-educated
Tung Chee-hwa the first Chief Executive. Tung had worked for
General Electric in Boston and San Francisco before returning to
Hong Kong in 1969 to join his father's Orient Overseas shipping
company. Prior to his selection questions had been raised over the
fact that, in 1986, he received what the press referred to as a $120
million "bailout" from Chinese investors to save his ailing firm.
Some found it unlikely that, in light of this favor, he would be
able to hold his own against the importunings of the Beijing government. He has also described himself as an admirer of Singapore's Lee Kwan Yew and the "Asian values" he espouses, which
has aroused concern among Hong Kong's democratic opposition,
with whom he is said to have little patience.

Meanwhile the short-term economic future of Hong Kong appears
promising. Performance figures for the economy are strong and
steady. Per capita gross domestic product is about fifteen thousand

dollars, the third highest in Asia (after Japan and Singapore), and the growth rate over the last ten years has averaged about 7 percent, a figure that pales only when compared with the growth rate of coastal China, which far outstrips it. Inflation has been averaging 10 percent. Unemployment is nearly negligible (the unemployment rate stands at just over 1 percent).

The trend to integrate the Hong Kong economy with that of Guangdong Province has accelerated. Today, about three-quarters of Guangdong's exports go to or through Hong Kong. More than five thousand factories in Guangdong are Hong Kong–owned. Double that number of factories operate as subcontractors for Hong Kong firms. In all, between two and three million workers in Guangdong are employed by Hong Kong–affiliated enterprises, well in excess of twice the number of blue-collar workers in Hong Kong itself.

About 80 percent of Guangdong's foreign direct investment comes from Hong Kong, most of it from Hong Kong investors but some of it Chinese capital channeled through Hong Kong investment companies in order to take advantage of special privileges accorded foreign investors. Hong Kong is also the point through which most of the legal trade and investment between Taiwan and the mainland passes. By Taiwan law, all economic activity with mainland China must take place through a third party, and in the majority of cases, Hong Kong is that third party. Taiwan investment in mainland China totals some $13 billion, and the official figure for two-way trade in 1995 is also estimated at $13 billion.

The gross domestic product of the now closely integrated economies of Taiwan, Hong Kong, and the mainland provinces of Guangdong and Fujian (where most of Taiwan and Hong Kong investments are situated) amounts to more than $467 billion, or two-thirds of the total gross national product of China as a whole.

The economic interdependence between Hong Kong and the southern provinces will have important political consequences in the years ahead. As noted above, one consequence has been to mute some voices in Hong Kong that might otherwise be critical of Beijing. It is also safe to assume that the southern provinces, recognizing their dependence on a strong and viable Hong Kong economy, would serve as advocates and allies of the Hong Kong Special Administrative Region in its post-1997 relationship with Beijing.

Many Hong Kong residents who lack confidence in the future of the territory have chosen to emigrate in the past decade. Before the negotiations, Hong Kong lost an average of 20,000 residents per year, but this was not a net loss: an equal or greater number moved into the territory each year. Since 1985, however, the number leaving Hong Kong has increased to a yearly average of 65,000, while the current rate of legal immigration from the mainland is 150 per day, for an annual total of more than 50,000. There is no accurate count of illegal immigration, but arrests of illegal immigrants are running just short of 100 per day.

Portugal handled the issue of Macao residents' nationality very differently from Britain's treatment of residents of Hong Kong. Macao reverts to Chinese sovereignty in 1998: all of its residents have been given the option of immigrating to Portugal with Portuguese citizenship. But the British government adopted a different policy with respect to residents in its overseas territories: a new British overseas passport entitled the bearer to visit Britain but not to take up residence there. A few Hong Kong residents hold regular British passports, but the vast majority were entitled only to these new overseas passports, which did not qualify them as British subjects. Given this situation, many Hong Kong people who can do so have decided to seek citizenship elsewhere—the United States, Canada, Australia, or New Zealand. Other countries have taken advantage of the situation by offering Hong Kong residents citizenship in exchange for a pledge to invest. Those who argued that Hong Kong citizens were being abandoned to an uncertain fate by the retreating colonial power brought pressure to bear on the British government after 1989, in response to which London offered to make available fifty thousand passports good for residence in Britain; up to two hundred thousand people, including dependents traveling on these passports, could be accommodated by this offer.

Most very wealthy people in Hong Kong have held foreign passports for years. Unlike the boat people who left Vietnam after the fall of their government, these "yacht people," as they are sometimes sarcastically called, will have no difficulty establishing residence outside Hong Kong when and if they choose to do so. But most members of Hong Kong's working class could not afford to emigrate even if they had the papers to do so. Hence the middle class is disproportionately represented among those who left in advance of the transfer of sovereignty. The mid-levels of most professions have been seriously affected by a brain drain. And these well-trained and experienced emigrants from Hong Kong are being replaced by immigrants, most of them from the mainland and nearly all of them less well-trained and experienced.

The Hong Kong government, eager to maintain confidence in the future of the territory, was quick to point out that many of those who left in the mid-1980s came back after having secured citizenship elsewhere, returning both because of the economic slowdown in Canada and the United States and because of Hong Kong's continuing growth and prosperity. They have an enviable position: they can take advantage of Hong Kong's good economic conditions and the excellent employment opportunities over the short term, and they can leave again if the situation deteriorates. The problem for the new government will be to keep this group in the territory, for without continuing strength in mid-level professions, there is little possibility of maintaining Hong Kong's position as the economic and financial center of East Asia.

There are adverse and perhaps unanticipated consequences of the decision by the British and Hong Kong governments to abandon the idea of a through train. Although Sino-British relations had improved enough by mid-1995 to allow for talks on issues critical to Hong Kong's future, the Chinese position hardened when they decided to form what they called a "second kitchen"—a shadow government composed of individuals acceptable to Beijing. This compounded the Hong Kong government's lame-duck status and, in the eyes of some observers, rendered the territory ungovernable for the remainder of the run-up.

The Chinese position of ignoring the Hong Kong government was worsened by the enormous amount of ill will the Chinese felt for Christopher Patten. The Chinese press called him virtually every uncomplimentary name their style sheets permit, including what Patten calls his favorite, a "tango dancer," and for years the Chinese ignored him on every possible occasion. He was not included on the schedule of Chinese officials visiting the territory, and he was not received by Chinese officials in Beijing. This tactic effectively dissuaded Hong Kong citizens from viewing their government as efficacious.

The Chinese also tried, somewhat less successfully, to discredit Hong Kong's democratic parties. Beijing has made it abundantly clear that participation in the post-1997 government by Martin Lee, Szeto Wah, or any of the other prominent and outspoken members of Hong Kong's democratic parties is unacceptable. They denounced the September 1995 elections for seats on the Legislative Council carried out under Patten's new electoral rules, and gave notice that the council seated by this election would be dismissed on 1 July 1997. Paradoxically, they also campaigned actively for a slate of pro-Beijing candidates, who, in the event, were soundly defeated at the polls. Voter participation, at 35 percent, was neither significantly lower nor significantly higher than in past elections.

This dispute has given rise to questions about the legality of the current Legislative Council. A decision adopted by the National People's Congress in 1990 stipulated that if the composition of the Legislative Council in office in June 1997 conformed with the Basic Law, it would remain in office after the transfer of sovereignty. Patten consistently argued that he had carefully crafted his electoral reforms to do just that, and he challenged the Chinese side to show where they did not conform correctly. Without giving details, the Chinese side declared that the reforms violated the Basic Law and proceeded to select a new Council, which took office on 1 July 1997. Tung Chee-hwa, coming to its support soon after he was named Chief Executive, disappointed those in Hong Kong who had hoped that he would uphold the results of the territory's eleventh-hour democratization. For their part, some members of the former Council threatened to mount a legal challenge to the legitimacy of the new body. Thus, whether or not it was their intention to do so, all parties involved contributed to the undermining of the new Hong Kong government's authority.

Two factors have made Hong Kong the successful financial center it is: the free flow of information and a careful adherence to the rule of law. Because neither of these is a characteristic of the People's Republic of China, both are in jeopardy.

Among the most serious legal issues to arise during the run-up was the post-1997 composition of the Final Court of Appeals. The original plan was that it would be composed of seven justices, three from the Hong Kong legal community, three from a panel of British Commonwealth judges with experience in common law, and a chief justice. The Chinese proposed only one external justice, to be drawn from either an international or a local panel. After extensive, unsuccessful negotiations, the British side agreed to this—but the Legislative Council rejected it. The Chinese subsequently conceded that more than one justice could be drawn from an international panel, but have adopted a very vague definition of the court's jurisdiction that leaves many cases to be decided by the National People's Congress. Reluctantly, and after much campaigning by the Hong Kong government, the Legislative Council ratified this proposal. Nonetheless, the episode raised serious doubts, within Hong Kong and in the international business community, as to the future integrity of Hong Kong's legal system.

Under pressure from those in Hong Kong and elsewhere who are concerned about human rights, the Hong Kong government belatedly adopted a Bill of Rights in 1991, intended to supplement protections provided in the Basic Law, but China denounced this as a violation of the Basic Law. At their March 1997 meeting the National People's Congress invalidated the Bill of Rights and some two dozen other laws and regulations. Here again Tung Chee-hwa disturbed many in Hong Kong with his unhesitating endorsement of the NPC's action. Without these changes, he said, Hong Kong risked becoming an "indulgent Western society."

With the substantial increase in economic relations between Hong Kong and mainland China, the frequency with which Hong Kong residents travel to the latter has of course increased significantly. In several well-publicized incidents, Hong Kong residents were detained by Chinese authorities, and, whereas foreigners arrested in China ordinarily have the assistance of a consular representative of their government, Hong Kong residents are not accorded this privilege but treated as Chinese citizens. The stories of how these individuals have fared at the hands of the Chinese system of justice have not inspired confidence about the future in the minds of the people of Hong Kong.

.    .    .

The constitution of the People's Republic of China guarantees Chinese citizens freedom of the press, yet, whenever the press oversteps the boundary of discourse deemed appropriate by the Party, it is brought back into line. The privately owned *World Economic Herald* in Shanghai, for example, was shut down by the authorities in 1989 when it continued to speak openly and favorably about the demands of the demonstrators in Tiananmen Square.

Hong Kong's Basic Law also guarantees freedom of the press and publication, and citizens are asked to take it on faith that the phrase in this context means something different than it does in the Chinese constitution. But their confidence was not strengthened by the case of Yang Xi, a reporter for the Hong Kong newspaper *Ming Pao*, who was arrested while reporting in China and sentenced to twelve years' imprisonment for stealing and publishing state secrets—the secrets in question being a change in the People's Bank of China interest rate, which Yang reported on before it was officially announced. Yet the media in Hong Kong are numerous, vibrant, and diverse, with nearly seventy daily newspapers and as many as six hundred periodicals, three television stations, two privately owned and one managed by the government, and two privately owned radio stations. People in the communications business in Hong Kong are skeptical about the extent of their freedom under the Basic Law, and some are hedging their bets, most frequently with a kind of voluntary self-censorship.

Self-censorship is often a business decision. In 1993 the British Broadcasting Corporation produced a documentary marking the centenary of the birth of Mao Zedong. Because it was critical of aspects of Mao's life in ways that went beyond those condoned by the Chinese Communist Party, the Chinese government demanded that it not be shown in Hong Kong. Rupert Murdoch's Star TV pulled the documentary from its broadcast schedule saying there had been insufficient time to accommodate it; subsequently, Murdoch removed BBC programming entirely from the cable service he was in the process of selling to mainland China.

In other cases, the decision to self-censor is less obviously business-driven. A number of Hong Kong Chinese-language newspapers, for example, have eliminated their editorial pages; in recent years, owners and editors evidently concluding that, in the minefield of Sino-British contention, there was no telling what might offend Chinese sensibilities and what the consequences of having offended them might be in the future. Expressing no opinion at all is the safest course, and the loss of the editorial page does not significantly affect circulation.

Hong Kong's effectiveness as a principal financial center in East Asia is predicated on the absolutely free flow of information, but it is hard to imagine the Chinese government, as currently configured, allowing that flow to continue uninterrupted in the Hong Kong SAR.

Hong Kong's negative image in Beijing is almost exclusively due to popular reaction in Hong Kong to the suppression of China's democracy movement. Christopher Patten's proposals to democratize the Hong Kong government and the rise of political parties opposed to the terms of the transfer of sovereignty both occurred after that suppression. Were the Beijing government to cease categorizing the Tiananmen demonstration as a counterrevolutionary rebellion, democracy in Hong Kong might seem less threatening.

Frustrated by glitches and difficulties in an otherwise remarkably well-functioning city, Hong Kong people sometimes complain that "Hong Kong is becoming more like China every day." But the reverse of that sarcastic comment is also true: China, and particularly its southern provinces, is in fact becoming more like Hong Kong every day. The more that marketization and liberalization spread through the Chinese system, the brighter is Hong Kong's future.

Even the darkest scenario for China's future—the weakening of central control and the breakup of the country into regional satrapies—is not the worst news for the future of Hong Kong. If the central Chinese government cannot impose its will on cities like Shanghai and Guangzhou, which have been under its close control for nearly a half century, why should we assume that it can do so with the Hong Kong SAR?

The key to Hong Kong's future lies in the quality of the people chosen to lead it after 1997. Optimists point to the truth that Hong Kong people have survived and thrived against what appeared to be insurmountable odds in the past: the settling of the unpromising island in the nineteenth century; the rebuilding of the colony after World War II; the dark days of the Cultural Revolution, when it seemed that sovereignty would be transferred under circumstances of violence, anarchy, and chaos. They believe it can happen again, and they may be right.

# Democratization on Taiwan: Model or Rival?

Taiwan, an island of about four thousand square miles that lies about 120 miles off the coast of Fujian province, in the East China Sea, is a province of China, though the government on the island calls itself the Republic of China and, until very recently, claimed sovereignty over all of China. In addition to the island of Taiwan, that government exercises sovereignty over three other tiny islands: Penghu, located in the Taiwan Strait about forty miles off the coast of Taiwan; Matsu, just a few miles off the coast of the mainland near the city of Fuzhou; and Jinmen (Quemoy), located even closer to shore near the city of Xiamen.

Taiwan, a little smaller than the state of Connecticut, has a population of twenty-four million, seven times that of Connecticut. The people of Taiwan enjoy a per capita gross national product of about twelve thousand dollars, which is fourth in Asia after Japan, Singapore, and Hong Kong and about twenty times the figure for mainland China. Its economy, now the world's nineteenth largest, is growing at a rate of about 6 percent per year; inflation stands at about 5 percent.

The question of the relationship between the government on Taiwan and the government of the People's Republic of China, unresolved for nearly fifty years, is a source of friction in both governments' relations with the United States. In the spring of 1996, it became a potential flash point that had many of China's East Asian neighbors concerned.

Those who believe that Taiwan should be unified with the mainland begin their argument by asserting that "Taiwan has always been an integral part of China." Despite the frequency with which this is repeated, the statement is a myth, not a fact. Only during the decade 1885–95 and in the three years immediately after the end of World War II was Taiwan governed as a province of China. At all other times, Taiwan has been largely independent of the control of a mainland Chinese government.

Prior to the seventeenth century, there was virtually no contact at all between Taiwan and the mainland. Sparsely inhabited by a population of Malay-Polynesian ethnic origin, the island was "discovered" during the sixteenth and seventeenth centuries by Portuguese explorers, who named it Formosa. Dutch settlers, who arrived on the island at about the same time as the Portuguese, set up fortified bases, and meanwhile, Japanese pirates had begun to use it as a base for coastal operations.

With the collapse of the Ming dynasty in 1644, loyalists to the fallen house, pursued by Manchu forces, retreated across the Taiwan Strait. Forty years later Qing dynasty forces finally brought Taiwan under their control, and it was placed under the administration of the governor of Fujian, where it remained for two hundred years. That control of the island population was something less than wholly effective is attested to by a Taiwanese saying: "Small rebellions every three years, big ones every five." Only in 1885 did Taiwan gain its own provincial administration—and that was short-lived. Ten years later, following China's defeat in the Sino-Japanese war of 1895, Taiwan was ceded in perpetuity to Japan. It remained under Japanese control for the next fifty years, administered as an agricultural colony, its principal crop being sugarcane. Japanese was adopted as its official language and was taught in the schools. Gradually, if reluctantly, Taiwan culture began to grow away from that of mainland China under the influence of its Japanese rulers.

At the Cairo Conference in December 1943, the Allied powers agreed that Taiwan would be returned to Chinese sovereignty after the defeat of Japan. Nationalist forces received the surrender of Japan on the island, and Taiwan began once again to be administered as a province of China, this time under the Nationalist government based in Nanjing. But on 28 February 1947, less than two years later, the local population rose up against the Nationalist forces occupying the island. The Nationalist government brutally suppressed this uprising, with the loss of many lives, and declared martial law, which was not lifted for forty years.

In much the same fashion as the Ming loyalists who, pursued by Manchus, had fled to Taiwan in 1644, Nationalist loyalists, pursued by the Red Army, fled to Taiwan in 1949—about two million of them, who then set up residence on the island. The population of Taiwan today includes the result of these two retreats. Descendants of the seventeenth-century influx, often referred to as "Taiwanese," make up about 85 percent of the population; the survivors and descendants of the twentieth-century influx, called "mainlanders," make up the remaining 15 percent. A very small number of the aboriginal population remain, amounting to less than 1 percent of the total.

A kind of modus vivendi was established on Taiwan in the years following the arrival of the mainlanders. Politics, the professions, and the armed forces were controlled by mainlanders; the economy was dominated by the Taiwanese. The political system, a highly authoritarian one based on a constitution adopted by the Nationalist forces when their Republic of China was still located on the mainland, began with a National Assembly and a legislature composed of representatives elected on the mainland in 1947.

The United States did not at first intend to protect Nationalist forces on Taiwan against attack from the Communist regime on the mainland, though the United States did not recognize the government in Beijing, instead tacitly supporting the Nationalists' claim to be the rightful government of China. The outbreak of war on the Korean peninsula altered that policy militarily, and the U.S. Seventh Fleet was ordered to begin patrolling the Taiwan Strait; a mutual defense treaty was signed. During the 1950s, the United States contributed some $2 billion in economic and military aid to Taiwan's postwar economic recovery and became deeply involved in the relationship between Taiwan and the mainland. Despite its best efforts to extricate itself, it remains deeply involved today.

Reunification with Taiwan, peaceful if possible, by force if necessary, is currently a very high priority of the Chinese Party-state. In pushing hard for this, it is not motivated in the first instance by economic interest. It could be argued, in fact, that China would stand to lose economically as a result of reunification. Rather, as is the case with Hong Kong and many other issues concerning the outside world, Beijing is driven by its conception of national sovereignty and its determination to gain face and avoid losing it.

Were economic logic to govern Beijing's position on Taiwan, it would dictate a maintenance of the status quo. Taiwan is now the fourth largest supplier of foreign direct investment to China, and there is a substantial two-way trade between them. It is unlikely that economic interaction could improve with reunification; indeed, there is a strong likelihood that it would deteriorate. As is the case with Hong Kong, even if the Chinese government wanted to keep its promise to leave the capitalist system on Taiwan intact for fifty years after reunification, the likelihood that it could do so is very slim. Authorities in Beijing have no experience in allowing a capitalist system to function without excessive regulation, and the situation in Taiwan, like that in Hong Kong, is far too sensitive for the authorities to let well enough alone.

But why is the Chinese concept of national sovereignty at stake? The senior leaders in Beijing believe their own myths: they *believe* that Taiwan has always been an integral part of China and that national sovereignty will be incomplete until they control the province. At one time it seemed as though only a handful of the oldest leaders in China took this hard-line position, and it was hoped that once they departed the political stage, younger successors would adopt a more flexible view, but the armed forces have weighed in decisively on the side of early reunification, and the politicians who depend on the army's support find that they cannot be flexible with respect to Taiwan.

Loss of face is at issue with respect to Taiwan in several ways. First is the long-standing rivalry between Chinese Communists and Nationalists: for the older generation in China, the revolution will be complete and face regained only when Taiwan is "liberated" from Nationalist hands. But there is also a link between reunification with Taiwan and regaining sovereignty over Hong Kong, since the "one country, two systems" arrangement negotiated with Britain for the future of Hong Kong is seen as a model for a future relationship with Taiwan. Taiwan also involves a potential loss or gain of face vis-à-vis the United States. Given recent history, Beijing refuses to believe that the United States can be a neutral party in the resolution of this issue, and they are confirmed in their views by the public statements of many influential Americans who feel strongly that it would be wrong for the United States to be neutral: were the Chinese government to retreat from its policy on reunification, then, it would be seen as a serious loss of face vis-à-vis the Americans.

Yet Beijing's unequivocal and public policy on Taiwan, re-affirmed so strongly in recent years, has only escalated the intensity of the conflict. Beijing believes that Lee Teng-hui, president of the government on Taiwan, is moving in the direction of independence. To discourage him from taking those steps, and at the same time to discourage Taiwan voters from reelecting him in March 1996, the People's Liberation Army (PLA) engaged in provocative military exercises, with live shells and missiles fired into the East China Sea near the coast of Taiwan. Under these circumstances, to effect reunification on mainland terms is to gain face, to accept any other arrangement is to lose face.

With this saber-rattling, the Chinese government is close to coming full circle. Thwarted in its initial effort in 1949 to cross the Taiwan Strait in pursuit of the defeated Nationalist forces, it set as a goal the eventual liberation of the island by force. China acted on this policy in 1954 and again in 1958, but it overestimated the support it would receive from its Soviet allies and underestimated American support for the Nationalists. When, in 1971, Mao decided to effect a rapprochement with the United States—a move designed to intimidate the now wary Soviet Union—the policy toward Taiwan became that of promoting "peaceful reunification." In response, the American government "acknowledged" (the Chinese translation of the Shanghai Communiqué on this subject read "recognized") that "all Chinese on either side of the Taiwan Strait maintain that there is but one China and that Taiwan is a part of China." The use of force was never renounced entirely but was now seen as a backup, not a first step.

This new policy (and, by implication, the Shanghai Communiqué itself) was based on a second enduring myth about Taiwan, which has it that the vast majority of the people of Taiwan—as contrasted with the tiny handful of their reactionary leaders—harbor a deep desire to be governed as a part of the People's

Republic of China. Countless opinion polls taken in Taiwan suggest that the reverse is the case: it is only a tiny handful, not the vast majority, who favor reunification. But this has done nothing to dispel the myth.

In 1978 Deng reiterated Mao's policy of peaceful reunification with Taiwan, and the priority assigned to it: quoting Mao, he said it didn't really matter "if it took a hundred years for Taiwan to return to the embrace of the motherland." But evidently not all Deng's elder colleagues agreed with this relaxed timetable. Theirs was, after all, the generation for whom Taiwan symbolized a revolution uncompleted. By 1980 Deng had begun talking about a decade instead of a century, and he said that he wanted to live to see the day when reunification had been achieved.

In 1981, Ye Jianying, a senior military officer with impeccable revolutionary credentials, was made the spokesman for a new proposal on Taiwan. His Nine Points document is the locus classicus for the concept of "one state, two systems." (It is worth noting that this was issued a full year before Margaret Thatcher's visit to Beijing, which precipitated the process of recouping sovereignty over Hong Kong.) The Nine Points called for the establishment of a special administrative region for Taiwan, within which its present political and economic system would remain intact for fifty years. Details were to be resolved in direct negotiations—not between the government in Beijing and the government on Taiwan but between the Chinese Communist Party and the Nationalist Party. This latter provision, delegitimizing the government of the Republic of China, also ignored the interests of the Taiwanese majority on the island who were then ill-represented in the Nationalist power structure. Ye Jianying's Nine Points also contained a critical caveat: were Taiwan to resist reunification, and particularly were it to declare independence, China reserved the right to use force to bring about reunification.

Chiang Kai-shek, who had led the Nationalists through their conflict with the Chinese Communists and the Japanese, had died three years before Mao and was eventually succeeded by his son, Chiang Ching-kuo, who now responded unequivocally to the Nine Points with a policy of Three Noes: Taiwan would engage in no official contact, would have no negotiations, and would make no concessions.

It was against this background that Beijing turned its attention to Hong Kong. The successful execution of the plan for recouping sovereignty over Hong Kong could serve as a model for the more critical and difficult case of Taiwan. Moreover, Taiwan had extensive business interests in Hong Kong, and a Hong Kong controlled by Beijing put the Taiwan authorities in a bind: they would either have to abandon their Hong Kong business interests or have to give up the Three Noes and come to the negotiating table. Hong Kong was thus both a model for Taiwan and a goad.

Until Taiwan president Lee Teng-hui's controversial visit to Cornell University in the summer of 1995, the American media had totally ignored one of the most stunning political transformations of the postwar period: although the Nationalists remained in power in Taiwan, the political system they controlled had been, during the previous decade, transformed from a highly authoritarian one-party state to a vibrant multiparty democracy. Chinese culture and democracy, said to be the oil and water of political practice, were a viable mixture after all.

The rough and tumble of Taiwan politics, with its vociferous and often disrespectful opposition, has given rise to frequent fist-fights in the legislature and occasional violent street demonstrations. It is a political style that belies several common assumptions about Chinese culture, such as its preference for harmony over chaos and its reverence for the elderly, and it elicits disdain from the starched and buttoned-down Singaporean Chinese. No doubt it also sends chills down elderly Communist spines in Beijing.

Among the forces that led to this startling change, three stand out as particularly important. The first is the person of Chiang Ching-kuo himself. Stricken with leukemia in the 1980s and given only a few years to live, he devoted himself to accomplishing two goals: democratizing Taiwan's political system and opening up contact with the mainland.

Chiang took the first step toward liberalizing his government in 1985, when he selected a Taiwanese rather than a mainlander as his vice presidential running mate: Lee Teng-hui, an American-educated agronomist who had made his career in Nationalist Party politics. The second step came the following year. Opposition parties had been outlawed on Taiwan, and opposition politicians campaigned as individuals (collectively known as *dangwai*, meaning outside the [Nationalist] party). In 1986, when the *dangwai* politicians organized themselves into a new opposition party, the Democratic Progressive Party (DPP), and campaigned on a party ticket, Chiang Ching-kuo decided not to prosecute them and not to disband their party but, rather, to repeal the law that banned opposition parties. A year later he lifted the martial law that had been in effect on Taiwan since 1947. With this move, political rights —guaranteed in the constitution but suspended by martial law— were restored to the citizens of Taiwan. His fourth and final step was taken in October 1987, when he lifted the ban on traveling to mainland China. Initial visits were made under the guise of being merely *tanqin*—visiting relatives—but soon the regulations were very liberally interpreted, and many Taiwanese went to China to observe, to sightsee, and ultimately to begin to do business. Chiang died the following year, having accomplished his goals and having put his legacy in place.

The second force that helped to transform Taiwan's political system was the courage and persistence of the *dangwai* politicians who, against all odds, brought about this political awakening. Harassed, beaten, imprisoned, and exiled by the authoritarian Nationalist government, they had persevered in their determination to be heard. Although Chiang's decisions were critically important, it is unlikely that he would have made them or that they alone would have had the effect they eventually did were it not for the boldness of the opposition.

Finally, a third force was the mainland government's calculated guess that the impending change of sovereignty in Hong Kong would help to make Taiwan more flexible about the reunification issue. When the Joint Declaration on Hong Kong was released in 1985 and the Taiwan government's initial reaction was to say that, given its terms, the policy of no contact would apply to Hong Kong as well after 1997, Taiwan businessmen immediately responded that this was not acceptable. Contact with Hong Kong was critical to their businesses and thus to the economic health of Taiwan. The government would have to come up with a new and more flexible policy. Beijing's goad had proved successful.

Liberalizing the political system on Taiwan involved four inter-related processes: bringing the Taiwanese majority into full political participation, legalizing a political opposition, reconstituting the government, and opening relations with the mainland.

Lee Teng-hui's election by the National Assembly as Chiang's vice president had been the culmination of a long, slow "Taiwan-ization" of the Nationalist Party and government. The informal division of labor between the Taiwanese majority and the main-lander minority in 1949 had largely excluded Taiwanese from politics, but over the years, Taiwanese were actively recruited for Nationalist Party membership and gradually rose to positions of leadership. Chiang's selection of Lee was taken by his mainlander senior colleagues to be no more than a symbolic gesture, but to their surprise, Lee not only succeeded to the presidency upon Chiang's death, but also was appointed head of the Nationalist Party. Very shortly thereafter, he was elected by the National Assembly to his own term as president, though mainlanders brought all their forces to bear against this happening, even enlisting the support of the elderly but determined Madame Chiang Kai-shek, who returned to Taiwan from her home in New York to lobby in favor of a mainlander. Their failure marked the real completion of the process of Taiwanization. Today more than three-quarters of the Nationalist Party are Taiwanese, and they hold virtually all the leading positions in the party and government.

In office, Lee kept to the policies of his predecessor. In legislative elections in 1991, the DPP adopted a platform plank that called for Taiwanese independence: advocacy of independence violates Taiwan law, and some demanded that the president arrest the leaders of the DPP and strip the party of its legal status. He refused to do so.

Reconstituting the government on Taiwan was more difficult. The legitimacy of the government's claim to sovereignty over all of China rested on the fact that the legislature and the National Assembly were initially made up of representatives of all of China's provinces, elected to office prior to the Nationalists' departure from the mainland. Almost fifty years later, though, these representatives were aged, ill, and infirm; supplementary elections held to increase the number of representatives from Taiwan were only a partial solution to the problem.

Shortly after he took office as president, Lee inaugurated discussions about reconstitution, and the government began a series of steps to alter the political system to conform to contemporary reality. A new, smaller National Assembly was elected in 1991. The following year, elderly legislators were forced to retire and elections were held for the posts they vacated. In 1993 and 1994, local elections were held for once-appointed mayors and other officials. In December 1994, mayoral elections were held in Taiwan's two largest cities, Taipei and Kaohsiung, and a gubernatorial election was held for the province of Taiwan. The final stage of the process was the March 1996 election in which the president was directly elected for the first time.

Through this process, the DPP gradually strengthened its position and a number of new political parties emerged. When the DPP campaigns on a platform of Taiwanese independence, it tends to lose support but otherwise garners about a third of the vote. As the table makes clear, its support is mostly in the cities; it does not fare well in small-town and rural elections. The New Party, formed in 1993, is a splinter of the Nationalist Party that has campaigned on an anticorruption and proreunification platform. In the December 1994 elections, Nationalist candidates were elected to office as governor of Taiwan and mayor of the large southern city of Kaohsiung. The mayor of Taipei, however, is a member of the DPP. In his position as mayor, he sits ex officio in the cabinet of the national government—the first opposition politician to do so.

## Results of Recent Elections on Taiwan
### (in percentages of votes cast)

| Election | Kuomintang | Democratic Progressive Party | New Party | Others |
|---|---|---|---|---|
| 12/89 Legislative Yuan | 59 | 30 | | 11 |
| 12/91 National Assembly | 71 | 24 | | 5 |
| 12/92 New Legislative Yuan | 53 | 31 | | 16 |
| 11/93 Medium-size city officials | 48 | 41 | 3 | 8 |
| 2/94 Small city officials | 69 | 7 | 5 | 19 |
| 12/94 Major city officials | 52 | 39 | 8 | 1 |
| 12/95 Legislative Yuan | 46 | 33 | 13 | 8 |
| 3/96 Presidential | 54 | 21 | 15 | 10 |

*(Sources: Asian Wall Street Journal and Far Eastern Economic Review)*

In 1991, though the Three Noes policy was technically still in force, President Lee put forward a proposal for a three-stage process of reunification with the mainland. The first stage had already begun, with the informal contacts initiated by Chiang Ching-kuo in 1987, and according to Lee's plan, it would feature a policy he called "flexible diplomacy" to break the international isolation imposed on Taiwan by China's insistence that any government recognizing Beijing must sever its ties with Taiwan.

Stage two in Lee's reunification plan would move the two sides from informal to formal state-to-state communications. Moving to this stage would require that China continue its economic reforms, renounce the use of force as a means of effecting reunification, and accept the government on Taiwan on an equal standing and as entitled to recognition in the world community. In the third and final stage, the two sides would engage in "long-term consultation and unification."

Informal contacts between the two sides have resulted in the development of substantial economic ties between Taiwan and China. Every year, more than a million Taiwan citizens visit China; Taiwan investors have put more than $25 billion into some thirty thousand enterprises (most of them in Guangdong and Fujian Provinces); and whole industries on Taiwan—such as shoe manufacturing—have moved their plants to China in search of inexpensive real estate and labor. Though direct trade with and investment in China are prohibited under Taiwan law—goods and capital must pass through a third party, in most instances in Hong Kong, as we have seen—this two-way trade exceeded $17 billion in 1995.

In 1993, Prime Minister Lien Chan of Taiwan proposed moving to the second stage of Lee Teng-hui's reunification process, though the preconditions laid down earlier had not been met. Still, some form of legal protection was needed for Taiwan's substantial mainland investments. A first step in this direction occurred at a meeting in Singapore in April 1993 between the heads of unofficial organizations set up by the two governments. The Strait Exchange Foundation (SEF) on the Taiwan side and the Association for Relations Across the Taiwan Strait (ARATS) followed up this initial Singapore meeting with subsequent meetings in Beijing and Taipei.

The talks were interrupted twice: once by the Taiwan side, after a group of Taiwan tourists were robbed and murdered on a pleasure boat in Qiandao Lake in Zhejiang Province, and the Taiwanese complained that the Chinese had engaged in a clumsy attempt to cover up the crime; and then once by Beijing, in protest against Lee Teng-hui's June 1995 visit to the United States. The two sides differ on what should be included on the agenda, in any case. The SEF has authority to discuss only economic and social matters; ARATS's mandate calls for it to introduce political issues. To date, the two sides have negotiated an agreement on the return of hijacked aircraft, procedures for dealing with illegal immigrants, and a settlement of fishing rights in the Taiwan Strait.

Meanwhile, Lee Teng-hui has actively pursued his policy of flexible diplomacy to secure some form of recognition for the government on Taiwan beyond the two dozen nations with whom it now has diplomatic relations. Adopting a plank from the opposition party's platform, his government is also seeking to return to membership in the United Nations—a position it lost in 1971, when the China seat was taken from it and given to the mainland government. Flexible diplomacy has made for a busy travel schedule, as Lee has made formal visits to the nations that still recognize his government, informal visits to others, and worked closely with a group of UN member states that, since 1993, have proposed that the issue of Taiwan's representation be added to the agenda of the General Assembly. In conducting this campaign, Lee has formally abandoned his predecessors' fiction that the government on Taiwan speaks for the whole of China. Countering the "one country, two systems" formula, Lee uses the phrase "one country, two governments," suggesting analogies with Germany and Korea. Lee and the Nationalist Party for whom he speaks continue to support reunification and to reject independence, but his articulation of this position is not entirely unequivocal. He describes his position as "conditional rejection" of the opposition's pro-independence stance, but there is no question that mainland authorities are skeptical of the firmness of his pro-reunification stance.

Because they have benefited so much from economic ties with Taiwan, the mainland authorities have enthusiastically supported them. And there is a group of influential individuals on Taiwan who have a vested interest in maintaining good cross-Strait ties. It is even possible that the Taiwan economy could become dependent on them for its continued health and growth. Indeed, shortly after his election in 1996 President Lee called for voluntary limits on Taiwan's investments in the mainland. He suggested that no more than 30 percent of Taiwan's total overseas investment should be placed in China and that China investments should amount to no more than a fifth of any Taiwan firm's domestic investments. The Chinese side denounced Lee's limits as creating obstacles to the free operation of market forces.

The authorities in Beijing have pushed to make the cross-Strait talks between the SEF and ARATS more substantive with respect to political issues, but Beijing is unequivocal in its denunciation of the opposition DPP and its advocacy of Taiwan independence —particularly as DPP candidates capture major posts in the government and more seats in the legislature. A far greater threat, however, is that the Nationalist Party, now firmly under the control of the Taiwanese majority, might pursue a policy of de facto independence, although no Nationalist is ready to describe his policy publicly in these terms. This arouses a strident response on the Chinese side, which includes conducting military exercises and weapons tests off the Taiwan coast. But Beijing's policy to intimidate Taiwanese voters appears to have backfired badly, only underscoring its naïveté in dealings with those whom it considers compatriots.

Beijing finds the policy of flexible diplomacy especially aggravating. That foreign governments should accord Taiwan or its representatives respect as anything other than a province of China is absolutely unacceptable. (The applications of Taiwan and China to join the World Trade Organization are especially contentious. Applying under the name "The Customs Territory of Taiwan, Penghu, Quemoy, and Matsu," Taiwan has pressed to be first, and of course Beijing insists on being approved first so that it can have a voice in deciding the terms under which Taiwan is admitted.) That foreign governments should sell arms to Taiwan, strengthening its ability to resist China's use of force to accomplish reunification, is equally unacceptable.

Successive American administrations since 1972 have taken the position that relations between Taiwan and the mainland can only be settled by the two sides themselves, a hands-off policy that a substantial group in the U.S. Congress has from the outset found unacceptable. With the congressional elections in 1994, Taiwan's supporters were able to muster a majority—in some cases, near unanimity—on questions affecting Taiwan, but Beijing was unsympathetic to the Clinton administration's protestations that its freedom to maneuver was severely limited by Congress.

Cross-Strait relations reached a low point during the period between President Lee's visit to the United States in the summer of 1995 and his election to the presidency in March 1996. China's leaders appear to believe that, despite his statements to the contrary, Lee is a closet advocate of independence for Taiwan, and they found the contrast between the rapid expansion of democracy on Taiwan and their own hardening resistance to political liberalization highly distasteful and potentially embarrassing. As a result, Beijing actively worked to bring about Lee's defeat in the presidential election or at least to cut the size of his majority. The official press carried blistering denunciations of him.

More alarming, the People's Liberation Army dropped hints to an American visitor to Beijing in December 1995 that, should Lee be elected, it would conduct daily missile strikes on the island for thirty days. Fueling the rumors, the PLA moved more than 150,000 troops into Fujian Province, opposite Taiwan, in late February 1996 and began a series of missile test firings into the Taiwan Strait in early March. A week later a series of war games was announced involving the use of live ammunition in a large sector of the Strait northwest of the island. The sites of these exercises were chosen to cause disruption in the sea lanes used for shipping in and out of Taiwan's major ports and to demonstrate China's capability to interrupt the island's maritime commerce. What was particularly disturbing about these measures was that the People's Liberation Army seemed to be calling the shots with very little interference from the civilian authorities.

Generally speaking, the reaction among the Taiwan population was the opposite of that anticipated by Beijing. Although Taiwan's stock market fluctuated even more wildly than usual and there were some who laid in a large supply of rice and other staples, support remained strong for Lee and even for those advocating a more extreme anti-Chinese position than he did. The United States government, though it did not take seriously the threat of actual attack on Taiwan, denounced the military exercises as "unnecessarily provocative and reckless," moved a carrier group into the vicinity of the island, and agreed to the sale to Taiwan of Stinger air defense missiles, advanced targeting and navigating systems for jet aircraft, and 300 additional M60-A3 tanks.

In the event, more than three-quarters of those eligible participated in the first direct election for the chief executive, giving Lee and Lien Chan, his vice presidential running mate, 54 percent of the vote. In fact, it was the first such election in any Chinese society and was regarded by many as a major milestone in the emergence of Chinese democracy. Lee campaigned on a de facto platform of independence from the mainland. Combining his share of the vote with the 21 percent garnered by Peng Ming-min, the opposition DPP candidate who campaigned on a platform of de jure independence, one could argue that three-quarters of the voters on Taiwan expressed their opposition to reunification with the mainland.

Beijing's interpretation of the election results was very different. Choosing to ignore Lee's covert support of independence and pointing to the decline in support for the DPP between the legislative elections in December 1995 (in which they received 41 percent of the vote) and the presidential elections, the Chinese press said that the election results offered irrefutable proof that the people of Taiwan had rejected independence. It advocated an early meeting between Lee Teng-hui and the Chinese president, Jiang Zemin, and the opening of direct air, shipping, and mail links across the Taiwan Strait. At his inauguration in May, President Lee, too, proposed an early meeting with President Jiang.

The events of 1995 and 1996 illustrate the strength of feeling in Beijing over the possibility of an independent Taiwan. They also illustrate the options available to the Chinese government to influence the authorities on Taiwan.

The Chinese armed forces have shown that they can pressure the civilian leadership to take a strong stand with respect to Taiwan. Short of military invasion, which the PLA is ill-equipped to carry out, there are several steps the Chinese government might choose to take if negotiations were to break down. Intimidation, such as the military exercises and tests conducted during 1995 and 1996, is one. Another might well be a reversion to the economic policy in force in the early 1970s, when firms doing business on Taiwan were not permitted to do business in China. A third step—well within the current capability of the PLA—might be to carry out a blockade of Quemoy and Matsu Islands, very close to the mainland coast. The two islands are guarded by a garrison of some hundred thousand troops: substantial pressure could be brought to bear on the Taiwan government were these troops held hostage by mainland forces.

A fourth step—a considerable escalation—would be to blockade Taiwan itself. This would immediately and adversely affect the Taiwan economy, but it would also invite international intervention in order to keep international shipping lanes open.

A final step to wring compliance from an intransigent Taiwan would be a direct attack on the island, but launching such an attack would be a high-risk maneuver. The PLA navy is ill-equipped and untrained to launch an amphibious attack, Taiwan is well-defended (its military budget is somewhat in excess of $10 billion per year, or about 6 percent of GNP, a third of the estimated actual budget for the PLA in dollar terms and about the same proportion of GNP), and although somewhat outdated compared to the most advanced American, European, and Russian capabilities, the Taiwan air force is better equipped and better trained than the PLA air force. Though it is not clear that Taiwan would win an armed conflict with China, it would at least make it a protracted and costly war, which would seriously damage the island's economy, the strength of which is one of the most important motivations for reunification, and the economy of the coastal provinces in which it has invested most heavily.

Armed conflict between Taiwan and the mainland could also trigger international intervention, notably from two of China's major trade and investment partners that have strong economic ties to Taiwan—Japan and the United States. Many Americans would favor military action on Taiwan's behalf. Whether either Japan or the United States would go to war with China to defend Taiwan is highly questionable, but at the very least they would feel compelled to adopt economic and military sanctions that would be certain to slow China's economic development.

Any of these steps is likely to have an effect on the Taiwan population that is the opposite of that desired. Threatened with blockade or outright attack, the people on Taiwan are likely to rally in support of their independence from the mainland. Even if beaten into submission, they would probably be at least as difficult to control from Beijing as were their Ming-loyalist ancestors three centuries ago.

One reason that the Taiwan issue touches such a raw nerve in Beijing is that Taiwan's democratization is a counter-model for the political repression that China's authoritarian leaders are trying to keep in place. The two governments once closely resembled each other, but now Taiwan has set aside its authoritarian practices in favor of a no-holds-barred democracy, while at the same time enjoying continued economic prosperity, and this is a thorn in Beijing's side.

The Taiwan model of political liberalization starts with an autocratic party holding a monopoly over the political system and enforcing its control by a heavy reliance on armed force. The transformation of that system occurred because of the coincidence of two key factors: the emergence of courageous individuals who, risking arrest and persecution, nonetheless actively campaigned against the autocratic party; and the forward-looking decision by the autocrat Chiang Ching-kuo to permit a political evolution. But there are key differences between Taiwan and mainland China that make the new Taiwan a questionable model. First and most obvious is the difference of scale. The people of Taiwan, for all their differences, are a highly integrated island population of 24 million.

China's people, for all their much-vaunted ethnic unity, are a
highly diverse population of 1.2 billion scattered over a very large
territory. A second important difference is in the levels of economic development. Taiwan's per capita GNP was about ten times
that of mainland China when its political transformation began. If
it is true that economic development produces a demand for political liberalization, then we should not expect that demand to be
made in China—particularly in its poorer areas—for some time
to come.

A third difference is that in mainland China there is no single
mobilizing issue. Gaining a political voice for the Taiwanese majority was an issue that united up to 85 percent of Taiwan's population, but, despite all the complaints that citizens of the People's
Republic have about their government, no single complaint has
the potential to mobilize a comparable opposition.

External pressure affected the political evolution of Taiwan, but
it is not clear that it could in China. When the liberalization process was inaugurated, Taiwan was at its most isolated internation-
ally, and democratization was a course of action that was certain
to elicit international support, though that support has been a long
time in coming. But since 1989, the Chinese government has dug
in its heels and become more repressive and more defiant, apparently presuming that an economically burgeoning China cannot be
ignored and will not long be isolated in the world economy.

Finally, there is a substantial difference between the senior
leaders on the two sides of the Taiwan Strait. Knowing death was
near, Chiang Ching-kuo had the political courage and vision to
open and revivify his government. Knowing death was near, Deng
Xiaoping demonstrated the limits to his political courage and vision by moving in the opposite direction.

# China's Foreign Relations

There were those who said that the collapse of the Soviet Union in 1991 marked the beginning of a new world order. There is no question that the sudden demise of the second superpower rearranged the familiar landmarks of international politics in the last half of the century, but if there is a new order in the re-arrangement, it has yet to become manifest. In the old order, China was equidistant from the two superpowers and, because of this position as a balancing force, could influence world politics out of all proportion to its national strength. Today, although China's national strength is growing, its strategic importance has declined. Like the United States, China has not yet defined the strategic role it hopes to play in a future world order or set the foreign policy goals that flow from that intended role.

Foreign policy questions, like domestic ones, are subject to the power grid of the Chinese political system, though this has not always been the case. The formulation of foreign policy used to be confined to a small number of people at the apex of the Party-state, and its implementation was the exclusive purview of the Foreign Ministry. But several changes during the 1980s opened the field to other players.

The first was the increasing dominance of economic issues. When China was largely cut off from the world economy, ideological and strategic issues dominated foreign policy. With the economic reforms, these have receded to the background, and a vastly expanded trade and investment, creating new links to the outside world, have become central.

A second, more recent change is the emergence of the People's Liberation Army as a principal player. During the last decade, as we have seen, the PLA has developed extensive international connections of its own, many of them economic rather than military or strategic. As a consequence, the PLA has interests that are often at variance with the interests of China's Party-state.

Finally, as the balance of power between the central government and the regions has shifted in the direction of the latter, they, too, have begun to affect foreign policy. But they do not speak with a single voice.

Still, the most important player remains the Party-state, and within it divergent views are held with respect to China's foreign policy goals. A small number of conservatives have a kind of "fortress China" mentality. They believe that Deng Xiaoping's open policy has resulted in dangerous dependencies and noxious influences. In their view, the country would be far better off if it returned to economic autarky and strategic disengagement. But the opposite point of view is also represented within the Party-state, by those who argue that there should be no limit to China's interaction with the world economy, that new sources of investment capital and technology should be sought, that new markets for Chinese goods should be actively cultivated, and that market forces should be allowed to determine foreign economic links and drive the domestic economy. Although they might not want to say so, it is an American model of international economic policy that they have in mind for China.

A third group within the Party-state takes a cautious middle position. They share the conservative minority's concern about China's becoming too dependent on foreign interests. But they are favorably impressed with the results of Japan's government-managed industrial policy and its carefully calculated penetration of foreign economies in search of markets, raw materials, and labor. They consider that this mercantilist approach to economic development has greater potential for China than one based exclusively on free trade.

As for the armed forces, which during 1995 and 1996 began to look as though they might be the dominant voice, they speak from several different perspectives. From the perspective of its strategic concerns, the PLA's goal is to have enough military strength to assert China's sovereignty, to secure and defend its national borders, and to guarantee access for China to offshore energy sources and shipping lanes. From the perspective of its varied and substantial economic interests, it wants to maintain open access to foreign capital and markets. From the perspective of its institutional self-interest, it is inclined to support a foreign policy that justifies military expansion—whether in the South China Sea, in Burma, or in dealing with Taiwan—and helps it to get more and better equipment and a larger budget. Also in its self-interest, however, is access to the expertise and technology of the most advanced military establishments, particularly that of the United States, and seeking to ensure that access may dampen the PLA's expansionist tendencies.

The horizontal components in China's power grid have their own foreign policy interests, too. The south China coast, for example, with its heavy concentration of Taiwan-invested enterprises, has its own point of view on relations with Taiwan. Similarly, Guangdong and its special economic zones, closely linked as they are to the Hong Kong economy, can be expected to advocate policies that foster a smooth transition and the preservation of Hong Kong's economic viability. In like fashion, the southeastern macroregion has close links with Burma and the former Indochinese states, Shandong Province is closely tied to Korea, the northeastern provinces to Russia and Japan. Each regional player is likely to act as an advocate for policies that foster its external ties. Although every effort is made to ensure that the PLA speaks with a single voice and is immune to power-grid politics, regional military commanders persist in cultivating local ties against these heavy odds. The connections they make with foreign powers serve both economic and military interests. In some cases, they appear to have been cultivated without the blessing of the central command.

Taking one or two steps back from the interests of specific nodes in the power grid, it is possible to discern some broad and generally accepted priorities in Chinese foreign policy in the post–Cold War world. The first priority is clearly that of pursuing policies that promote China's economic development.

China was a late arrival in the modern global economy but in a very short period has become a highly important contestant, deeply involved in the game. On a price-parity basis, China's is the world's third largest economy after those of the United States and Japan. Were it to maintain its current rate of growth into the next century, it would surpass both Japan and the United States by 2050. Its foreign trade is growing at 20 percent per year— nearly twice the growth rate of the economy itself. Total two-way trade in 1995 was $280 billion, which amounts to 40 percent of gross domestic product (about double the ratio of the United States' trade to its GDP). Foreign direct investment totaled $37 billion in 1995, and is increasing at an average annual rate of about 15 percent. A cumulative total of foreign investment in China's economy is approximately $100 billion, coming from Hong Kong (about two-thirds of the total), Japan (somewhat less than one-fifth), Taiwan (somewhat more than one-tenth), and the United States (just behind Taiwan).

Certain constraints could prevent the Chinese economy from realizing its potential, as we have seen, notably the drain on the national budget and on bank credit created by the state-owned enterprises' mounting losses; the shortage of arable land, and the limits that places on China's ability to feed its population without resorting to massive grain imports; its inability to slow its population growth; the growing income inequality compounded by rampant and apparently uncontrollable corruption; and the possibility of regional fragmentation. Still, it is likely that China's foreign trade will continue to grow, albeit at a slower pace. China's trading partners are very likely to develop protectionist measures to defend their own domestic industries against competition from less expensive Chinese products. Moreover, as production costs rise at home, Chinese products will begin to lose their early competitive lead. China is likely to continue to look to foreign capital markets as a source of investment capital, particularly as a means to fund major public works projects and to resolve the crisis in the state-owned sector of the economy.

China's economy is remarkably open by comparison with those of other Asian nations and is likely to continue to be so. Closed economies tend to restrict imports, but the Chinese import substantial quantities of goods (to the point of running up trade deficits in ten of the last fifteen years), have placed few restrictions on foreign investors, and have tried to put in place regulations and incentives to encourage foreign participation in Chinese economic development. A measure of their success is the fact that exports of goods produced in foreign-invested enterprises made up a quarter of China's total exports in 1994. Exports from foreign-invested firms are growing five times as fast as exports from domestically owned firms.

## China's Economic Interaction with Selected Nations, 1995
### (in billions of U.S. dollars)

|  | Incoming investment | Total two-way trade | China's exports | China's imports |
|---|---|---|---|---|
| Britain | 0.92 | 4.76 | 2.79 | 1.97 |
| Burma | 0.00 | 0.77 | 0.62 | 0.15 |
| France | 0.29 | 4.49 | 1.84 | 2.65 |
| Germany | 0.39 | 13.71 | 5.67 | 8.04 |
| Hong Kong | 20.19 | 44.57 | 35.98 | 8.59 |
| Japan | 3.21 | 57.47 | 28.46 | 29.00 |
| North Korea | 0.01 | 0.55 | 0.49 | 0.06 |
| Philippines | 0.11 | 1.31 | 1.03 | 0.28 |
| Russia | 0.02 | 5.46 | 1.66 | 3.80 |
| Singapore | 1.86 | 6.90 | 3.50 | 3.40 |
| South Korea | 1.05 | 16.98 | 6.69 | 10.29 |
| Taiwan | 3.17 | 17.88 | 3.10 | 14.78 |
| United States | 3.08 | 40.83 | 24.71 | 16.12 |
| Vietnam | 0.03 | 1.05 | 0.72 | 0.33 |
| Total all countries (including those not listed) | 37.81 | 280.85 | 148.77 | 132.08 |

*(Source: China Statistical Yearbook 1996)*

The offshore components of Greater China—Taiwan, Hong Kong, Singapore, and the overseas Chinese communities in North America and Europe—are likely to continue to be the most reliable and lucrative sources of investment capital, and this constrains Chinese policy on delicate issues of sovereignty. The Chinese authorities probably find rattling sabers in the Taiwan Strait and venting spleen against Hong Kong democrats highly gratifying in the short term, but soberer heads in Beijing are well aware that the continuing viability of the economies of Taiwan and Hong

Kong is indispensable to the continuing economic growth of mainland China.

The Japanese were among the first to trade with the newly opened and reforming China, but they have been slow to invest there, though Japan is now second after Hong Kong as a source of foreign capital. China's economic policy with respect to Japan is to encourage additional investment while trying to balance its trade.

China's trade with South Korea has grown rapidly and now vastly outweighs the economic connections with North Korea, though because it shares a border as well as, nominally speaking, a political ideology with North Korea, China is not interested in alienating that government. Moreover, its ability to communicate with Pyongyang is a unique asset that can be used with other nations, the United States among them, as a bargaining chip. On the other hand, there are limits to China's willingness to oblige North Korea, and Beijing has made it clear that it will not take up the slack in foreign assistance that resulted from the collapse of the Soviet Union. Knowing that reunification of North and South Korea would divert South Korea's trade and investment potential, China has not strongly advocated a settlement but instead has encouraged South Koreans to invest in China, particularly in neighboring Shandong Province, and has actively promoted Sino-Korean trade.

China's foreign economic policy often puts a damper on the natural instincts of Chinese leaders with respect to the United States. Concerns about sovereignty and face, taken alone, would surely lead them to cut themselves off from annoying American criticism, but they cannot be taken alone, and economic interests dictate caution. It would be possible but difficult for China to find better or other markets for its goods, other sources of capital and technology, and thus it is prepared to grant concessions in order to keep Sino-American links open and functioning. Some Chinese decision makers believe that, from an economic perspective, the United States needs Chinese markets, labor power, and investment opportunities more than China needs the United States. This group is more likely to bring issues of sovereignty and face to the fore and is willing to grant concessions only grudgingly and at the eleventh hour.

In Europe, China finds trading partners and potential investors who are much more relaxed about difficult questions of human rights than Americans are. And while in some fields, high technology can be found only in the United States, European substitutes for American goods are usually acceptable and often much easier to acquire.

A second goal of Chinese foreign economic policy is to develop new markets for Chinese goods in order to balance with exports the demand for costly high-tech imports. In years past, it was the Third World to which China turned: China's championing of the cause of less developed countries in Africa, Asia, and Latin America was motivated in part by its interest in finding buyers for the low-end manufactured goods it turned out in such great quantity. More recently, Russia has become an avid customer; some of this export business moves through ordinary trade channels, some of it is cross-border trade involving barter arrangements, and Chinese goods also make their way to Russian consumers via duffel bags carried on the Trans-Siberian Railroad by Russian and Chinese merchants in search of a fast profit. But Russia is likely to be only a temporary market for Chinese consumer goods, since soon the latter will be replaced by goods produced in Russian factories.

Chinese factories are now turning out more and more high-quality, sophisticated products, for which new markets must be sought, most likely in developed countries. Expanding this market will help to bring China's trade with Japan into balance but only exacerbate the already serious problem of a trade surplus with the

United States. It is also likely to elicit protectionist reactions from manufacturers within the developed world.

A third goal of China's foreign economic policy, to curb its competition, is of longer term significance. As China's economy develops, what are now complementary and symbiotic relationships are likely to become fraught. The relationship with Taiwan is an excellent example: China's need for investment capital and Taiwan's need for cheap labor and real estate for its manufacturing sector make for mutually beneficial relations. But as costs rise on the mainland, it will no longer serve Taiwan's needs to locate manufacturing operations there, and as China's products become more sophisticated, they will compete in foreign markets with goods produced on Taiwan.

China's most immediate source of competition is the newly opened economy of Vietnam. Although on a smaller scale, Vietnam has been just as aggressive in pursuit of foreign investors as China, and its production costs are, for the moment, considerably lower than in China's coastal provinces.

During the Cold War, the strategic triangle in East Asia was made up of the United States, the Soviet Union, and China. In economic and military terms, China was not in the same league with the other two (only much later did we learn that the Soviet Union wasn't either), but it served the interests of the two superpowers to use China as a makeweight against the other. Today, Japan has taken the place of the Soviet Union in the East Asian strategic triangle, and the gaps between the world's three largest economies are narrowing rapidly, though in strategic terms, the relationships are far from parity. Despite computer simulations that show China besting the United States in military conflicts under certain circumstances, the Chinese armed forces are far outmatched in equipment, training, and logistics by the Americans. Japan, prevented by its constitution from creating an offensive military capability, nonetheless now spends just over 1 percent of its GNP on its military establishment under the rubric of "self-defense forces." And the Chinese have long voiced concern about the revival of Japanese militarism. Having borne the brunt of that militarism through much of the first half of the twentieth century, they are not persuaded that it was ended once and for all with Japan's defeat in 1945. Until very recently, the Chinese argument seemed counterintuitive: the Japanese were prevented from rearming by their constitution; so long as the United States was prepared to serve as a shield for Japan, it would be economically foolish for the Japanese government to take over that responsibility; and Japanese public opinion has consistently opposed rearmament in any form.

But recently reasons to question all these safeguards have lent more credence to the Chinese view. There is talk in Japanese political circles of the need to reconsider the constitution. Some argue that it is time for Japan once again to become a "normal nation," by which is meant a nation with a full-scale defense establishment. The American shield was designed to protect Japan from Soviet aggression, but today a threat to Japan's national security is unlikely to come from Russia, and Japanese (and American) planners question whether American forces would leap reliably to Japan's defense in any other case. Moreover, the United States has for some years pressured the Japanese to bear a greater share of the cost of their defense, and recent public opinion polls show that a majority of Japanese citizens agree that it is time for their country to have a full-scale military force.

Japan's potential military expansion serves as a rationale for the expansion of the People's Liberation Army. The growth of Chinese military capability, in turn, serves as an argument for those in Japan favoring its becoming a normal nation. The Sino-Japanese relationship, focused on economic issues almost exclusively since

1972, must at some point in the near term concentrate on strategic concerns as well.

If China's goal is to reduce the possibility of the reemergence of Japanese militarism, two steps are called for that the Chinese may find difficult to take. One is active encouragement of a continued U.S. presence in East Asia. Unfortunately, the Chinese have persuaded themselves that American policy makers are trying once again to encircle China and thwart its emergence as a world power. Given this mind-set, Chinese strategic planners find it hard to separate what they believe are the baneful effects on China of the American presence in East Asia from its beneficial effects on Japan.

Second, China should not do anything that can be construed as military expansionism, since Japan would use this as a pretext for its own military buildup. But the PLA's institutional self-interest, which is so influential in policy making, leads it to seek out external situations that will justify a larger, technologically more sophisticated military establishment.

Sovereignty and national security also figure importantly in China's relations with Russia and the other former Soviet republics. Sino-Soviet hostility reached the point of armed conflict in 1969, but the two sides did not begin the long process of reconstructing their relationship until the early 1980s. Mikhail Gorbachev's visit to China, which unexpectedly coincided with and was engulfed by the Tiananmen demonstrations in 1989, marked the culmination of that process of rapprochement. With the collapse of the Soviet Union and its Communist Party two years later, however, Russia again became an unpredictable and potentially dangerous neighbor. Once, the Soviet Union was a strong and heavily armed source of Communist heterodoxy; today, Russia is a weak and heavily armed source of democratic heterodoxy. In particular, the border area remains heavily armed. Although the two sides negotiated an agreement to demilitarize their borders, Russia has been unable to carry it out for lack of resources to cover the cost of troop relocation.

Boris Yeltsin has paid three visits to China, the most recent in 1996 just prior to the Russian presidential election. Both sides are eager to expand their trade relations. The Russians have offered technical assistance for the Three Gorges Dam project, and the Chinese have been ready buyers of excess Russian military equipment. But China remains concerned that the government in Moscow will either lose control or be taken over by Russian nationalists who would profit from reviving the conflict with China. As for the Mongol, Kazakh, and Kirghiz ethnic minorities who live in China's far west, adjacent to their ethnic cousins in Mongolia, Russia, and the Central Asian republics, the Chinese are interested in avoiding at all costs collaboration among ethnic separatists arguing for national self-determination. Indeed, during his 1996 visit, Yeltsin and Jiang Zemin, together with representatives from Kazakhstan, Kirgyzstan and Tajikistan, signed agreements that resolved long-standing differences over their common borders.

Meanwhile the Russians are worried about the 2 million-odd Chinese entrepreneurs living and working in Siberia. Although it is likely that they only mean to make money and go back to the somewhat more hospitable clime of their homes, their presence seems to resurrect Russian fears of a "yellow horde" engulfing Mother Russia.

China's actions in the South China Sea continue to be a serious concern for its neighbors in East and Southeast Asia. The Chinese claim that the Spratly Island chain, which lies in the South China Sea between Vietnam, the Philippines, and the island of Borneo, is Chinese territory, while the Philippines, Vietnam, Malaysia, Brunei, and Taiwan make rival claims to sovereignty over it. By its very liberal reading of the Law of the Sea Convention of 1982 (which it signed but has not ratified), China not only owns the islands but controls the twelve-mile contiguous zone and the two-hundred-mile "exclusive economic zone" around each island. Laws passed by the National People's Congress in 1992 refer to the area as China's "territorial sea" and claim the right to "take all necessary measures" to assert and protect its sovereignty.

It has long been assumed that the principal reason for interest in the islands is the possibility that there are substantial offshore oil deposits in the island chain; control over fishing rights is also at issue, though the sea has been heavily overfished. Finally, the South China Sea is regarded by other countries as a critical international maritime passage, open access to which they would be prepared to defend.

China began to enforce its claim to the islands in 1988, when it captured six atolls from the Vietnamese in the Johnson Reef area. Since then, it has established outposts on a number of the islands, and Chinese naval vessels have had frequent encounters with those of the other claimants. Pressed by Vietnam to state its intentions, China proposed that the two sides pursue a policy of "joint exploitation first" and leave awkward questions of sovereignty to be resolved later. But these intentions were called abruptly into question in the spring of 1995, when it was discovered that China had built an outpost on one island located only 135 miles off the Philippines coast. The boldness of this move, in the context of a substantial increase in military spending and the acquisition of much new equipment designed to strengthen the Chinese navy, raised many questions about China's intentions in the area. The initial American reaction was to say that the question must be settled between the Chinese and Philippine governments, but then Washington said it was prepared to intervene if the international right of free passage was interrupted.

China's actions in the South China Sea are on the face expansionist. There was no Chinese presence in the area in the past and now there is. Is this a harbinger of a broader expansionist policy? Is this a policy on which there is general agreement in Beijing, or is it an initiative undertaken by the Chinese navy to strengthen its claim on scarce budget dollars?

As we have seen, China's foreign-policy decisions are driven by a desire to enhance the respect that other nations show for China—to gain face—and an equally strong desire to avoid situations in which the strength and competence of China and its political leaders are publicly called into question.

It took the government of the People's Republic three decades to obtain the recognition of other governments. Securing representation in the United Nations was a particularly important goal, and China has taken its participation in that organization very seriously. Although it resists the incursions on its sovereignty that such participation might entail and consistently favors backstairs negotiations over public sanctions as a means of resolving international disputes, it nonetheless savors the status that derives from permanent membership on the Security Council. A measure of the importance it still accords to UN membership is the vigor with which it opposes Taiwan's participation.

Membership in the newly formed World Trade Organization (WTO) is high on the Chinese agenda. China had expected to be offered membership in the General Agreement on Tariffs and Trade (GATT) before that organization became the WTO in January 1995, since it was one of the original contracting parties to GATT in 1948, though the Nationalist government withdrew its membership four years later. Beijing began applying for membership in 1988. The United States took the lead in making the case that China should have no special treatment, and the other leading members of GATT supported this position, but China saw it as one more indication of a concerted anti-China policy. At issue were China's policies protecting state-owned enterprises and its lack of transparency in trade and investment regulations. China sought membership as a developing country; the United States and others responded that the Chinese economy was already too large and well developed for that category to be appropriate. The question of China's membership in WTO is complicated by the fact that Taiwan's application is being considered simultaneously.

China takes its role as a regional power seriously and actively participates in several new international groupings, such as the Association of Southeast Asian Nations (ASEAN) Regional Forum on Security, which includes the ASEAN states (Brunei, Indonesia, Malaysia, the Philippines, Singapore, Thailand, and, as of 1995, Vietnam) plus Australia, Cambodia, Canada, the European Union, Japan, Laos, New Zealand, Papua New Guinea, Russia, South Korea, and the United States. At the meeting of the Regional Forum in August 1995, the issue of China's actions in the South China Sea was taken up. It was a measure of Chinese respect for the forum and for its membership in it that China came to the table with a conciliatory approach, agreeing to multilateral negotiations.

A slightly different configuration of members makes up the Asian Pacific Economic Cooperation (APEC) Forum, which excludes Cambodia, Laos, the European Union, Papua New Guinea, and Russia but includes Taiwan and Hong Kong. Although the agenda of APEC Forum meetings is intended to focus on Pacific rim economic issues, its meetings ordinarily include a session of its Eminent Persons Group, the agenda for which is more far-ranging.

China is also involved in a proposal to set up an Asian common market, the European Union being the model. The proposed membership for the Community of Asian Nations (CAN), much more extensive than any existing economic and security organizations in the region, is to include all the APEC states (excluding the United States and Canada), as well as Mongolia, North Korea, Laos, Cambodia, Burma, India, Afghanistan, Bhutan, Nepal, Sri Lanka, Bangladesh, Pakistan, and the Maldives.

.　　.　　.

As the new century begins, the key strategic relationship in East
Asia—among China, Japan, and the United States—should be the
central focus of American foreign policy toward China. China
needs concrete reassurances that isolating it is not the goal of
American foreign policy. China and Japan need to come to a long-
term strategic understanding, which the United States is in a good
position to facilitate.

To be able to reassure China, the United States needs, in the
first instance, a clear and consistent policy, and Congress needs
to take a calmer view. Currently, when Congress is not agitated
about China's human rights record or treatment of Taiwan, it is
agitated over China's rapidly developing trade surplus, which
threatens to become a perennial sore point, as Japan's trade surplus is in our relations with that country. In the early 1980s, the
United States enjoyed a modest annual trade surplus with China.
The situation was reversed in 1983, when China realized a $68
million surplus in total two-way trade of just over $4 billion. Ac-
cording to American figures, the surplus had grown to $30 billion
by 1995, nearly half the size of Japan's surplus. China and the
United States differ in their methods of calculating trade figures,
since the United States counts goods from China transshipped
through Hong Kong as imports from China, while China counts
them as exports to Hong Kong. Although other factors are also
involved, the result is that U.S. trade data show a surplus in China's favor more than double the size of that surplus shown in
Chinese trade data.

Another factor needs to be taken into account: as Taiwan and
Hong Kong manufacturers have relocated their production facilities to mainland China, goods produced in those facilities and
exported to the United States count in American trade statistics
as exports from China, not from Taiwan or Hong Kong, and our
trade deficits with Taiwan and Hong Kong show a decrease as the
one with China increases. Our trade deficit with China increased

by a factor of more than six between 1987 and 1992, but if one adds in Taiwan and Hong Kong, the growth in the deficit drops to just under 10 percent.

A second step toward de-escalating tensions between the United States and China would be to grant China permanent most-favored-nation status, removing the issue of renewal from the annual agenda. The law under which annual renewal is mandated—the Jackson-Vanik amendment to the trade act of 1974—was originally written so as to encourage the Soviet government to permit the free emigration of Russian Jews. Since China is now allowing more Chinese to leave for the United States than the United States is prepared to admit, free emigration is not really at issue. Congress will be reluctant to relinquish what it regards as one of its few levers in dealing with China, though the lever is inappropriate for the purposes to which it is put.

A third step toward improving Sino-American relations would be to use multilateral forums rather than bilateral negotiations to influence Chinese behavior whenever feasible. Although most nations do not share the intense American feeling about human rights abuses in China, they do share America's concern over nuclear proliferation and weapons sales; American concerns about these issues should be voiced through regional and international forums where pressure brought to bear on China is not unilateral.

A fourth step is to work toward the early entry of China into the WTO. While the obstacles to China's entry are not exclusively of American making, Beijing sees Washington as its principal opponent standing in the way of membership. Finally, we should actively pursue contact at all levels of the Chinese government— particularly with the People's Liberation Army. Contacts with the Chinese side developed rapidly after normalization of relations in 1979, but virtually all these were interrupted after the Tiananmen massacre. Although the expression of American—and international—outrage was appropriate at the time, our being out of contact has become counterproductive, especially when China's armed forces exert such a strong influence on the political system and may be nursing dreams of military expansion.

There are lessons to be learned from our century and a half of dealing with China, lest we repeat our past mistakes. First, despite the increasing veneer of Westernization, China's culture is still based on premises very different from our own. Second, we should bear in mind that, although we have tried hard over the years to change China after our image, we have never succeeded in doing so. In the nineteenth century we tried to Christianize China; in the twentieth century we tried to democratize China; currently we are eager to transform China after American economic and technological models. We are very likely to be unsuccessful once again.

It seems paradoxical that there are more active Chinese Christians today than there were when the American missionary movement was at its height, early in this century. Although no one would mistake China for a fully functioning democracy, there are more elements of grassroots democracy in the political system today than there were when American political influence was at its height in the 1930s and 1940s. And economic, scientific, and technological progress is occurring at a startlingly rapid rate. All of these changes, however, have come about as a result of Chinese decisions to change, not because of American pressure on China to change.

A final point: we need to be less passionate and more neutral about the American relationship with China, however special it is. China is neither the utopia we thought it was when we "rediscovered" it in the 1970s, nor is it the unmitigatedly evil place we sometimes think of its being in the 1990s. If we can be more realistic about our expectations for China, we are likely to be less frequently disappointed.

# Conclusion:
# China in the Next Century

This book set out to consider three questions: What are the principal problems confronting China today? What is the capacity of the Chinese political system to address those problems successfully? And, given the problems and government's capacity, what is the outcome likely to be?

Preceding chapters have described the formidable challenges to which the Chinese Party-state must respond in order to restore its authority, maintain public order, and create the conditions under which continued economic development can occur. I have also tried to show how that Party-state is seriously weakened by a lack of public confidence, a habit of corruption, and a rigidity in the face of change. Now we must ask, What is China's near-term future likely to be?

It may be useful to begin by offering some scenarios that are *not* likely and then to consider more probable ones. Least likely of all, I believe, is more of the same.

Deng Xiaoping adopted a unique method of overseeing China's entry into the modern world. Nearly seventy-five years old when he returned to power and launched the economic reforms, Deng had succession on his mind from the outset. It was his plan to avoid assuming the most senior positions in the Party-state himself and to appoint individuals to them whom he thought he could trust to carry on his reform program. If the process had worked as planned, he would gradually have retired and vanished like Lewis Carroll's cat, "quite slowly, beginning with the end of the tail, and ending with the grin, which remained some time after the rest of it had gone." But the process did not work as he planned: he did retire from office and become an éminence grise, whispering into his successors' ears from behind the curtain, but all too quickly, he lost confidence in the men he had appointed and intervened either to replace them or to reverse what he believed was their incorrect course. This continued until the eve of his ninety-first birthday when, emerging from a coma and stepping back from the brink of death, he is alleged to have called Jiang Zemin to his bedside for a heart-to-heart talk about Taiwan and the United States.

With his vision, his revolutionary credentials, and his clout, Deng was an indispensable element of the political machine he put in place to change China. He was also irreplaceable. None of his contemporaries possess his special combination of qualities, and China's political system cannot function in the same way following his death that it did while he was still active.

Equally unlikely, in my view, is a reversal of course and the reestablishment of a centrally planned economy built around a strong state-owned sector cut off from the outside world. First, no one in China of any consequence advocates such a reversal. Second, twenty years of reform have created far too many interests vested in the growth of the Chinese economy—its collective and private sectors—and in linking it to the world economy. It would take a massive turn in China's economic fortunes or in the world economy as a whole to make rebuilding a Soviet-style socialist economy seem sensible, and it would take a political revolution to implement that.

Taiwanization is a third scenario, very unlikely in the near term, but it is my hope that it might be realized over the longer term. By "Taiwanization" I mean the duplication on mainland China of the political transformation that occurred on Taiwan: a relaxation of political repression, the emergence of a viable political opposition, and the reconstitution of the government so that a number of different parties might become the ruling one. Indispensable to this transformation are, as we have seen, a forward-looking leader with the political power to carry out his plans, courageous politicians willing to take risks to express opposition, and an electorate interested in and enthusiastic about democracy. A fledgling democracy is often somewhat chaotic and occasionally ineffective. One needs economic prosperity and the absence of serious political challenges to allow for tranquillity while a new system tries its wings.

At the moment, there are no signs in China of a visionary and powerful leader ready to launch a move toward democratization. Nor are there bold politicians prepared to form an opposition movement. Most of them have been imprisoned, placed under house arrest, or thoroughly intimidated. Also lacking is a strong commitment to democracy on the part of a politically aware and active public. In fact, among the politically conscious citizenry there is widespread skepticism about democracy. Many of them argue that democracy is ill-suited to China, either because of its history and culture or because of its size and ungovernability. Others believe that democracy may be appropriate for China at some future date but not now, when China needs honest authoritarianism. Therefore, a political liberalization of the Chinese government similar to Taiwan's seems a highly unlikely scenario in the near term.

Somewhat more likely, I think, is an abrupt collapse of the Party-state, similar to what happened in the Soviet Union in the summer of 1991. There are ample reasons in China today for popular dissatisfaction with the Party-state. The problems that brought people into the streets in 1989—inflation and corruption—are unresolved: although the inflation rate is dropping, the incidence of corruption is mounting rapidly. And, unlike the situation in 1989, there is reason to believe that the level of anger among the rural population is even higher than that in the cities. Country people have shown no hesitation in taking their grievances to the village streets, even in today's repressive political atmosphere.

What is the spark that might set off a conflagration that brings down the government? Students might act as a vanguard, as they did in the late 1980s, though the reservoir of idealism and political activism in the student community seems well below the high-water mark then. Or rural protests over excess taxes, a shortage of cash to pay for harvested crops, or egregious examples of corruption might become more numerous, less isolated, and spread from the hinterlands to the cities. More likely, I think, is urban workers being the first to rise. Laid off or furloughed in the state sector and unable to find jobs in the collective or private sector, workers may take to the streets, and if they do, their protests will quickly be echoed in the surrounding countryside. A nation in the streets is surely beyond the capability of the weakened Party-state to control. A rapid meltdown of the Chinese Communist Party and the government it controls is plausible under these circumstances.

Or the process may be slower, triggered not by aggrieved citizens but by dissident regions. Assuming that simultaneous weakening of central authority and strengthening of local authority continues, interregional conflicts are sure to arise, and the central government will no longer be in a position to mediate or end those conflicts. Some observers have called this situation "economic warlordism," using a term meant to remind us of the period between the collapse of dynastic authority and the reassertion of a strong central authority under the Chinese Communist Party in 1949 during which the warlord who happened to control Beijing and its environs at any given time claimed that he spoke for the government of China but, apart from receiving foreign envoys, had no effective national power. If one wanted to do business in Shanghai or settle a claim in Guangzhou, one addressed oneself to the local warlord, not to Beijing. Disputes between warlords were settled by armed conflict between the troops loyal to each. A repeat of this collapse of civil order and central control is certainly a possibility in the near term.

Were either of these last two sets of circumstances to come about, there is no question that the People's Liberation Army would intervene, but in neither instance to prop up the existing incumbents of the weakened Party-state. Rather, I believe, it would intervene in the name of Chinese patriotism and in defense of the Chinese national entity, resulting in a de facto military caretaker government. Given the strengths and weaknesses of the PLA as potential praetorians, such a government is more likely to be successful in the first set of circumstances—citizens on the streets—than with regional dissidence. It could very likely gain substantial popular support if it refused to support a discredited civilian leadership and set itself apart as an alternative to weakened and corrupted institutions. A promise to restore order to city streets and village roads would appeal to the people's natural distaste for anarchy and chaos.

An optimistic conclusion assumes that the PLA succeeds in restoring order, finds new and uncorrupted civilian leaders, rebuilds the power of the central government, and begins to address the nation's agenda of problems. It also assumes that military professionalism is stronger than the pleasures of politics and that the army returns to its barracks at an early date. A pessimistic conclusion assumes that the PLA, like the Party, cannot restore the credibility of central authority and that personal and institutional self-interest preclude a successful political reconstitution.

Ending civil war among competing economic warlords would be a substantially more formidable challenge. The PLA would be stretched very thin, and even if some of its units were not actually involved as combatants, its own regional interests would not be easy to separate from patriotism. Chiang Kai-shek spent twenty years trying to create a national entity out of a patchwork of regional fiefdoms. In the end he created a web of tenuous alliances among warlords, not a strong central state, which came only as a result of a revolution that won popular support by its appeal to nationalism and its promise to run an honest government and improve living standards. That process can hardly be accomplished by the PLA acting on its own.

In sum, regardless of which of these or other circumstances comes to pass, China has a protracted and problematical time ahead, in which the army will be heavily involved in the political process. The extraordinary growth of its economy may slow down during this transitional period, and China's best endowed regions are likely to weather this more successfully than the others. Because perceived threats from outside are always effective in creating national unity, we can expect China's national ego to be especially sensitive.

Understanding China is a necessity if we hope to be able to deal effectively with it during this sensitive period. To do so requires that we keep in the closest possible touch with a broad spectrum of Chinese people and institutions, for that is the only way to keep ourselves as well informed as we can be about the changes taking place there. It also requires sensitivity and flexibility in responding to the changes we observe. It requires that we bear in mind our past experience. We have, over the years, exerted a great deal of influence on China indirectly, rather than directly, and we have been most successful in doing so when we have taught by example, least successful when we have tried to teach through sanctions.

To understand China is not to hold it to a standard of its own and to exempt it from the standards to which we hold ourselves and other nations. It is to suggest that since it had very little to do with setting those standards in the past, it may have difficulty in living up to them in the present. To understand China is not necessarily to love it, but understanding China is a prerequisite to dealing with it effectively in the years ahead. And, given its size and its potential, and given the degree to which the rest of the world has become linked with it both economically and politically, there is no avoiding the necessity to deal with China in the years ahead.

# Bibliography

## Introduction

Kristof, Nicholas D. and Sheryl Wudunn. *China Wakes: The Struggle for the Soul of a Rising Power.* New York: New York Times Books, 1994.

Tyson, James and Ann Tyson. *Chinese Awakenings: Life Stories from the Unofficial China.* Boulder, Colorado: Westview, 1995.

## I. Geographical Inequalities

Blunden, Caroline and Mark Elvin. *Cultural Atlas of China.* London: Phaidon, 1983.

Cannon, Terry and Alan Jenkins, eds. *The Geography of Contemporary China: The Impact of Deng Xiaoping's Decade.* London: Routledge, 1990.

Gedlan, P. J. and D. C. Twitchett, eds. *The Times Atlas of China.* London: Times Books, 1974.

Skinner, G. William. "Marketing and Social Structure in Rural China," *Journal of Asian Studies* 24 (1965), pp. 1–3.

Smil, Vaclav. *Energy in China's Modernization: Advances and Limitations.* Armonk, New York: M. E. Sharpe, 1988.

Smith, Christopher J. *China: People and Places in the Land of One Billion.* Boulder, Colorado: Westview, 1990.

Van Slyke, Lyman P. *Yangtze: Nature, History and the River.* New York: Addison Wesley, 1988.

## II. Patterns from the Past

Chang Jung. *Wild Swans: Three Daughters of China.* New York: Simon & Schuster, 1991.

Cheng, Nien. *Life and Death in Shanghai.* New York: Grove Press, 1986.

Fairbank, John K. *China: A New History.* Cambridge, Massachusetts: Harvard University Press, 1992.

———— and Albert Feuerwerker, eds. *Cambridge History of China, Volume 13: Republican China, 1912–49.* Cambridge: Cambridge University Press, 1984.

———— and Roderick MacFarquhar, eds. *Cambridge History of China, Volumes 14–15: The People's Republic of China, 1949–79.* Cambridge: Cambridge University Press, 1985.

Jenner, W.J.F. *The Tyranny of History: The Roots of China's Crisis.* New York: Penguin, 1992.

Spence, Jonathan D. *The Search for Modern China.* New York: W. W. Norton, 1990.

Su Xiaokang, Wang Luxiang, and Xia Jun. *Deathsong of the River: A Reader's Guide to the Chinese TV Series "He Shang."* Ithaca, New York: Cornell University East Asia Program, 1991.

## III. China's Political System

Goldman, Merle. *Sowing the Seeds of Democracy in China: Political Reform in the Deng Xiaoping Era.* Cambridge, Massachusetts: Harvard University Press, 1994.

Gong Ting. *The Politics of Corruption in Contemporary China: An*

*Analysis of Policy Outcomes.* Westport, Connecticut: Praeger, 1994.

Jia Hao and Lin Zhimin, eds. *Changing Central-Local Relations in China: Reform and State Capacity.* Boulder, Colorado: Westview, 1994.

Levy, Richard. "Corruption, Economic Crime and the Social Transformation since the Reforms," *Australian Journal of Chinese Affairs* 33 (1995), pp. 183–216.

Lieberthal, Kenneth. *Governing China: From Revolution through Reform.* New York: W. W. Norton, 1995.

———— and David M. Lampton, eds. *Bureaucracy, Politics and Decision-making in Post-Mao China.* Berkeley and Los Angeles: University of California Press, 1992.

———— and Michel Oksenberg, eds. *Policy Making in China: Leaders, Structures and Processes.* Princeton, New Jersey: Princeton University Press, 1990.

MacFarquhar, Roderick, ed. *The Politics of China, 1949–1989.* New York and Cambridge: Cambridge University Press, 1993.

Nathan, Andrew J. *Chinese Democracy.* New York: Alfred A. Knopf, 1985.

O'Brien, Kevin J. *Reform without Liberalization: China's National People's Congress and the Politics of Institutional Change.* New York and Cambridge: Cambridge University Press, 1990.

Shambaugh, David L. "Losing Control: The Erosion of State Authority in China," *Current History* 93 (1993), pp. 253–59.

Shue, Vivienne. *The Reach of the State: Sketches of the Chinese Body Politic.* Stanford, California: Stanford University Press, 1988.

White, Gordon, ed. *The Chinese State in the Era of Economic Reform: The Road to Crisis.* Armonk, New York: M. E. Sharpe, 1991.

Yang, Mayfair Mei-hui. *Gifts, Favors, and Banquets: The Art of*

*Social Relationships in China*. Ithaca, New York: Cornell University Press, 1994.

## IV. China's Economy

Cheng Tiejun and Mark Selden. "The Origins and Social Consequences of China's *hukou* System." *China Quarterly* 139 (1994), pp. 644–68.

Cheng Yuk-shing and Tsang Shu-ki. "The Changing Grain Marketing System in China," *China Quarterly* 140 (1994), pp. 1080–1104.

Findlay, Christopher, Andrew Watson, and Wu, Harry X., eds. *Rural Enterprises in China*. New York: St. Martin's Press, 1994.

Kelliher, Daniel. *Peasant Power in China: The Era of Rural Reform, 1979–89*. New Haven: Yale University Press, 1992.

Kueh, Y. Y. and Robert Ash, eds. *Economic Trends in Chinese Agriculture: The Impact of the Post-Mao Reforms*. Oxford: Clarendon Press, 1993.

McKinley, Terry. *The Distribution of Wealth in Rural China*. Armonk, New York: M. E. Sharpe, 1995.

Naughton, Barry. *Growing Out of the Plan: Chinese Economic Reform 1978–1993*. New York and Cambridge: Cambridge University Press, 1995.

———. "China's Macroeconomy in Transition," *China Quarterly* 144 (1995), pp. 1083–1104.

Putterman, Louis. "The Role of Ownership and Property Rights in China's Economic Transition," *China Quarterly* 144 (1995), pp. 1047–64.

Shirk, Susan L. *The Political Logic of Economic Reform in China*. Berkeley and Los Angeles: University of California Press, 1993.

Sicular, Terry. "Redefining State, Plan and Market: China's Reforms in Agricultural Commerce," *China Quarterly* 144 (1995), pp. 1020–46.

Walder, Andrew G. "China's Transitional Economy: Interpreting Its Significance," *China Quarterly* 144 (1995), pp. 963–79.

World Bank. *China: Internal Market Development and Regulation.* Washington, D.C.: The World Bank, 1994.

## V. The Chinese Armed Forces

Bickford, Thomas J. "The Chinese Military and Its Business Operations: The People's Libertion Army as Entrepreneur," *Asian Survey* 34:5 (1994), pp. 460–74.

Bitzinger, Richard A. "Arms to Go: Chinese Arms Sales to the Third World," *International Security* (Fall 1992), pp. 84–111.

Lewis, John Wilson and Xue Litai. *China's Strategic Seapower: The Politics of Force Modernization in the Nuclear Age.* Stanford, California: Stanford University Press, 1994.

McNamara, Robert S., David E. Jeremiah, James P. McCarthy, William R. Richardson, Jimmy D. Ross, David M. Lampton, and June Mei. *Sino-American Military Relations: Mutual Responsibilities in the Post-Cold War Era.* New York: National Committee on U.S.–China Relations, 1994.

Nelsen, Harvey W. *The Chinese Military System: An Organizational Study of the Chinese People's Liberation Army,* 2nd ed. Boulder, Colorado: Westview, 1981.

Segal, Gerald. *Defending China.* New York and Oxford: Oxford University Press, 1985.

Swaine, Michael D. *The Military and Political Succession in China: Leadership, Institutions and Beliefs.* Los Angeles, California: Rand Corporation, 1992.

Yang, Richard H., ed. *China's Military: The PLA in 1992–93.* Boulder, Colorado: Westview, 1993.

## VI. Sources of Rural Discontent

Burns, John P. *Political Participation in Rural China.* Berkeley and Los Angeles: University of California Press, 1988.

Carter, Colin A. and Zhong Fu-ning. *China's Grain Production and Trade: An Economic Analysis*. Boulder, Colorado: Westview, 1988.

Howard, Pat. *Breaking the Iron Ricebowl: Prospects for Socialism in China's Countryside*. Armonk, New York: M. E. Sharpe, 1988.

Jacka, Tamara. *Women's Work in Rural China: Change and Continuity in an Era of Reform*. New York and Cambridge: Cambridge University Press, 1997.

Knapp, Ronald G. *China's Traditional Rural Architecture: A Cultural Geography of the Common House*. Honolulu: University of Hawaii Press, 1987.

Oi, Jean C. *State and Peasant in Contemporary China: The Political Economy of Village Government*. Berkeley and Los Angeles: University of California Press, 1989.

Parish, William L., ed. *Chinese Rural Development*. Armonk, New York: M. E. Sharpe, 1985.

————, Zhe Xiaoye, and Li Fang. "Nonfarm Work and Marketization of the Chinese Countryside," *China Quarterly* 143 (1995), pp. 697–730.

Putterman, Louis. *Continuity and Change in China's Rural Development: The Collective and Reform Eras in Perspective*. New York and Oxford: Oxford University Press, 1992.

Siu, Helen, ed. *Furrows: Peasants, Intellectuals and the State*. Stanford, California: Stanford University Press, 1990.

Yan Yunxiang. *The Flow of Gifts: Reciprocity and Social Networks in a Chinese Village*. Stanford, California: Stanford University Press, 1996.

## VII. China's Cities

Bian Yanjie. *Work and Inequality in Urban China*. New York: State University of New York Press, 1994.

Davis, Deborah and Stevan Harrell, eds. *Chinese Families in the*

*Post-Mao Era.* Berkeley and Los Angeles: University of California Press, 1993.

Davis, Deborah, Richard Kraus, Barry Naughton, and Elizabeth Perry, eds. *Urban Spaces in Contemporary China: The Potential for Autonomy and Community in Post-Mao China.* New York and Cambridge: Cambridge University Press, 1995.

Davis, Deborah and Ezra Vogel, eds. *Chinese Society on the Eve of Tiananmen: The Impact of Reform.* Cambridge, Massachusetts: Harvard University Press, 1990.

Day, Lincoln H., ed. *Migration and Urbanization in China.* Armonk, New York: M. E. Sharpe, 1994.

Kirkby, R.J.R. *Urbanization in China: Town and Country in a Developing Economy, 1949–2000 A.D.* New York: Columbia University Press, 1985.

Kwok, R. Yin-wang, William L. Parish, et al., eds. *Chinese Urban Reform: What Model Now?* Armonk, New York: M. E. Sharpe, 1990.

Lewis, John W., ed. *The City in Communist China.* Stanford, California: Stanford University Press, 1971.

Sit, Victor F.S., ed. *Chinese Cities: The Growth of the Metropolis since 1949.* New York and Oxford: Oxford University Press, 1988.

### VIII. The Centrifugal Forces of Regionalism

Ash, Robert and Y. Y. Kueh. "Economic Integration within Greater China: Trade and Investment Flows between China, Hong Kong and Taiwan," *China Quarterly* 136 (1993), pp. 711–45.

Goodman, David S.G., ed. *China's Regional Development.* London: Routledge, 1989.

———. *The Evolution of Greater China and What It Means for America.* New York: National Committee for United States–China Relations, 1994.

Segal, Gerald. *China Changes Shape: Regionalism and Foreign Policy*. London: International Institute for Strategic Studies, Adelphi Papers, 1994.

Shambaugh, David L., ed. *Greater China: The Next Superpower*. New York and Oxford: Oxford University Press, 1995.

Skinner, G. William, ed. *The City in Late Imperial China*. Stanford, California: Stanford University Press, 1977.

Yahuda, Michael. "The Foreign Relations of Greater China," *China Quarterly* 136 (1993), pp. 687–710.

Yeung Yue-man and Hu Xu-wei. *China's Coastal Cities: Catalysts for Modernization*. Honolulu: University of Hawaii Press, 1992.

## IX. The Challenge of Environmental Degradation

Edmonds, Richard Louis. *Patterns of China's Lost Harmony: A Survey of Environmental Degradation and Protection*. London: Routledge, 1994.

Luk Shui-hung and Joseph Whitney, eds. *Megaproject: A Case Study of China's Three Gorges Project*. Armonk, New York: M. E. Sharpe, 1993.

Qu Geping and Li Jinchang. *Population and the Environment in China*. Boulder, Colorado: Lynne Rienner, 1994.

Robinson, Thomas W., ed. *The Foreign Relations of China's Environment Policy*. Washington, D.C.: American Enterprise Institute, 1992.

Smil, Vaclav. *The Bad Earth: Environmental Degradation in China*. Armonk, New York: M. E. Sharpe, 1984.

―――. *China's Environmental Crisis: An Inquiry into the Limits of National Development*. Armonk, New York: M. E. Sharpe, 1993.

## X. One Billion Plus

Aird, John S. *Slaughter of the Innocents: Coercive Birth Control in China*. Lanham, Maryland: University Press of America, 1990.

Brown, Lester and H. Kane. *Full House.* New York: W. W. Norton, 1994.

Harrell, Stevan. *Chinese Historical Microdemography.* Berkeley and Los Angeles: University of California Press, 1995.

Peng Xizhe. *Demographic Transition in China: Fertility Trends since the 1950s.* Oxford: Clarendon Press, 1991.

Tien, H. Yuan. *China's Strategic Demographic Initiative.* Westport, Connecticut: Praeger, 1991.

### XI. Human Rights and the Rule of Law

Alford, William P. *To Steal a Book Is an Elegant Offense: Intellectual Property Rights in Chinese Civilization.* Stanford, California: Stanford University Press, 1995.

————. "Tasseled Loafers for Barefoot Lawyers: Transformation and Tension in Chinese Legal Work," *China Quarterly* 141 (1995), pp. 22–38.

Barmé, Geremie and John Minford. *Seeds of Fire: Chinese Voices of Conscience.* New York: Hill and Wang, 1989.

Brook, Timothy. *Quelling the People: The Military Suppression of the Beijing Democracy Movement.* New York and London: Oxford University Press, 1992.

Chiu Hungdah and Leng Shao-chuan. *Criminal Justice in Post-Mao China.* New York: State University of New York Press, 1985.

Clarke, Donald C. and James V. Feinerman. "Antagonistic Contradictions: Criminal Law and Human Rights in China," *China Quarterly* 141 (1995), pp. 135–54.

Copper, John Franklin and Lee Ta-ling. *Tiananmen Aftermath: Human Rights in the People's Republic of China, 1990.* College Park: University of Maryland Press, 1992.

Davis, Michael C., ed. *Human Rights and Chinese Values: Legal, Philosophical, and Political Perspectives.* Hong Kong: Oxford University Press, 1995.

Gilmartin, Christina K., Gail Hershatter, Lisa Rofel, and Tyrene White, eds. *Engendering China: Women, Culture and the State*. Cambridge, Massachusetts: Harvard University Press, 1994.

Jones, William C., ed. *Basic Principles of Civil Law in China*. Armonk, New York: M. E. Sharpe, 1989.

Kent, Ann. *Between Freedom and Subsistence: China and Human Rights*. Hong Kong: Oxford University Press, 1993.

Lubman, Stanley B. "The Future of Chinese Law," *China Quarterly* 141 (1995), pp. 1–21.

Nathan, Andrew J. "Human Rights in Chinese Foreign Policy," *China Quarterly* 139 (1994), pp. 622–43.

Potter, Pitman B. *The Economic Contract Law of C: Legitimation and Contract Antonomy in the PRC*. Seattle: University of Washington Press, 1992.

————, ed. *Domestic Law Reforms in Post-Mao China*. Armonk, New York: M. E. Sharpe, 1994.

Tanner, Murray Scot. "The Erosion of Communist Party Control over Lawmaking in China," *China Quarterly* 138 (1994), pp. 344–72.

## XII. Intellectual Freedom and Chinese Education

Fang Lizhi. *Bringing Down the Great Wall: Writings on Science, Culture and Democracy in China*. New York: W. W. Norton, 1992.

Hayhoe, Ruth, ed. *Education and Modernization: The Chinese Experience*. New York: Pergamon, 1992.

Lin Jing. *Education in Post-Mao China*. Westport, Connecticut: Praeger, 1993.

Link, Perry. *Evening Chats in Beijing*. New York: W. W. Norton, 1992.

Liu Binyan. *China's Crisis, China's Hope*. Cambridge, Massachusetts: Harvard University Press, 1990.

Ogden, Suzanne, Kathleen Hartford, and Lawrence Sullivan. *China's *Search for Democracy: The Student and Mass Movement of 1989*. Armonk, New York: M. E. Sharpe, 1992.

Pepper, Suzanne. *China's Education Reform in the 1980's: Policies, Issues and Historical Perspectives*. Berkeley and Los Angeles: University of California Press, 1990.

————. *Radicalism and Education Reform in 20th Century China*. Hong Kong: Cambridge University Press, 1996.

Schoenhals, Martin. *The Paradox of Power in a PRC Middle School*. Armonk, New York: M. E. Sharpe, 1993.

Yan Jiaqi. *Toward a Democratic China: The Intellectual Autobiography of Yan Jiaqi*. Trans. by David S.K. Hong and Denis C. Mair. Honolulu: University of Hawaii Press, 1992.

### XIII. Artistic Freedom and China's Contemporary Culture

Andrews, Julia. *Painters and Politics in the People's Republic of China 1949–79*. Berkeley and Los Angeles: University of California Press, 1994.

Barlow, Tani E., ed. *Gender Politics in Modern China: Writing and Feminism*. Durham, North Carolina: Duke University Press, 1993.

Browne, Nick, Paul G. Pickowicz, Vivian Sobchack, and Esther Yau, eds. *New Chinese Cinemas: Forms, Identities, Politics*. New York and Cambridge: Cambridge University Press, 1994.

Chang Tsong-zung, Valerie C. Doran, et al. *China's New Art Post 1989*. Seattle: University of Washington Press, 1994.

Chow, Rey. *Primitive Passions: Visuality, Sexuality, Ethnography and Contemporary Chinese Cinema*. New York: Columbia University Press, 1995.

Cohen, Joan Lebold. *The New Chinese Painting, 1949–86*. New York: Harry N. Abrams, 1987.

Duke, Michael S., ed. *Modern Chinese Women Writers*. Armonk, New York: M. E. Sharpe, 1990.

Gold, Thomas B. "Go with Your Feelings: Hong Kong and Taiwan

Popular Culture in Greater China," *China Quarterly* 136 (1993), pp. 907–25.

Goldblatt, Howard, ed. *Chairman Mao Would Not Be Amused: Fiction from Today's China.* New York: Grove/Atlantic, 1996.

Holm, David. *Art and Ideology in Revolutionary China.* Hong Kong: Oxford University Press, 1991.

Jones, Andrew F. *Like a Knife: Ideology and Genre in Contemporary Chinese Popular Music.* Ithaca, New York: Cornell University Press, 1992.

Kolatch, Jonathan. *Is the Moon in China Just as Round? Sporting Life and Sundry Scenes.* London: Jonathan David, 1992.

Kraus, Richard Curt. *Brushes with Power: Modern Politics and the Chinese Art of Calligraphy.* Berkeley and Los Angeles: University of California Press, 1991.

Leung Laifong. *Morning Sun: Interviews with Post-Mao Chinese Writers.* Armonk, New York: M. E. Sharpe, 1993.

Riley, Jo. *Chinese Theatre and the Actor in Performance.* New York and Cambridge: Cambridge University Press, 1997.

Semsel, George S., Hou Jianping, and Xia Hong, eds. *Chinese Film Theory: A Guide to the New Era.* Westport, Connecticut: Praeger, 1990.

Sullivan, Michael. *Art and Artists of Twentieth-Century China.* Berkeley and Los Angeles: University of California Press, 1997.

Wang, David Der-Wei and Jeanne Tai, eds. *Running Wild: New Chinese Writers.* New York: Columbia University Press, 1994.

Wang Jing. *High Culture Fever: Politics, Aesthetics and Ideology in Deng's China.* Berkeley and Los Angeles: University of California Press, 1997.

Widmer, Ellen and David Der-Wei Wang, eds. *From May Fourth to June Fourth: Fiction and Film in Twentieth Century China.* Cambridge, Massachusetts: Harvard University Press, 1993.

Zha Jianying. *China Pop: How Soap Operas, Tabloids and Best-*

*sellers Are Transforming a Culture.* New York: The New Press, 1995.

Zhao, Henry Y.H. *The Uneasy Narrator: Chinese Fiction from the Traditional to the Modern.* New York and Oxford: Oxford University Press, 1995.


### XIV. Hong Kong: Beyond 1997

Cameron, Nigel. *An Illustrated History of Hong Kong.* Hong Kong: Oxford University Press, 1991.

Chan, Ming K. and Gerard Postiglione, eds. *The Hong Kong Reader: Passage to Chinese Sovereignty.* Armonk, New York: M. E. Sharpe, 1996.

Chiu Hungdah. *Hong Kong's Transition to 1997: Background, Problems and Prospects.* College Park: University of Maryland School of Law, 1993.

Ho Yin-ping. *Trade, Industrial Restructuring and Development in Hong Kong.* Honolulu: University of Hawaii Press, 1992.

Hsu, Berry Fong-chung. *The Common Law System in Chinese Context: Hong Kong in Transition.* Armonk, New York: M. E. Sharpe, 1992.

Lane, Kevin P. *Sovereignty and the Status Quo: The Historical Roots of China's Hong Kong Policy.* Boulder, Colorado: Westview, 1990.

Leung, Benjamin K.P. *Perspectives on Hong Kong Society.* Hong Kong: Oxford University Press, 1996.

McMillen, Donald H. and Michael E. DeGolyer, eds. *One Culture, Many Systems: Politics in the Reunification of China.* Hong Kong: Chinese University of Hong Kong Press, 1993.

Postiglione, Gerard A., ed. *Education and Society in Hong Kong: Toward One Country and Two Systems.* Armonk, New York: M. E. Sharpe, 1991.

Segal, Gerald. *The Fate of Hong Kong*. London: St. Martin's Press, 1993.

Wang Enbao. *Hong Kong, 1997: The Politics of Transition*. Boulder, Colorado: Lynne Rienner, 1995.

Welsh, Frank. *A Borrowed Place: A History of Hong Kong*. New York: Hill and Wang, 1994.

Yahuda, Michael. *Hong Kong: China's Challenge*. London: Routledge, 1996.

## XV. Democratization on Taiwan?

Aberbach, Joel D., David Dollar, and Kenneth J. Sokoloff. *The Role of the State in Taiwan's Development*. Armonk, New York: M. E. Sharpe, 1994.

Chang, Parris H. and Martin L. Lasater. *If the People's Republic of China Crosses the Taiwan Strait: An International Response*. Lanham, Maryland: University Press of America, 1993.

Chao, Linda and Ramon H. Myers. "The First Chinese Democracy: Political Development of the Republic of China on Taiwan, 1986–94," *Asian Survey* 34:3 (1994), pp. 213–30.

Cheng Tun-jen and Stephan Haggard, eds. *Political Change in Taiwan*. Boulder, Colorado: Lynne Rienner, 1992.

———, Chi Huang, and Samuel S.G. Wu. *Inherited Rivalry: Conflict across the Taiwan Straits*. Boulder, Colorado: Lynne Rienner, 1995.

Clough, Ralph N. *Reaching across the Taiwan Strait: People to People Diplomacy*. Boulder, Colorado: Westview, 1993.

Harrell, Stevan and Huang Chun-chieh, eds. *Cultural Change in Postwar Taiwan*. Boulder, Colorado: Westview, 1994.

Hickey, Dennis Van Vranken. *Taiwan's Security in the Changing International System*. Boulder, Colorado: Lynne Rienner, 1997.

Hughes, Christopher. *Taiwan and Chinese Nationalism: National Identity and Status in International Society*. London: Routledge, 1997.

Lasater, Martin L. *U.S. Interests in the New Taiwan*. Boulder, Colorado: Westview, 1993.

Leng Shao-chuan and Lin Cheng-yi. "Political Change on Taiwan: Transition to Democracy?" *China Quarterly* 136 (1993), pp. 805–39.

Moody, Peter R., Jr. *Political Change on Taiwan: A Study of Ruling Party Adaptability*. Westport, Connecticut: Praeger, 1991.

Myers, Ramon H. *Two Societies in Opposition: The Republic of China and the People's Republic of China after Forty Years*. Stanford, California: Hoover Institution, 1991.

Qi Luo and Christopher Howe. "Direct Investment and Economic Integration in the Asia Pacific: The Case of Taiwan Investment in Xiamen," *China Quarterly* 136 (1993), pp. 746–69.

Simon, Denis Fred and Michael Ying-mao Kau, eds. *Taiwan: Beyond the Economic Miracle*. Armonk, New York: M. E. Sharpe, 1992.

Sutter, Robert G. and William R. Johnson, eds. *Taiwan in World Affairs*. Boulder, Colorado: Westview, 1994.

Thornton, Arland and Lin Hui-sheng. *Social Change and the Family in Taiwan*. Chicago: University of Chicago Press, 1994.

Tien Hung-mao and Cheng Tun-jen. "Crafting Democratic Institutions in Taiwan," *China Journal* 37 (1997), pp. 1–30.

Tsang, Steve, ed. *In the Shadow of China: Political Developments in Taiwan since 1949*. Honolulu: University of Hawaii Press, 1994.

Tucker, Nancy Bernkopf. *Taiwan, Hong Kong and the U.S., 1945–92: Uncertain Friendships*. London and New York: Twayne, 1994.

Wachman, Alan M. *Taiwan: National Identity and Democratization*. Armonk, New York: M. E. Sharpe, 1994.

Wang, N. T., ed. *Taiwan Enterprises in Global Perspective*. Armonk, New York: M. E. Sharpe, 1992.

Wu, Jaushieh Joseph. *Taiwan's Democratization: Forces behind the New Momentum.* New York and Oxford: Oxford University Press, 1995.

Wu Hsin-hsing. *Bridging the Strait: Taiwan, China and the Prospects for Reunification.* Hong Kong: Oxford University Press, 1994.

### XVI. China's Foreign Relations

Cohen, Warren I. and Akira Iriye, eds. *The Great Powers in East Asia.* New York: Columbia University Press, 1990.

Copper, John Franklin. *China Diplomacy: The Washington–Taipei–Beijing Triangle.* Boulder, Colorado: Westview, 1992.

Dittmer, Lowell and Samuel S. Kim, eds. *China's Quest for National Identity.* Ithaca, New York: Cornell University Press, 1993.

Faust, John R. and Judith F. Kornberg. *China in World Politics.* Boulder, Colorado: Lynne Rienner, 1995.

Foot, Rosemary. *The Practice of Power: U.S. Relations with China since 1949.* Hong Kong: Oxford University Press, 1995.

Garver, John W. *Foreign Relations of the People's Republic of China.* Englewood Cliffs, New Jersey: Prentice-Hall, 1993.

Goodman, David S.G. and Gerald Segal, eds. *China Rising: Nationalism and Interdependence.* London: Routledge, 1997.

Greenfield, Jeanette. *China's Practice in the Law of the Sea.* Oxford: Clarendon Press, 1992.

Harding, Harry. *A Fragile Relationship: The United States and China since 1972.* Washington, D.C.: Brookings Institution, 1992.

Hartland-Thunberg, Penelope. *China, Hong Kong, Taiwan and the World Trading System.* London: Macmillan, 1990.

Kim, Samuel S. *China and the World: Chinese Foreign Policy in the Post-Mao Era,* 3rd ed. Boulder, Colorado: Westview, 1994.

Lampton, David M. and Alfred D. Wilhelm, Jr., eds. *United States and China Relations at a Crossroads.* Lanham, Maryland: University Press of America, 1995.

Lardy, Nicholas R. *China in the World Economy.* Washington, D.C.: Institute for International Economics, 1994.

Madsen, Richard. *China and the American Dream: A Moral Inquiry.* Berkeley and Los Angeles: University of California Press, 1995.

Robinson, Thomas W. and David Shambaugh, eds. *Chinese Foreign Policy: Theory and Practice.* Oxford and New York: Oxford University Press, 1994.

Ross, Robert S. *Negotiating Cooperation: The U.S. and China, 1969–1989.* Stanford, California: Stanford University Press, 1995.

Sutter, Robert G. and Shirley Kan. *China as a Security Concern in Asia: Perceptions, Assessment and U.S. Options.* Washington, D.C.: Congressional Research Service, 1994.

Tan Qingshan. *The Making of U.S. China Policy: From Normalization to the Post-Cold War Era.* Boulder, Colorado: Lynne Rienner, 1992.

Unger, Jonathan, ed. *Chinese Nationalism.* Armonk, New York: M. E. Sharpe, 1996.

Whiting, Allen S. "Chinese Nationalism and Foreign Policy after Deng," *China Quarterly* 142 (1995), pp. 295–316.

Zhang Ming. *Major Powers at a Crossroads: Economic Interdependence and an Asian Pacific Security Community.* Boulder, Colorado: Lynne Rienner, 1995.

# Index

Fang Lizhi, 210f
feudalism, 52
floating workers, 9, 71, 84, 87, 90,
    116, 122f, 144f, 148, 162, 193
food supply, 11, 41, 123–25, 147,
    205, 291
foreign direct investment, *see* invest-
    ment, foreign
foreign joint ventures, 83, 86, 93,
    103, 141, 143, 170, 203, 210
foreign relations, 17, 46, 66, 74, 113,
    181f, 210, 281, 287–304
foreign trade, 4, 13, 92f, 147, 166,
    203, 212, 269, 278, 284, 288–94,
    302, 306
France, 41, 112
Fujian Province, 37, 41, 93, 156,
    257, 266, 282
Fuzhou, 32, 266

# G

Gang of Four, 201
Gansu Province, 25, 181
GATT, *see* World Trade Organization
gentry, 45–51
Gezhouba Dam, 175
Gorbachev, Mikhail, 243, 297
government, 66f, 73, 86, 109, 137f,
    149, 153, 163, 176, 207, 242,
    282; *see also* Party-state
Great Leap Forward, 64, 89f, 115,
    118, 120, 186, 205
Great Wall, 23, 43, 56
Guangan County, Sichuan Province,
    189

Guangdong Province, 21, 37, 40,
    43, 93, 156, 161, 248, 252, 257,
    289
Guangzhou, 21, 31f, 35, 156, 247,
    251, 265, 309
*guanxi* (networking), 76, 127f
Gulf War, 108
Guo Shixing, 235

# H

Hainan Province, 93
Han Dongfang, 228
Han dynasty, 54
Han Fei, 198
Han River, 171
health care, 66, 80, 85–87, 92, 94f,
    138f, 141, 144, 204–6, 218
Heilongjiang Province, 25, 41
Hong Kong, 12, 18, 21, 40, 147,
    211, 232, 241, 246–66, 269f, 272,
    275, 289–93, 302
hospitals, *see* health care
household responsibility system,
    82–85, 91, 115, 118f, 121,
    124, 126, 135, 183, 188, 206,
    225
housing, 9, 81, 86f, 93f, 115, 122,
    125, 138–41, 143, 148
Hubei Province, 162, 171, 177
human rights, 17, 63, 184, 190,
    195, 197, 204–12, 261–64,
    294, 302f
Hunan Province, 35, 134, 161f,
    177
Hundred Flowers Campaign, 63

84, 86, 89, 92–95, 103, 120, 129,
137f, 140–43, 147, 155, 157f,
180, 234, 291, 306
Stern, Isaac, 232
students, *see* education
Su Rui, 233
Sun Yat-sen, 173
Supreme People's Court, *see* court
system
Szeto Wah, 252, 254, 260

# T

Taipei, 276
Taiping Rebellion, 55, 152
Taiwan, 12f, 18, 41, 44, 70,
232f, 241, 246, 250, 257,
266–86, 289, 291f, 295, 298,
300–2, 306f
Tan Dun, 233
Tang dynasty, 32
Tarim Basin, 25
taxation, 10, 53, 72, 80, 92, 127,
137f, 154–58, 163, 175, 180,
308
technology, 90, 93, 98, 100, 109,
135f, 159, 174f, 178, 207f, 244f,
289, 294, 297f, 304
Thatcher, Margaret, 248f, 272
Third World, 294
Three Gorges Dam, 21, 26, 162,
173–80, 298
Tian Zhuangzhuang, 239f
Tiananmen Square (June 4, 1989), 4,
8, 12f, 15, 17, 65f, 74, 99, 105f,
116, 132, 140, 145f, 165, 201,

203f, 210, 227f, 234,
242–44, 252, 254, 255, 264, 297,
303
Tianjin, 32, 35, 70, 157, 171
Tibet Autonomous Region, 21, 44,
74, 106
township and village enterprises
(TVE), *see* rural industry
trade, *see* foreign trade
transportation, 30–32, 81, 125, 148,
150, 170, 174, 176, 289
Tung Chee-hwa, 256, 261f

# U

Ukraine, 112
unemployment, *see* employment
"unit" (*danwei*), 71, 81, 117, 200
United Nations, 279, 300
United States, 3, 13, 18f, 23, 25f,
32, 41, 101, 103, 108, 220, 223,
232, 235, 258f, 269–71, 281f,
284f, 288–91, 293f, 297, 299f,
302
United States–China relations, 18, 32,
41, 101, 197, 211, 267, 269–71,
281f, 285, 289, 293f, 302–4, 306,
310
United States–China trade relations,
13, 284, 291, 302; *see also* most-
favored-nation status

# V

Vietnam, 33, 43, 100, 108, 110, 259,
295, 298f